W9-AWM-446

rreverent guides

New Orleans

St. Philip

other irreverent guides: Amsterdam • Boston • Chicago
London • Manhattan • Miami • Paris • San Francisco
Santa Fe • Virgin Islands • Washington, D.C.

irreverent

New

guides

Orleans

BY

GUY LEBLANC

A BALLIETT & FITZGERALD BOOK

MACMILLAN • USA

Where to let the *bons temps roulez*...

New Orleans Jazz and Heritage Festival, see Diversions

Breakfast like a Southern belle...

Madewood Plantation, see Diversions

Dress for Mardi Gras...

Mardi Gras, see Diversions

Search for the yellow-toothed nutria...

Swamp tours, see Getting Outside

Get hit by a Hurricane...

Pat O'Brien's, see Nightlife

Find a deal in the French Quarter...

Le Richelieu, see Accommodations

Dine on oysters Rockefeller...

Antoine's Restaurant, see Dining

Roll along with Old Man River...

Delta Queen Steamboat Company, see Diversions

Order your first warm muffuletta...

Napoleon House, see Dining

Buy influence in the spirit world.

Voodoo, see You Probably Didn't Know

what's so irreverent?

It's up to you.

You can buy a traditional guidebook with its fluff, its promotional hype, its let's-find-something-nice-to-say-about-everything point of view. Or you can buy an Irreverent guide.

What the Irreverents give you is the lowdown, the inside story. They have nothing to sell but the truth, which includes a balance of good and bad. They praise, they trash, they weigh, and leave the final decisions up to you. No tourist board, no chamber of commerce will ever recommend them.

Our writers are insiders, who feel passionate about the cities they live in, and have strong opinions they want to share with you. They take a special pleasure leading you where other guides fear to tread.

How irreverent are they? One of our authors insisted on writing under a pseudonym. "I couldn't show my face in town again if I used my own name," she told me. "My friends would never speak to me." Such is the price of honesty. She, like you, should know she'll always have a friend at Frommer's.

Warm regards,

Michael Spring

Michael Spring
Publisher

a disclaimer

Prices fluctuate in the course of time, and travel information changes under the impact of the varied and volatile factors that influence the travel industry. Neither the author nor the publisher can be held responsible for the experiences of readers while traveling. Readers are invited to write to the publisher with ideas, comments, and suggestions for future editions.

about the author

Guy LeBlanc is as mysterious as Marie Laveau, as daring as pirate Jean Lafitte, and as eccentric as the Crescent City itself.

photo credits

Page 1: courtesy of Louisiana Office of Tourism; Page 2: courtesy of Louisiana Office of Tourism; Page 4, top: © Syndey Byrd, bottom: courtesy of Louisiana Office of Tourism; Page 5: © Syndey Byrd; Page 6, top: courtesy of Louisiana Office of Tourism, bottom: courtesy of Louisiana Office of Tourism; Page 7, top: courtesy of Le Richelieu, middle: courtesy of Louisiana Office of Tourism, bottom: © 1995 The Delta Steamboat Company; Page 8, top: © Michael Terranova, bottom © Syndey Byrd.

Balliett & Fitzgerald, Inc.
Series editor: Holly Hughes / Executive editor: Tom Dyja / Managing editor: Duncan Bock / Production editor: Howard Slatkin / Line editor: David Low / Photo editors: Rachel Florman, Sue Canavan / Assistant editor: Maria Fernandez / Editorial assistants: Sam Weinman, Jennifer Leben
Macmillan Travel Art director: Michele Laseau

Design by Tsang Seymour Design Studio

All maps © Simon & Schuster, Inc.

Air travel assistance courtesy of Continental Airlines

MACMILLAN TRAVEL
A Simon & Schuster Macmillan Company
1633 Broadway
New York, NY 10019

ISBN 0-02-860652-3
ISSN 1085-4762

special sales

Bulk purchase (10+ copies) of Frommer's Travel Guides are available to corporations at special discounts. The Special Sales Department can produce custom editions to be used as premiums and/or for sales promotions to suit individual needs. Existing editions can be produced with custom cover imprints such as corporate logos. For more information write to: Special Sales, Simon & Schuster, 1633 Broadway, New York, NY 10019.

Manufactured in the United States of America

contents

introduction

There's something both poignant and fascinating about watching the attempted mall-ification of the City that Care Forgot by Nineties corporate types. And make no mistake about it. They are trying. In fact, the way things are going, New Orleans could end up like any other American city.

For the past half-century or so, people have come to New Orleans because it's different. Different from any other Southern city, different from anyplace else in the country. Despite its thriving world-class port, New Orleans has always been at heart a lazy little town, a sleepy Caribbeanesque village that came by its quirkiness naturally. Until recently, there was nothing of a "big-city" feel to New Orleans, no crackle and zip in the air (except during Mardi Gras, when there has always been plenty). The subtropical climate seduced visitors and natives alike to loll around and fritter away their time. The temptations were many, and in this climate, who could work up the energy to resist?

People came to New Orleans to get a taste of its very particular charms (not to mention, to get roaring drunk on Bourbon Street, and go hog-wild during Mardi Gras). To this day, they expect to see an eccentric little French Creole party-town—even though it isn't really French anymore, and most visitors don't have a clue what "Creole" means. Actually not many natives know what it means either (see page nine for an explanation).

Now, some things haven't changed, may never change. Tourists or no, New Orleanians still look for any excuse for a party, and there are almost monthly festivals, with an emphasis on food and music. The French Quarter is still here, the peeling paint still carefully preserved, the flag-stones still cracked as ever. It's not gotten any cooler in the summer, and it's still a superb place for frittering away your time. But, in other ways, this city has started to move at a different pace.

I first started to sense a "big-city" crackle in the air back in 1984, the year New Orleans began to lurch uneasily into the 20th century. That was the year of the World's Fair—the second one (the first one was in 1884). In preparation for that event, high tech hotels began shooting up all over the Central Business District. The Convention Center was built—the ever-expanding Convention Center, which goes through more phases than a hormonally-driven adolescent—and New Orleans dusted itself off and geared up to become one of the country's favorite destinations for hordes of conventioneers. Then, after the Fair, the "riverfront development" began, and tourism took off big time. Renovated buildings that had housed pavilions for the Fair were renovated again, and Riverwalk was built—a Rouse Company "festival market-place" like the company's riverfront developments in New York and Baltimore.

There are now 200 or so trendy shops and restaurants in Riverwalk, and another slew of them in the Canal Place mall, built the same year. French Quarter merchants have started to feel the pinch, and locally-owned shops in quaint little 19th-century buildings are suddenly struggling to compete with the likes of Saks Fifth Avenue. Several small businesses that were evicted from the Jax Brewery after the building was purchased by Planet Hollywood have not reopened.

Casinos have also cropped up all over town—out on the water and in Armstrong Park, so far—and they've ripped down the Rivergate Exhibition Hall in the CBD, and begun construction on the "world's largest casino" on the site. They're even talking about converting some of those charm-ing hidden courtyards into parking garages to take care of all the traffic. Imagine uprooting banana trees to make way for compact cars!

Used to be, New Orleans tourist brochures were all about the French Quarter and Mardi Gras, because the French Quarter and Mardi Gras were all that New Orleans was about. "America's European Masterpiece," the brochures called the Quarter, ignoring the fact that there isn't anything quite like it in Europe, either. Nowadays, the tourist brochures tout the latest addition to the aquarium, and count all the roulette wheels in the newest casino. Hell, with all those attractions, the French Quarter may eventually become obsolete. Oh, not to the 5,000 or so people (like me) who live in it, of course — people who dearly love it, are accustomed to tripping over all the tourists, and hate the changes that are taking place in and around it. But even the fabled French Creole cuisine has fallen prey to change. Girded for the ongoing nationwide battle against cholesterol, toques all over town are cooking something called "nouvelle Creole"—i. e., they're throwing out the bacon fat and substituting "light" stuff for lard. Is nothing sacred?

No. Because, of course, Planet Hollywood has opened in the French Quarter—in the French Quarter!!—joining the Hard Rock Cafe and the House of Blues. Well, the House of Blues is actually okay; its $7 million restored factory fits in well here on Decatur Street. The worst problem with HOB is that it's putting a big business dent in Tipitina's, a New Orleans institution if ever there was one. But the House of Bruce and Demi and Sly and Arnold? Give us a break.

Most visitors won't notice the changes in Mardi Gras, but it, too, is different now, and probably will become even more so. Local Mardi Gras traditionalists sorely miss the parade of the Mystick Krewe of Comus—the oldest Carnival organization. The Comus parade was always the last of Carnival, a beautiful and romantic torch-lit procession. But Comus has now withdrawn, and so have two of the other very old, very traditional Carnival organizations, Proteus and Momus. The reason: they are no longer politically correct. In 1991, the city council passed a hotly debated ordinance dictating that the parading krewes sign an anti-discrimination oath, and the men-only secret societies opted to stop. Rex—the krewe of the King of Carnival—signed the pledge and still parades, but a lot of people expect that Rex and other krewes will eventually have to knuckle under to economic pressures and take on corporate sponsors. Orleanians see it coming: The Virginia Slims Rex Parade, or the Trojans Condoms Zulu Parade. The 60 or so current krewes are civic-cum-social clubs

NEW ORLEANS | INTRODUCTION

that "put on" and pay for Carnival every year, traditionally raising money via bingo games to defray the costs of parading and buying all those "throws"—the souvenirs tossed out to the crowds along the parade routes. But the casinos have taken a big bite out of bingo, making fund-raising a problem for the organizations.

Even the oft-misunderstood "Creole" is going by the wayside. December being an off month, the city launched "A Creole Christmas" as a promotional gimmick to try to lure people to town. This city-wide series of festivities includes Papa Noel parading into town, restaurants offering versions of Creole "Reveillon" dinners—a Creole custom of midnight dinner after mass—and hotels offering discounted "Papa Noel" rates. Only now the celebration is called "A New Orleans Christmas." Seems that "Creole", too, is somehow now politically incorrect. Next thing you know the whole thing will become a promotion for Disney.

But for all of the unenlightened chamber-of-commerce effort to haul this city into what ironically seems to be the late-1970s (elsewhere, where it's the mid-1990s, preservation has become the byword), the essential soul of this town is still miraculously oblivious to the craven attempts to kill it. That is what is both so poignant and so fascinating. Because that very obliviousness—which these days seems more like a form of innocence—reveals a soul which couldn't care less about the conquest developers are attempting.

And maybe, with a climate which can slow down the most driven careerist, New Orleans can absorb this latest attempt on its virtue. Maybe humid entropy can still absorb frantic development, and make rampant Nineties-style commercialism stagger down Bourbon Street, pockets picked, like any other unsuspecting tourist. Bring it into the fold, so to speak. On the other hand, plastic is pretty much immune to humidity. The jury's still out (taking their time, just can't make it, deepest regrets).

In the meantime, you can still look out over the slanted rooftops and dormer windows, and almost kid yourself that you're somewhere in Paris. The plant-filled courtyards and sweeping archways are still redolent of Spain (they were, after all, designed by the Spanish back in the 19th century.) And the Mississippi River still slides quietly through the city, mesmerizing you, charming you, seducing you to languish on a park bench beside it and do absolutely nothing. The giant live oak trees, lavished with Spanish moss, the tall tropical palms, and the pale-green banana trees vie with the river, luring you to drop everything, and relax beneath them for a spell. The air is so thick with moisture you can almost drink it, and for most of the year it's simply too hot to do anything much more energetic than slather on sunscreen, knock back another Dixie beer and suck on some crawfish heads.

See it while you can.

New Orleans Neighborhoods

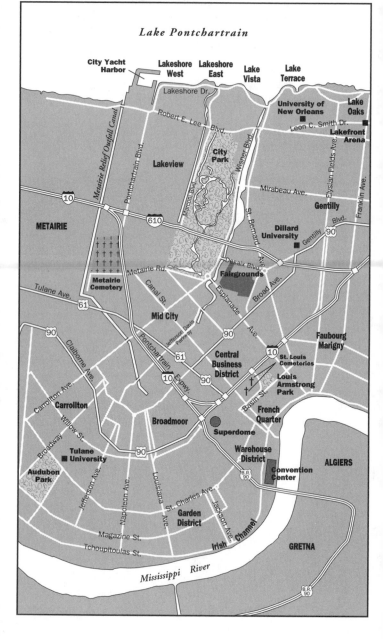

you
probably
didn't know

Where does novelist Anne Rice live?... The author of
the wildly popular Vampire Chronicles, not to mention
other novels like *Exit to Eden* (under the pen name Anne
Rampling) and porn novels like *The Claiming of Sleeping
Beauty* (under the name A. N. Roquelaure), Anne Rice lives
at 1239 First Street in the Garden District, a ritzy residential section upriver of the French Quarter. Try calling her at
504/522–8634, her published answering machine number.
Recently, there's been no answer sometimes, which may be
related to Rice's announcement in February 1995 that
"Lestat has left me." She claims to have been married to
this vampire hero of hers (wonder what her real-life hubby,
Stan, thinks of all that), and now that she's bereft, rather
than wearing widow's weeds she dresses in old wedding
dresses for book signings and other public appearances.
(She collects wedding dresses, among other things.) Get
the idea that she's a tad eccentric? She actually owns several Garden District mansions, including a former orphanage
that she bought to house her doll collection, word has it.
That's the house where the annual Memnoch Ball, a
Halloween coven party, is held, Memnoch being the protagonist of what she insists is the final book in the Lestat

chronicles. If you finally get through on her phone line, you'll hear Rice's voice talk about sundry things, such as how to get on the mailing list for her newsletter "Commotion Strange" (write to Vampire Lestat Fan Club, Box 58277, New Orleans LA 70158–8277), how to find her house ("F-i-r-s-t" Street, corner of Chestnut, "but please don't disturb our privacy"), her "strange passion" for writing, ideas for new novels, and occasional epiphanies. The recordings run 10 minutes or so, and at the proverbial beep you can leave a message for her. Don't expect to chat her up, though.

What is the French Quarter, and why is it so famous?... Today this part of town is a far cry from the canebrakes and squishy swamplands the French Creoles fashioned into a colony back in 1718. Locals call it "the Quarter," but the exit off I-10 reads "Vieux Carré"—i.e., "Old Square," *en français*. The Quarter is home to about 5,000 Orleanians, but it's also the city's biggest tourist draw. For a whole slew of visitors, the Quarter means only one thing: Bourbon Street—named for the 18th-century French royals and not, as it may seem from its scent and reputation, for the adult beverage. Locals know that Bourbon is hardly the be-all of the Quarter, though. For them, the Quarter means breakfasting on croissants and café au lait at Croissant d'Or and lunching at Galatoire's; grocery shopping at the Royal Street A&P or Matassa's; picking over fresh produce at the Old Farmers' Market; tending to the profusion of subtropical plants in their courtyards; browsing through the musty old books at the Librairie or Beckham's; having a gin-based Pimm's Cup cocktail at the Napoleon House; maintaining as much privacy as possible in a major tourist center; and, lately, worrying about how their neighborhood and their lives will be affected by the new casinos. The key word for the Quarter is "quaint"—narrow streets overhung with lacy, wrought-iron balconies; little 18th- and 19th-century buildings and cottages with gables, dormers, French windows, and shutters; and hidden courtyards bursting with banana trees and subtropical blooms. Skyrocketing rents in the Quarter are already beginning to force some longtime residents out. Most recently, there have been rumblings about converting some Quarter courtyards and buildings into parking lots to make way for all those millions of cars bringing gamblers into the casinos. There is reason for Quarterites to worry. Those original French Creole colonists would turn over in their graves if they knew.

And what are French Creoles?... The word "creole" has been bandied about so much over the years that these days it means almost anything indigenous to the New Orleans region. You may hear tell of creole tomatoes, creole cottages, and even a creole mustard, but they are not much different from tomatoes, cottages, and mustard elsewhere—they're simply homegrown south Louisiana specimens. But during the colonial period, a Creole (capitalized) was a person—a child born in the colonies to parents of the same national origins. Thus, a French Creole was the child of a French mother and a French father. The word was gallicized from the Spanish word *Crillo*, which simply distinguished a full-blooded child born in the colonies from one born of mixed parentage. Somewhere along the way it came to mean a French-Spanish aristocrat, and there are still some folks around today who boast of their Creole French–Spanish lineage.

Who lives in the French Quarter?... Behind those batten or louvered shutters and

Code Words

Orleanians use a slew of code words and pronunciations—if you don't bone up on them, you'll give yourself away as an outsider. Names of thoroughfares can be tricky. Chartres Street is locally pronounced like "charters," Conti Street is con-TIE (though the same word in Musée Conti Wax Museum is usually said con-TEE). The second syllable of Burgundy is emphasized, and so are the first syllables of Calliope, Melpomene, and, mercilessly, Terpsichore. Tchoupitoulas rolls off the tongue as Chop-a-TOO-lus, or, often, Chap-a-TOO-lus. Carondelet Street, named not for a Frenchman but a Spaniard, emphasizes the final "let." And Pitot—as in the Pitot House museum—rhymes with teapot.

lacy iron balconies, Quarterites are happily at home in various sleek condos, creaky attics, chic town houses, and quaint gingerbread cottages. The live-and-let-live ambiance of the neighborhood attracts not only a sizable and visible gay community, but also celebrities who are allowed to live in relative peace and quiet. Homeowners include Delta Burke and Gerald McRaney, Francis Ford Coppola, and Taylor Hackford. (Brandon Tartikoff's house is in Metairie.) Lindy Boggs, former United States congresswoman, has a lovely home in the Quarter on

Bourbon Street. There are also local artists and musicians, a slew of writers, and waiters, doctors, lawyers—probably even a few candlemakers.

Is New Orleans a city of aristocrats or low-lifes?... It's both. Uptown, the Garden District (including St. Charles Avenue), and parts of the lakefront area are all bastions of old-line, old-money Orleanians. It is those folks who turn up, for the most part, on the society pages of the *Times-Picayune* and who uphold the rituals of the city's most revered blow-out. During Mardi Gras, flags of various kings and queens of Carnival are displayed on palatial mansions along St. Charles Avenue, symbols of the "royalty" that reside within. It is these clubby, staid, and stolid business professionals who don sequins, plumes, capes, and masks in order to toss trinkets and bikinis from three-story-high floats lurching along Canal Street. The Quarter is a whole different story, a mixed bag of politicians, professionals, ordinary folk, and sundry street people who make the word "diversity" seem stilted. Skinheads hang out in Jackson Square and sleep on its park benches. Course, that's not all who lives in the Quarter (see above...).

Do they speak French in the French Quarter?... Sure, there are some fine French and French Creole restaurants, and the city as a whole prides itself on its French heritage. Truth to tell, though, you hear much more Italian than French. Thousands of Italians, mostly Sicilian, migrated to New Orleans in the late 19th century, and at the turn of the century the French Quarter was an Italian neighborhood. Stop in Angelo Brocato's on Jackson Square, an old-fashioned ice cream parlor that's been there for 85 years or so, or the Central Grocery Store on Decatur Street. You'll think you're in the heart of Rome. You'll hear a lot of Spanish around nowadays, too, but that's because New Orleans has such a huge Honduran population—some say larger than Honduras itself. Street signs in the Quarter come in three languages—English, French, and Spanish—which is a blessing, since outside of the downtown area it is almost impossible to find the names of streets. Look closely for small, rectangular white signs painted on telephone poles, with street names usually printed vertically.

What's meant by the "Mardi Gras mentality"?... This may or may not be pejorative, depending upon who's doing the talking. For example, an out-of-state hotel developer might fume, "We're running six months late and four gazillion dollars over budget, all because of that (expletive deleted) Mardi Gras mentality in this town!" On the other hand, it's the Mardi Gras mentality that created...well, Mardi Gras, and a general propensity to party long and hard.

Where can you meet locals during Mardi Gras?...
Try Perdido Bay, Alabama. Or head for the slopes in Colorado. So many Orleanians go skiing they've formed a Krewe of Vail and a Krewe of Aspen (a "krewe" being one of the social–cum–civic clubs that stage, and pay for, Carnival events). Anything to get away from the Mardi Gras mobs.

How do locals pronounce the name of the city?...
That's hard to say. Literally. For some reason, the town lately has been virtually papered with various promos, ads, and such in which the word "N'Awlins" appears. That's fairly close. There are roughly two and a half syllables, with the most emphasis on "aw" —pronounced aw-wuh. Mind, if you say Noo Or-*leens*, you may as well have a large, red letter *Y* branded on your forehead, you Yankee. But to further complicate things for outsiders, Orleans Street and Orleans Parish are both pronounced Or-*leens*. Not fair, is it? Incidentally, don't expect everyone in the Big Easy to have a stereotypical southern accent. And note that locals tend not to use the terms "Crescent City," "Big Easy," and certainly not "The City That Care Forgot," though you'll certainly hear the local media use (and overuse) those nicknames.

What the devil is voodoo, and how do you do it?... Do not be misled by film fantasies such as *Angel Heart*. Voodoo, as promoted by the Historic Voodoo Museum on Dumaine Street, is a prime tourist attraction, but you'd be hard-pressed to find true voodoo when you visit. It's estimated there may be some 20,000 believers in voodoo in the New Orleans area, the overwhelming majority of them African Americans, but the uninitiated are *never* privy to secret rites. The believers do consider voodoo a religion, and those who practice it take it very seriously. Originating centuries ago in the West African province of Dahomey (now the Republic of Benin), voodoo was transported to these shores by slaves in the late 18th and early 19th centuries. Following the slave uprisings in Saint-Domingue (now Haiti) at the turn of the 19th century, voodooists flooded into New Orleans and south Louisiana, its pulsating drumbeats, blood sacrifices, snakes, and frenetic dancing instilling terror in the hearts of whites. There are some shops that sell potions, oils, and the voodoo charms called *gris-gris* (pronounced gree-gree), which you can find in the Shopping chapter. But don't expect to see anything very authentic.

Where can you rent the gaudiest Mardi Gras costumes?... For New Orleanians, Carnival is a family event. They'll spend weeks, if not months, making costumes for all the kids and cousins, then get all dolled up and take picnics to the parade routes. So you won't exactly have to get in line at the rental shops. If you want to get properly (or improperly) prepared for Fat Tuesday, board the St. Charles Streetcar and in five minutes you'll arrive at **MGM Costume Rentals** (tel 504/581–3999, 1617 St. Charles Ave.), which has thousands of costumes from the old MGM studio in Hollywood. (This should be done as far in advance of Fat Tuesday as possible.) In the unlikely event you can't satisfy that suppressed desire there, you can search for your boas, beads, and Big Birds at **Patty's** (tel 504/837–3833, 2020 Veterans Blvd.) or at **Broadway Bound Costumes, Inc.** (tel 504/821–1000, 2737 Canal St.), which sell as well as rent costumes (see Shopping). If you're really creative—and here you will have stiff local competition—sign up for the Mardi Gras Mask-A-Thon. The annual locally televised contest takes place on Fat Tuesday morn, with various dancing raisins and walking crawfish sashaying across a stage on Canal Street. (If all you want is a bit of face paint, stop by the French Market, where several street artists set up shop.)

What's so jazzy about the Jazz Fest, and how do you get the most out of it?... First of all, put a sponge on your head—no kidding, soak a big, fat sponge in cold water and plop it on your head to keep you cool. Sun-shielding headgear is highly important at this annual music blowout, as is sunscreen. By the last weekend in April, when the fest kicks off, it's sizzling hot in the city, and the temperature is only going to climb during the 10-day bash. For local music lovers, and a large number of international visitors, Jazz Fest is the event of the entire year. During the two weekends, the main venue is the infield of the Fair Grounds, where tents and stages are set up and some seventy thousand fans per day swarm over the grounds, juking, jiving, and second-lining to the likes of the Neville Brothers, Ray Charles, Chuck Berry, Dr. John, Wynton and Branford Marsalis, Wilson Pickett, Gladys Knight, and a few thousand other top-name entertainers. Be in the gospel tent on the final Sunday night, when Aaron Neville traditionally chimes in with the Famous Zion Harmonizers in a soulful show that brings down the tent. Figuratively speaking. Officially called the New Orleans Jazz and Heritage Festival, the shebang features not only music but also crafts and, of course, food—this is, after all, New Orleans.

What is zydeco, and who cares?...

New Orleanians love Cajun music and its red-hot cousin, zydeco, which you may have been turned on to by the soundtracks of movies such as *The Big Easy* and *Passion Fish*. Black Creoles of French Louisiana developed zydeco; the late Clifton Chenier was an early proponent. The word derives from the French word for snap beans: say *les haricots* fast and it comes out, roughly, "zydeco." According to lore, some folks snapped beans on country back porches while other folks practiced the snappy music on their fiddles and *frottoirs* (washtubs).

Code Words

Where y'at? is the Ninth Warders' favorite greeting. It means "Hey, how're ya doin'?" If it can be said that there's an indigenous New Orleans accent, the natives of this sprawling working-class neighborhood speak it. The accent is a softer, slightly slurred version of Brooklynese—the "dese," "dat," and "dose" are the same, only less harsh. The Ninth Ward is "who dat" country, as in "Who dat say dey gonna beat dem Saints?" Ninth Warders tend to be rabid Saints fans, locally nicknamed Yats, derived from "Where y'at?"

Are there sharks in them thar swamps?...

Louisiana seems to breed, and often elect to high office, wheelers and dealers of all, shall we say, stripes. New Orleans, in particular, seems to have more than its share of shady characters. Perhaps it shouldn't be surprising, given that the town was founded by a crook—a French-Canadian fellow with the highfalutin moniker Pierre Le Moyne, Sieur d'Iberville. He physically staked out the colony, but he did so on orders of a wheeler-dealer named John Law, a Scotsman who fled England after killing a man and settled in France, where he gained the confidence of Philippe, Duc d'Orleans, regent to young Louis XV. Law was the protagonist of a plot that came to be called the Mississippi Bubble, a major land scam in which he exploited the Louisiana Territory and eventually threw France into bankruptcy. It was he who named New Orleans (after his friend Philippe), and he who persuaded scores of gullible Europeans to emigrate to a no-man's-land mired in swamps, tortured by hurricanes, and infested with alligators. Bienville and his hardy French Creoles deserve all the credit for pulling things together, and Law has been swept under the carpet. Don't look for any monuments dedicated to him.

Where are the hippest art galleries?... Royal Street is famous for its century-old antique shops and snazzy art galleries, but local aficionados haunt the contemporary galleries in the renovated warehouses of the Warehouse District. The Contemporary Arts Center on Camp Street is the mother of all such galleries, and the scene of the big blowout that concludes fall's Art for Art's Sake openings.

Which renowned music club is strictly for tourists?... The only locals who hang out at the world-famous Preservation Hall are musicians and friends of musicians. That's because the music preserved in the Hall is traditional jazz, while most locals are moved by New Orleans funk, R&B, and Cajun licks. (Although the traditional jazz legends are greatly revered; the death of a famed old-timer is front-page news, and jazz funerals see him off to his reward.) This is not to say the Hall should be avoided. It's a great, grungy place that draws a diverse crowd of tourists from around the globe. Legends of the traditional jazz genre play nightly, and nobody does it better. It's fun, too, to watch the rapt faces of international tourists. Be forewarned, though: Sets are only about 20 minutes long (though you can stay for more), there's virtually no seating, and the Hall gets *very* crowded.

What is The Split, and why should it be avoided?... Coming into the city from the west, I-610 splits off from I-10 and goes its merry way north of the French Quarter. There is actually no way to avoid this juncture and still get downtown, but the wise driver will steer clear of it during morning and afternoon rush hours. Traffic jams are nightmarish.

What's the best way to get around town?... The areas you'll probably spend most of your time in—the

Quarter, the CBD, and the Garden District—are all best seen on foot. To reach the Garden District from the Quarter and the CBD, where most visitors stay, take the St. Charles streetcar, which will also deliver you to Audubon Park and the zoo. You can roll up to the New Orleans Museum of Art in City Park on the Esplanade bus. Beyond these areas, New Orleans sprawls out all over the place, and even locals get confused about which way north, south, east, and west are. It's not safe to wander away from the well-known areas, especially not late at night—seedy neighborhoods border the Quarter, St. Charles Avenue, and the Garden District (though boarded-up Rampart Street on the lakeside fringe of the Quarter is now the site of Harrah's casino, opened in 1995, and the city has spent several million dollars beefing up police protection in its vicinity). When it gets late, do what carless Orleanians do: "Don't get excited, called United"— that's United Cab Company (tel 504/522–9771).

Where do you find the swells on Friday?... Without a doubt, Galatoire's is aburst with old-line Orleanians at noon every Friday. The stately bistro is smack on Bourbon Street, just a few steps from some of the Quarter's most outré niteries. But once inside you're on a different planet: a small, stylish room with mirrored walls, slowly whirling ceiling fans, white-clothed tables, and tuxedo-clad waiters, all very genteel. Established in 1905, Galatoire's is famed for seafood (crawfish étouffée is an off-the-menu special), chicken, steaks, and French Creole fare. Sunday afternoons are also popular here, but Fridays seem to bring out the very best in people, so to speak. You'll have to stand in line outside for a table. And incidentally, you'll not only be embarrassed if you turn up in jeans—you'll be turned away.

Where does Fats Domino live?... The R&B icon lives in the big pink and yellow house at 5525 Marais Street, on the corner of Marais and Caffin Avenue in the working-class Ninth Ward downriver of the French Quarter. It's his private home, and can be ogled only from the street.

How can you avoid all the tourists?... Stay holed up in a North Shore B&B. It's the only way.

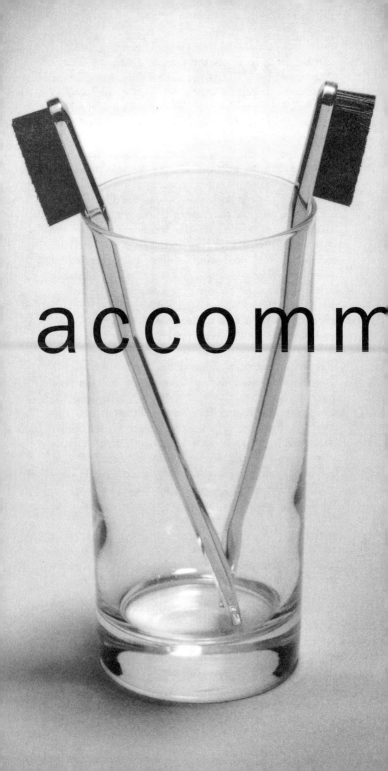

accomm

1

odations

The first thing to
know about
choosing a place
to stay down here
is that any hotel
or guest house
that didn't have

air-conditioning would fold in about 10 minutes. The second thing is that hotel rates are extremely whimsical—there's no high or low season, as there are in, say, the Caribbean. New Orleans's "high season," when rates can sometimes double, occurs anytime a lot of people are looking for a place to stay: for Mardi Gras, Jazz Fest, Sugar Bowl, or even a big convention. During such special events, many hotels require a three- to five-day minimum; some even want full payment up front. Once upon a time most hotels would practically *give* you a room during the long, hot summer, but that was before the Convention Center expanded and all those casinos opened. Summers are no cooler these days, but you can't even depend on hot weather anymore to keep the hordes away and hotel rates low. Many hotels don't even publish rack rates and won't give you a quote until you tell them the exact dates you're coming. And then they charge whatever the traffic will bear. A few years ago the City Council made a laughable attempt to control price gouging, but the ordinance was pretty much ignored. Most people have forgotten it ever even existed.

Whatever your bill, the bottom line will increase to the tune of 11%, courtesy of the city and state—plus another city tax of $1 to $3 per night, depending upon the size of the hotel (this from the same City Council that worries about price gouging). Now, about Mardi Gras. Thousands of people come to New Orleans for the big blowout—a term used advisedly— with the great hordes usually pouring in for the final weekend of Carnival. People tend to, shall we say, let their hair down during the windup, and behavior is often absolutely outrageous. Hotel staffs are used to battening down the hatches, and they do a heroic job just staying open in the face of the onslaught. Get a concierge or a desk clerk going, and he or she can tell you hundreds of stories. A few years ago, for example, in one of the upscale French Quarter hotels, one inmate—that is, guest—attempted to take a bidet home as a souvenir. He managed to get it unscrewed, and his ploy was discovered only when the ceiling downstairs began to flood. No one knows how he thought he could get the thing through the lobby and onto the plane. Just be aware that nothing runs quite smoothly during Mardi Gras.

Winning the Reservations Game
When you call to reserve, ask about package deals and corporate or any other special rates. For example, during December's month-long "Christmas in New Orleans"—né

"A Creole Christmas"—most hotels offer special Papa Noel rates, discounted by about 30%. Summertime rates have traditionally been low-low, but that was before the expansion of the Ernest N. Morial Convention Center and the influx of conventioneers. Almost all major hotels (but few guest houses) offer some sort of deal when business is on the slow side. Packages usually include, say, a two- to four-night deal with some meals thrown in, plus perhaps a breakfast at Brennan's, a carriage ride, a night on the town, or a sightseeing outing on a riverboat, at the aquarium, or the zoo. New Orleans's tour operators that package up Mardi Gras, Sugar Bowl, Superbowl, and Jazz Fest include: **Tours by Andrea** (tel 504/942–5708 or 800/535–2732, 2838 Touro St., New Orleans, LA 70122), **Travel New Orleans** (tel 504/561–8747, 434 Dauphine St., New Orleans, LA 70112), and **Evans Travel** (tel 504/581–6811, 615 Baronne St., New Orleans, LA 70112). If you can't find a room on your own, call **Room Finders** (tel 504/456–7077 or 800/473–7829; 4241 Veterans Blvd., Metairie, LA 70006). With their blocks of rooms, this outfit can usually find a place even when the hotels say they're full.

> **What's in a name?**
> *The pen names "Mark Twain" and "O. Henry" were both adopted in New Orleans when the two writers were working in the city as journalists. As a riverboat pilot, Samuel Clemens spent a lot of time in New Orleans. He first wrote under the name Mark Twain in 1857, in a piece he wrote for the New Orleans Crescent. And in 1896 William S. Porter lived here and wrote for the New Orleans Item. According to local lore, he was nursing a drink in a bar when someone summoned the bartender—"Oh, Henry"—and the name O. Henry was born.*

Is There a Right Neighborhood?

For many people, the **French Quarter** is the only place to stay. That's where most visitors spend their time anyway, exploring and overeating. There's lodging for almost every taste, from large luxury hotels awash with restaurants, bars, and music clubs, to little family-run guest houses with minimal services. The **Central Business District** (CBD) is adjacent to the French Quarter, on the west side of Canal Street and within an easy stroll of Quarter sights, eats, and music clubs. In addition to a whole slew of high-rise hotels, the CBD is home to the Superdome, the Convention Center, upscale shopping malls, and Spanish Plaza, where sightseeing riverboats dock and the big free Lundi Gras bash is held the night before Fat Tuesday. Most of the CBD hotels are boxlike modern high-rises, many of them are chains, and their cookie-cutter rooms tend to attract convention and tour- group business.

Staying anywhere else in town means some travel time. The **Garden District**, southwest of the CBD along a bend in the river, is only about five minutes by streetcar, however, and a lot less by cab. If you have business reasons or some dark hidden secret that compels you to stay in a hotel or motel in **east New Orleans**, where there is virtually nothing to do, or on the **West Bank**, where there are a couple of top restaurants (Mosca's and Kelsey's—see Dining chapter) and not much else, you'll be a 20- to 30-minute drive away from the French Quarter action. There are plenty of motels scattered all over town—in the Quarter, in the CBD, on the West Bank, near the airport—that are not much different from those anywhere else in the country. If you like an idyllic country setting—tall pine trees, rolling hills, ponds, and peace and quiet—there are some charming bed-and-breakfasts on the North Shore of Lake Pontchartrain, but you'll have to cross the 24-mile-long causeway to reach them. They're anywhere from 45 minutes to an hour from downtown and the French Quarter; however, they're handy to the Global Wildlife Center near Folsom and they're near La Provence and Sal and Judy's, two recommended eateries (see Dining). If you opt for Kenner, you'll be near the airport. Period.

The Lowdown

Haunted houses... New Orleans is alive with ghosts—it's that kind of town. There are any number of haunted houses, all with the requisite horror stories, and some of them are French Quarter guest houses. Housekeepers at the **Lafitte Guest House** think the ghost who, um, lives in room 40 was probably the lady of the house when it was built as a home in 1849. The parlor is Victorian right down to the fringed lampshades, and guest rooms are done up with testers, half-testers, and marbletop tables. At the **Olivier House Hotel**, several guests have been startled by the appearance in their rooms of a peripatetic pair—a woman in antebellum garb chatting it up with a Confederate soldier. The 42-room guest house, built in 1836 as a town house for the widow of a Creole planter, rambles around two courtyards and has a mix of antiques, reproductions, and contemporary furnishings. Don't expect biscuits at the **Biscuit Palace**; the name comes from the advertisement for Uneeda Biscuits painted in huge letters on the high gable. This, too, was an 1830s private residence, now offering modestly furnished apartments around a flowery courtyard; it has its original spiral staircase and, possibly, an original tenant—a pale, petite female apparition who the staff considers benevolent, albeit transparent.

Suite deals... Those who need more space than a mere room provides can strew their things about in one of the all-suites hotels. Top of the line in that category is the **Windsor Court**—*the* luxury hotel in the city, loaded with artworks, liveried staff, and enough flowers to stock a fair-sized florist shop. Most of its rooms are posh suites, done up with wet bars, phones in each room (including, of course, the oversized marble baths), canopied or four-poster beds, and cushy furnishings. In the mid-range, **Embassy Suites** is a zebra-striped balconied building that rises above the somewhat bleak cityscape of the Warehouse District, New Orleans's answer to New York's SoHo (at least as SoHo was a few years ago). The two-room suites offer creature comforts such as microwave ovens and coffee makers, and guests may partake of a full breakfast, included in the rate. And at the low end, **Comfort Suites** is a good buy for budget travelers. It's in a restored 1904 CBD office building whose lobby is minimalist, to say the most. Nothing at all fancy, but the price is excellent for the CBD and they do have a spa and sauna.

Take me to the river... The romantic appeal of the Mississippi has not been lost on local hotel developers. In the CBD, a brace of high-rise hotels boast spectacular views of Old Man River. Top honors go to the **Westin**, whose large Carrara marble lobby on the 11th floor of the Canal Place mall has two-story arched windows that frame the great bend in the Mississippi and the rooftops of the Quarter. Every guest room has a view either of the river or the Quarter; go for the spectacular river vistas over the Quarter ones, which are marred by the sprawling parking lot. Glass elevators purr upward above the mall's splashing fountain. Rooms in the **New Orleans Hilton**

Riverside's riverside also offer unobstructed Mississippi views. Above the 10th floor, riverside rooms of the **Windsor Court**, **Le Meridien**, the **Doubletree**, the **Marriott**, and the **Sheraton** also offer great Mississippi panoramas. The 200 or so shops and restaurants in the Riverwalk mall are a spitting distance, so to speak, from all of these hotels.

Pools with a view... New Orleans's hot and humid weather is nothing if not conducive to poolside lounging. In the CBD, both the **Westin** and **Le Meridien** have 30th-floor rooftop outdoor pools with panoramic views of the river and the city. The 16-story **Monteleone**, the tallest building in the Quarter, has a pool on its roof, too; from it you can see the river 3 blocks away, the CBD 2 blocks away, and the Quarter, which sprawls down below. The **Omni Royal Orleans**, known to locals as the Royal O., smack in the middle of the French Quarter, has the rooftop La Riviera Club, with pool and snack bar; though it's only six stories high, it allows a closer-up view of the Quarter's shingles and dormers.

Casino royale... For those who want to be near the action, there are some respectable lodging choices: Smack across Rampart Street from the casino, the **Maison Dupuy** occupies renovated 19th-century townhouses, with rooms built around one of the city's prettiest courtyards. There's also the **French Quarter Courtyard**, a 33-room guest house on Rampart Street, which was built in the 19th century as a private mansion but has been many things in its century-plus career; in the 1980s it was a popular gay bar. For access to riverboat casinos, the **New Orleans Hilton Riverside** has a prime location: the *Flamingo*, a four-deck gambling boat on the Mississippi, docks almost at its door, with a second-floor gangway connecting them.

Superdome domains... The **Hyatt Regency** zooms and sprawls over a considerable portion of the Superdome area in the CBD: It isn't possible to sleep any closer to the Superdome unless you pitch a tent in front of it. Built around the chain's signature atrium, in this case lit by sky-high, steel-frame windows, the Hyatt is a part of the Poydras Plaza and New Orleans Center complex, with a glass-enclosed walkway connecting the hotel and the sports arena. Less pricey, and less luxurious, digs are in the **Holiday Inn Downtown Superdome**, an aptly named motel with Holiday Inn–type rooms. There is only the one lone restaurant, but the parking is on-site, as in the Hyatt. Gracious **Le Pavillon**—a very good CBD buy—is also close to the Superdome.

Luscious love nests... You need wheels and a certain amount of flexibility if you opt for the **House on Bayou Road**, but this is one of the city's best B&Bs. You'll only be about a 10-minute cab ride from the Quarter, but don't expect to stroll out the front door and be in the middle of anything except a nondescript residential neighborhood. A 19th-century house on an historic portage road, it has only three guest rooms plus a private cottage, and you'll swear you're waking up somewhere in the peaceful French countryside. Even farther afield, **Woods Hole Inn** on the north shore of Lake Pontchartrain is hidden amid tall trees and lush foliage, so private it has its own driveway. It's a single cottage, discreetly far from the proprietors' house; you could lay in a supply of food and hole up for days on end. Not far from there, **Riverside Hills Farm**, on the 14 acres of an erstwhile turkey farm, is a similar retreat lazing on the banks of the Tchefuncte River; it's a three-bedroom cottage with rustic decor in a wooded setting laced with nature trails. If fresh country air and crickets make you crazy, opt for a suite or private cottages at **Lanaux House**, an Italianate mansion across the street from the French Quarter. Gleaming chandeliers, huge carved-wood beds and other antiques, plus a pretty plant-filled private courtyard dispel the notion that you're staying in a hotel; for those who don't want to leave their love nest, kitchenettes are stocked with croissants, cold cereals, juices, and the makings for coffee and tea.

If you think bigger is better... New Orleans assiduously courts the convention trade, and offers big hotels to service it—we're talking *big*, with more than a thousand guest rooms each. The **New Orleans Hilton Riverside**, one of the Gulf South's biggest hotels, is absolutely loaded with restaurants, cafes, bars, lounges, nightclubs, even a floating casino bobbing on the river right at the side door. There's a quarter-mile jogging track on the roof, as well as tennis courts, a golf clinic, and a health club. Only somewhat smaller are the **New Orleans Marriott** and the **ITT Sheraton**, which face each other across Canal Street. Both offer the whole laundry list of amenities—pool, health club, restaurants, lounges, and big lobbies. Despite its size, the Sheraton manages a somewhat warmer, cozier ambience than the Marriott, and the service is unbeatable. Not nearly as big as these modern chain hotels, but still big and splashy in a 19th-century way, is the **Chateau Sonesta**, which opened in 1995 as sister to the Quarter's Royal Sonesta; its handsome building was once the D. H. Holmes department store, one of the Gulf South's finest.

Dignified grande dames... The **Monteleone** has been the top French Quarter hotel almost since it opened in 1886, and the old girl continues to maintain her charms. Blimp-sized chandeliers hang from a sky-high ceiling and shine over a large, bustling lobby where liveried staff roll carts piled high with tour groups' luggage. The Carousel Bar—one of several bars and restaurants just off the lobby—is done up like an old-fashioned merry-go-round (though there are bar chairs instead of horses), and slo-o-wly revolves while you imbibe. Descendants of Antonio Monteleone, the Sicilian cobbler who founded it, still own and operate the hotel. Her CBD counterpart is the **Fairmont**, a grand old hotel, circa 1893, which many locals still call the Roosevelt. Fairmont rooms are oversized, beds have four down pillows apiece, and bathrooms have tub clotheslines, electric shoe polishers, and—a wicked twist for this hard-eating town—bathroom scales. The Fairmont's Sazerac restaurant (see Dining) serves the kind of rich food a classic hotel dining room ought to serve. The Garden District entry is the estimable **Pontchartrain**, a comparative youngster—it opened in 1927 as a posh residential hotel—notable for its celebrity-named suites. A high-vaulted ceiling soars over the Pontchartrain's smallish marbled lobby, with its Oriental carpeting and potted palms. The Caribbean Room (see Dining), one of the city's finest eating establishments, is just off the lobby, all rose and green and dolled up with murals of Caribbean scenes.

For gourmets who hate hotel restaurants... Your average picky gourmet generally turns a nose up at hotel dining rooms, but every kitchen in New Orleans is up against stiff competition. Locals rub shoulders with the tourists and visiting swells in the **Windsor Court**'s Grill Room and the **Pelham**'s Graham's. The **Hotel de la Poste**, basically an upmarket motel with cookie-cutter rooms, offers room service from Bacco (see Dining), Ralph and Cindy Brennan's sophisticated Italian restaurant. Rooms in the **Saint Louis Hotel**, built in the 1960s, fail to deliver on the promise of beauty held out by the glorious courtyard—a standout in a city designed around banana trees and magnolias. But its Louis XVI is a fine French restaurant, and breakfast is served out there around the glamorous stone fountain. The **Lafayette Hotel**, a French-country-style boutique hotel with a surprising amount of charm for the CBD, offers Mike's on the Avenue, one of the city's standouts.

Inn the mood... The limo dispatched by the **Melrose Mansion** to meet you at the airport delivers you to a big white Victorian Gothic, with veranda, leaded-glass door, turrets, and the works—even a library tucked away in a turret and an exercise room in what was once the attic. The breakfast portion of this B&B is more than croissants and coffee, an ever-changing selection from eggs Benedict to crepes and quiches, and the cocktail hour brings a stunning array of edibles and potables to be enjoyed around the pool. There's no restaurant, but all of those French Quarter restaurants are just a few blocks away. Not far from the Melrose, and actually within the Quarter, the **Soniat House** is a complex of 19th-century town houses, furnished now with Louisiana and European antiques. A small hotel in a noisy French Quarter block (just off Bourbon Street and across from three after-hours clubs), the **Hotel Maison de Ville & Audubon Cottages** strives for the ambience of a French-country inn, and would succeed were it not for those noisy nearby clubs. The main house, with its attached restored slave quarters, is where the noise is, on Toulouse Street; quieter digs are in the very elegant Audubon Cottages, 2 blocks away on Dauphine Street.

Homes away from home... A big Italianate mansion, replete with white columns, is home to the **Josephine Guest House**. Elaborate European antiques—called by owners Dan and Mary Ann Fuselier "Creole Baroque"—include a really awesome bed, black as night and inlaid with bone and ivory. And your fresh breads for breakfast, homemade by Mary Ann, come to you on Wedgwood china. At the **House on Bayou Road**, which sits on two acres of lawns and gardens, you have the option of staying in one of the antiques-filled rooms in the big West Indian–style house or you can take a cottage. If you've always wanted to stay in a glamorous Queen Anne mansion, head for the **Sully Mansion** in the Garden District. It's one of the few houses in that posh residential district that visitors can actually enter. The house, with its turret, veranda, and gingerbread froufrou, is tucked away behind an iron picket fence and shaded by big trees. Designed and built in the 1890s by 19th-century New Orleans architect Thomas Sully, it has 12-foot cove ceilings, original stained glass, and a grand piano in the foyer. Continental breakfast, included in the rate, is served informally in a formal dining room. In the French Quarter, directly across the street from the Croissant d'Or patisserie, the **Hotel Villa Convento** is a modest place operated by the friendly Campo family, who readily confess that the furnishings are reproductions. It was built in 1832 for a Spaniard named Fernandez, and local carriage drivers perpetuate the myth that this was the fabled House of the Rising Sun (the Campos haven't a clue how that rumor got started), famous in local legend as the house to which young men in the olden days were supposedly taken by their fathers to, um, become men.

Taking care of business... Business is business, and the main business of the CBD hotels is convention and business travelers. It's a highly competitive trade, with the **Hyatt Regency**, the **Inter-Continental**, the **Westin**—in fact, all of the chain high-rises—vying to see which can install more modems. In any suite of the **Windsor Court**, you're never more than a few inches from a phone or a few feet from a two-line phone with computer hookups, and all of the suites in the **Fairmont** have their own fax machines. Business is no less dull in the French Quarter, with top honors going to the **Royal Sonesta**, the **Omni Royal Orleans**, and the **Monte-leone**. However, if you'd rather combine business with small-hotel charm, check out the **Soniat House**, which has 20th-century services in a 19th-century setting, including a 24-hour concierge to take care of nuisances like faxing and photocopying.

Gym dandies... The **Hilton Riverside**'s rooftop Rivercenter Racquet and Health Club has a masseur, whirlpool, and tanning bed to soothe you after workouts on the tennis, racquetball, squash, and basketball courts, laps in the pool, aerobicsand exercise, and jogging on the quarter-mile path. **ITT Sheraton**, **Hyatt Regency**, **Marriott**, and **Le Meridien** hotels all have the usual complement of facilities you'd expect from a large chain hotel. If you'd rather stay in a charming place in the Quarter, though, try the **Dauphine Orleans** for its small exercise room off a rear courtyard.

Low-tech and low-key... Any of the inns or guest houses mentioned above—**Olivier House**, **Hotel Villa Convento**, **Lafitte Guest House**, **Sully Mansion**, **Josephine Guest House**, **Parkview Guest House**—have the kind of low-tech charm that distinctly forbids Stairmasters and Nautilus machines. You will get plenty of exercise scaling the awesome stairs at the **Rue Royal Inn**, tucked amid the galleries and shops on Royal Street, but apart from that the ambience is definitely lazy and low-key. Rue Royal is an unassuming guest house that rambles around a leafy courtyard; rooms are large, if somewhat darkish, and one suite has a Jacuzzi.

Sleeping cheap... The **Marquette House**, one of the nation's biggest youth hostels, has the usual bunk beds associated with such places, but also several apartments and a few private rooms with bath. It's very popular, and reservations are essential. The **International Center YMCA** is better located—at Lee Circle, right on the St. Charles Streetcar line; if you book early enough you may be able to get a room overlooking St. Charles, an ideal vantage point from which to watch Mardi Gras parades. In the Lower Garden District, the **St. Charles Guest House** has long been known as an oasis for budgeteers and backpackers. Rooms are merely functional in decor, but there is a pool and a big sundeck, and your morning coffee, juice, and pastries come with the bargain. **The Hampton Inn** may be in a homely high-rise, but it will look very good, indeed, to budgeteers in search of a good buy in the CBD.

Most French Quarterly of hotels outside the French Quarter... Every hotel in town attempts to convince guests that it's actually in the Quarter, or at least "within minutes" of the main tourist attraction. But some hotels that claim to be within the Quarter actually are not, given that the Vieux Carré Commission technically has jurisdiction only over the section bordered by Iberville Street (not Canal Street), the river side of Rampart Street, the upriver border of Esplanade Avenue, and Decatur Street. Sure, the restrictions are rigid, but then the Vieux Carré Commission is not locally noted for flexibility. Given those parameters, the **French Quarter Courtyard**—which sits on the lake side of Rampart Street—gets the nod. Like many of the French Quarter guest houses, it's a big 19th-century abode (painted pink in this case), with the green shutters, the rear courtyard, the polished wood floors, the works. Also technically outside the Quarter, the Italianate **Lanaux House** has a front balcony overlooking the big leafy trees on Esplanade Avenue and another one in the rear, with an almost bucolic view of the courtyard.

Least French Quarterly of hotels outside the French Quarter... Every high-tech high-rise in town qualifies as un–French Quarterly, given that most Quarter hotels are small two- and three-story affairs. The CBD's posh Windsor Court rates much higher than those on the charm scale, but it's decidedly British rather than French in flavor, sporting a House of Windsor theme carried out with some $7 million in oil paintings, sculpture, and objets d'art. And remember, the French Quarter really is more Spanish than French, anyway....

Mom-and-pop properties... The Campo family, who operate the little **Hotel Villa Convento** guest house in the Quarter, know the city inside out, and cheerfully offer their advice on what's where and what's not. You can't really call **The St. Charles Guest House** a mom-and-pop, since owners Joanne and Dennis Hilton let their staff runs things day to day, but it is a simple unpretentious place, with serve-yourself breakfast (Styrofoam cups set out around a big coffeemaker with plates of pastries in a room overlooking the pool) and a copy of the owners' own "survival manual" provided for navigating the wilds of New Orleans.

The most for your money... A splendid little gem in the quiet residential section of the Quarter, **Le Richelieu** occupies five white row houses. The lobby is small, with black-and-white tile floors, a glistening chandelier, and a restaurant and lounge overlooking the pool and courtyard. Service is highly personal, rooms are individually decorated, and guests are provided with extras such as ironing boards, and amenity packets that include a miniature (though quite adequate) sewing kit—a nice surprise.

When you've got a plane to catch... Near the airport, the boxlike **Holiday Inn & Holidome** is built around an enclosed dome with a pool and a slew of activities—about all it lacks is a bowling alley and stock-car races. The rooms are pretty much what you'd expect in a Holiday Inn. The **New Orleans Airport Hilton & Conference Center**, a more attractive building of pink masonry, has a big luxurious lobby with tile floors, area rugs, and several discreetly placed conversation groupings, and the rooms have all the comforts of a Hilton anywhere.

The Index

$$$$$	Over $200
$$$$	$125–$200
$$$	$90–$125
$$	$50–$90
$	Under $50

Biscuit Palace. Just 2 blocks off Jackson Square, the some-what rustic apartments of the not-quite-aptly-named Biscuit Palace (a fading sign advertising Uneeda Biscuits is painted on the gable) overlook a flowery courtyard. It doesn't have a pool and doesn't need a restaurant because there are dozens of eateries nearby. You can stock your kitchen with breakfast croissants from nearby Croissant d'Or (see Dining).... *Tel 504/525–9949, fax 504/525–9949. 730 Dumaine St. 70116. 4 rms., 2 suites. $$$*

Chateau Sonesta. A large, upscale hotel, the Sonesta is technically in the CBD, but it faces Canal Street and has the French Quarter at its back door. Front rooms have big windows overlooking Canal Street. Rooms are not overly large, but they are designed in interesting configurations, with nooks and crannies, and have minibars and the usual amenities: hairdryers, toiletries, the works. There are courtyards inside and out.... *Tel 504/586–0800, 800/766–3782, fax 504/524–1770. 800 Iberville St. 70112. 244 rms., 11 suites. $$$$*

Comfort Suites. The little two-room suites in this converted CBD office building won't win any decorator awards, but they come with hairdryers, in-room safes, high-tech phones, minifridges, and microwaves. Continental breakfast is included in the rate, and there's even a sauna and spa.... *Tel 504/524–1140, 800/221–2222, fax 504/524–4444. 346 Baronne St. 70112. 102 suites. $$*

Dauphine Orleans. You get a lot for your money here—no restaurant, but continental breakfast (accompanied by the morning paper) is included in the rate, and all rooms have safes, minibars, and hairdryers. The most interesting rooms are those in the rear of the main building, with exposed brick-between-posts walls and Jacuzzi baths. There's a charge for parking, but it's on-site and secured, and you may get your car washed. A small exercise room is just off the rear courtyard.... *Tel 504/586–1800, 800/521–7111, fax 504/586–1409. 415 Dauphine St. 70112. 111 rms. $$*

Doubletree Hotel. If this luxury high-rise, which soars like a stone tree straight up out of the foot of Canal Street, were any closer to Harrah's Canal Street, casino guests could play blackjack without getting out of bed. Fresh flowers and chocolate-chip cookies grace the small marble lobby, along with crowds of chewing and chatting conventioneers. Blond woods and pastel colors make the French-country-style rooms seem larger than they actually are. There is a pool, coffee shop, restaurant, and coin-operated Laundromat; the shops of Riverwalk are a three-minute stroll away.... *Tel 504/581–1300, 800/528–0444, fax 504/522–4100. 300 Canal St. 70130. 363 rms., 5 suites. $$$$*

Embassy Suites. Mercifully, you don't have to look at this building when you're in your room. In the Warehouse District, close to contemporary art galleries, the Convention Center, Harrah's, and Riverwalk, this link in the Embassy chain is in a really hideous zebra-striped building—no offense to zebras. All rooms are two-room suites; a full breakfast is served in a plant-filled brick room with skylights. There's also a full-service restaurant and an outdoor pool.... *Tel 504/525–1993, 800/ 362–2779, fax 504/522–3044. 315 Julia St. 70130. 253 suites. $$$$*

Fairmont Hotel. A row of crystal chandeliers runs slap through the block-long lobby, shining on gilded pillars, marbled floors, and a motley crew of conventioneers, movie stars, and heads of state. Scenes from both *Blaze* and *The Pelican Brief* were shot in the Sazerac Bar, a hangout for movers and shakers; the adjoining Sazerac Restaurant (see Dining) is a room to swoon over, all dressed up in velvet and lace. Rooms are extra large, and suites are sufficient for entertaining a fair-sized dinner party.... *Tel 504/529–7111, 800/527–4727, fax 504/522–2303. 123 Baronne St. 70130. 660 rms., 72 suites. $$$$*

French Quarter Courtyard. On iffy Rampart Street, but only a block and a half from Harrah's Armstrong Park casino, this small guest house occupies a building with a colorful past. It was built as a private mansion in the mid-19th century— there are high ceilings and polished wood floors throughout; in the late 1980s it was a wildly popular gay bar. No restaurant, but there is a courtyard, as the name promises.... *Tel 504/522–7333, 800/290–4233, fax 504/522–3908. 1101 N. Rampart St. 70116. 33 rms. $$$*

Hampton Inn. One of the best buys for budgeteers the CBD has to offer, this is only 2 blocks from Bourbon Street, and a short walk from all the goings-on at the foot of Canal Street. There's also an interior walkway to the shops and fast-food restaurants in Place St. Charles, a high-rise office complex with a ground-floor mall. Rooms are extra large, and each has a hairdryer and amenity packet. Some suites have whirlpools, and there is even an exercise room. Valet parking, free local calls, and a continental breakfast (included in the rate) are other lures for budget-watchers....

Tel. 504/529–9990, 800/426–7866, fax 504/529–9996. 226 Carondelet St. 70130. 186 rms. $$$

Holiday Inn Downtown Superdome. True to its name, the Holiday Inn Downtown Superdome is downtown, in the CBD, and near the overgrown Superdome. The rooftop pool is heated, as are the indoor restaurant and lounge—and rooms, of course, which offer no surprises.... *Tel 504/581–1600, 800/535–7830, fax 504/586–0833. 330 Loyola Ave. 70112. 291 rms., 4 minisuites, 3 suites. $$$*

Holiday Inn & Holidome-New Orleans Airport. This is one of those big inns with an enclosed dome full of Ping-Pong tables, pool, sauna, exercise rooms, and all sorts of activities to keep the kids occupied. Free parking is another enticement.... *Tel. 504/467–5611, 800/465–4329, fax 504/469–4915. 2929 Williams Blvd., Kenner, 70062. 302 rms., 1 suite. $$$*

Hotel de la Poste. In a prime location, near Jackson Square and Canal Street, the de la Poste is hardly more than a glorified motel—the registration area is straight off a turnpike. However, the draperies and quilted spreads match, and there is a splendid courtyard with pool and umbrella tables for lazing. The main attraction is Ristorante Bacco (see Dining), a posh Italian place operated by the Brennan family.... *Tel 504/581–2300, 800/448–4927, fax 504/522–3208. 316 Chartres St. 70130. 87 rms., 13 suites. $$$*

Hotel Inter-Continental. The local rendition of this upmarket chain is in a rose-granite building in which escalators roll up to a second-floor lobby with fresh flowers, recessed lighting, and artworks by local contemporary artists. The surprisingly tasteful sculpture garden on the fifth floor is a pleasant place for reading and quietly contemplating your life. The hotel is geared toward business travelers, so there is a whole slew of high-tech gadgets, including teleconferencing. The Veranda (see Dining), reminiscent of a Southern plantation home, is a draw for locals as well as visitors.... *Tel 504/525–5566, 800/332–4246, fax 504/523–7310. 444 St. Charles Ave. 70130. 480 rms., 32 suites. $$$$*

Hotel Maison de Ville & Audubon Cottages. One of the city's best-known small hotels, the Maison de Ville has luxurious rooms and suites in the main hotel, as well as in the cottages 2 blocks away. Rooms are furnished with antiques, but those in the main house are really quite small for such a high price. Baths, though outfitted with brass fixtures and marble vanities, are just plain tiny. Rooms in the restored slave quarters are quaint, with antiques and rustic cypress beams, but all open onto the courtyard; to have any privacy, draw the drapes. Best bets—though hardly a cheap alternative—are the Audubon Cottages, little two-story affairs with terra-cotta floors, private patios, and kitchens. The pool is at the cottages, in a peaceful courtyard. Continental breakfast is included in the rate, and there is an excellent restaurant, the Bistro (see Dining).... *Tel 504/561–5858, 800/634–1600, fax 504/528–9939. 727 Toulouse St. 70130. 14 rms., 2 suites, 7 cottages. $$$$*

Hotel Villa Convento. In the lower Quarter, near the Old Ursuline Convent, this little family-run guest house isn't luxurious, and doesn't have a pool or a restaurant, but the Campo family makes it terrifically friendly. The three-story hotel, built as a town house in the 19th century, has pale green ironwork and front balconies overlooking Ursulines Street and the nearby Old Ursuline Convent. The average-sized rooms, which could do with some freshening up, are furnished with reproductions of 19th-century antiques. A continental breakfast, served in the shaded courtyard, is included in the rate. The Croissant d'Or patisserie is directly across the street, and the French Market is a block away.... *Tel 504/522–1793, fax 504/524–1902. 616 Ursulines St. 70116. 25 rms. $*

House on Bayou Road. When Dan Aykroyd was in town opening the House of Blues, he stayed at this small outlying bed-and-breakfast. Peace, country quiet, rocking chairs, wind chimes, antique four-posters, and a gourmet breakfast give it its charm. The private cottage is splendid, with skylight, scads of books, and a Jacuzzi in which to relax and not give a hang that there's no pool or restaurant.... *Tel 504/945–0992 or 504/949–7711, 800/882–2968, fax 504/945–0993. 2275 Bayou Rd. 70119. 4 rms., 1 suite. D, DC not accepted. $$$$*

Hyatt Regency Hotel. Big, splashy, and over-stuffed with creature comforts, the Hyatt is in a complex of massive modern concrete that includes Poydras Plaza, New Orleans Center, and the Superdome, plus there's a shuttle to tool you over to the French Quarter and back. The extra perks—concierge services, private key–access elevator—are in the Regency Club. Otherwise, rooms and suites are scattered in various low- and high-rise sections. The Hyatt is home to the city's only revolving restaurant; Top of the Dome has a splendid view of the cityscape, and kids go hog-wild over the nightly Chocoholic Bar.... *Tel 504/561–1234, 800/233–1234, fax 504/587–4141. 500 Poydras Plaza. 70140. 1,184 rms., 100 suites. $$$$*

ITT Sheraton New Orleans. True, the lobby is usually crowded with conventioneers and tour groups, but the high-rise Sheraton somehow seems to rise above it all. A huge plate-glass window facing Canal Street allows plenty of light into the splashy lobby, where a handsome spiral staircase winds up to the mezzanine from a sunken lounge, and a deli turns out big thick sandwiches. Above-average rooms, plus excellent health club, a pool, restaurants, and lounges. It's in the CBD, directly across the street from the Marriott.... *Tel 504/525–2500, 800/325–3535, fax 504/561–0178. 500 Canal St. 70130. 1047 rms., 53 suites. $$$$*

Josephine Guest House. In the Garden District, a block from the streetcar line, the Josephine is an Italianate mansion, dating from 1870, and filled with handsome antiques. Continental breakfast is included in the rate. There is neither restaurant nor pool.... *Tel 504/524–6361, 800/779–6361, fax 504/523–6484. 1450 Josephine St. 70130. $$*

Lafayette Hotel. Like Le Meridien, the chic little Lafayette tries hard to perpetuate the myth that New Orleans is a French city. The switchboard operator answers with "Bonjour" and "Bon soir." Rooms and suites have high ceilings, lovely millwork, marble baths with brass fittings and bidets, and cushy easy chairs and chaises longues, as well as bookshelves filled with books. It's in the CBD, roughly midway between Lee Circle and Canal Street; the ground-floor restaurant, Mike's on the Avenue, is excellent (see Dining).... *Tel 504/524–4441, 800/733–4754, fax 504/523–7326. 600 St. Charles Ave. 70130. 24 rms., 20 suites. $$$$*

Lafitte Guest House. One of the most charming of the Quarter's guest houses, this Victorian-decor spot has no restaurant or pool, but continental breakfast and afternoon cocktails are included in the rate. It's on the quiet end of Bourbon Street.... *Tel 504/581–2678, 800/331–7971. 1003 Bourbon St. 70116. 14 rooms. $$$$*

Lanaux House. On the edge of the Quarter, in Faubourg Marigny, this Italianate mansion near the French Market offers complete privacy in elegant suites and cottages. No pool or restaurant, but continental breakfast fixings are provided, and you prepare it at your leisure.... *Tel 504/488–4640, 800/729–4640, fax 504/488–4639. 547 Esplanade Ave. 70116. Cash only. $$$$*

Le Meridien. This is a sleek, 30-story modern high-rise with a stunning atrium, a trickling waterfall in the lobby opposite the concierge desk, and a shopping arcade. Attuned to conventions, Le Meridien has both so-so rooms and sumptuous split-level suites, plus rooftop pool and tanning salon, restaurant, and lounge with nightly jazz.... *Tel 504/525–6500, 800/543–4300, fax 504/586–1543. 614 Canal St. 70130. 488 rms., 7 suites. $$$$*

Le Pavilion. Close to the Superdome and New Orleans Center shops, this upmarket property offers a lot for your money, including an open-air rooftop pool with cabanas and a restaurant with one of the city's best bargain-lunch buffets in the Gold Room (see Dining). Outside are awnings and a porte-cochère with massive Corinthian columns; inside, the European-style lobby is lovely, with oil paintings, lots of marble, and crystal chandeliers imported from Czechoslovakia. True, the rooms are identical, with traditional mahogany furnishings, though some have big bay windows, but the suites are sumptuous, all decked out in satins and velvet.... *Tel 504/581–3111, 800/535–9095, fax 504/522–5543. 833 Poydras St. 70140. 220 rms., 7 suites. $$$*

Le Richelieu. Without a doubt, this is the best buy in town. It's a small hotel in the lower Quarter, with rooms and suites all done up differently, and extra features such as walk-in closets, ceiling fans, and mirrored walls. The restaurant and bar are just off the courtyard and pool, and parking is on-site in a patrolled parking lot.... *Tel 504/529–2492, 800/535–9653, fax 504/524–8179. 1234 Chartres St. 70116. 60 rms., 17 suites. $$*

Maison Dupuy Hotel. If you want to be near Harrah's casino in Armstrong Park, you can't get closer than this. Rooms are not really anything to get all excited about, but the courtyard is spectacular, with an elaborate, oft-photographed fountain. There's a pool, a restaurant, and a lounge with evening entertainment.... *Tel 504/586–8000, 800/535–9177, fax 504/525–5334. 1001 Toulouse St. 70112. 185 rms., 13 suites. $$$$$*

Marquette House International Hostel. Strictly for budgeteers, this uptown youth hostel is one of the nation's largest. Lodging is in dormitory rooms or apartments and there's no restaurant, though there are two community kitchens, where you can stash your snacks, and picnic tables in a leafy patio where you can enjoy them. The price is rock-bottom.... *Tel 504/523–3014, fax 504/529–5933. 2253 Carondelet St. 70130. 160 dorm beds, 5 rms., 12 apartments. D, DC not accepted. $*

Melrose Mansion. The cost of an overnight stay matches the sky-high ceilings in this splendid Victorian Gothic house in Faubourg Marigny. The 19th-century antique furnishings wear brocade, velvet, and lace; hardwood floors are polished to a high sheen; and bedrooms have four-posters with delicate crocheted coverlets, wet bars, and private patios. Breakfast and afternoon cocktails and hors d'oeuvres are included in the rate, and there's a pool and exercise room. On the downside, you won't be right in the middle of things, and the neighborhood around here is iffy.... *Tel 504/944–2255, fax 504/945–1794. 937 Esplanade Ave. 70116. 4 rms., 4 suites. D, DC not accepted. $$$$$*

Monteleone Hotel. The Quarter's oldest and tallest hotel, the 16-story Monteleone wears her 100-plus years well, though she has had a number of facelifts. There are several restaurants and a rooftop pool and health club. Each of the rooms and suites is decorated differently, but all feature handsome antiques or reproductions and four-poster beds.... *Tel 504/523–3341, 800/535–9595, fax 504/528–1019. 214 Royal St. 70140. 600 rms., 35 suites. $$$*

New Orleans Airport Hilton & Conference Center. If you must stay across the street from the airport, you won't go wrong in this big luxury motel.... *Tel 504/469–5000, 800/*

445–8667, fax 504/465–1101. 901 Airline Hwy., Kenner, 70131. 312 rms., 2 suites. $$$

New Orleans Hilton Riverside. Near the convention center in the CBD, the Hilton is one of the biggest and splashiest of the convention-cum-tour-group hotels. The Flamingo casino docks at the side door, with its gangway via the second-floor lobby, and Pete Fountain's club is on the third floor. You can wear yourself completely out in the rooftop Rivercenter Racquet and Health Club, or you can just flop down and fatten up in the various restaurants, lounges, and bars.... *Tel 504/561–0500, 800/445–8667, fax 504/568–1721. 2 Poydras St. 70140. 1,602 rms., 89 suites. $$$$*

New Orleans Marriott. This is a major CBD convention hotel, but it's not to be confused with one of the Marriott's luxurious resorts. And you'll be shelling out a lot for a place that could as well be in Kansas City. But it comes with the works: pool, health club, lounges, coffee shop, and a lobby the size of a football field.... *Tel 504/581–1000, 800/228–9290, fax 504/581–5749. 555 Canal St. 70140. 1236 rms., 54 suites. $$$$*

Olivier House Hotel. This is a somewhat quirky family-run guest house that's well located in the Quarter, and whose loyal repeat guests eschew the big luxury hotels in favor of the very laid-back style. The general ambience might be termed Caribbean–cum–southern Italy. The assortment of rooms and suites includes a secluded cottage just off the courtyard and pool, and a rear courtyard that's been enclosed and transformed into a large two-story suite, with a skylight and a fountain. Others range from split-level suites and lofts to small darkish inside rooms with old-brick walls. Almost all have microwaves and some sort of kitchen facilities; there's no restaurant, but Antoine's is only a block and a half away.... *Tel 504/525–8456, fax 504/529–2006. 828 Toulouse St. 70112. 42 rms. $$$$*

Omni Royal Orleans. Smack in the center of the Quarter, the Royal O. is an upmarket hotel in which gilded statues guard marbled halls laid with Oriental rugs and hung with immense crystal chandeliers. Suites here are knee-weakening, with canopied beds only slightly smaller than your average Boy Scout tent, but regular rooms are on the smallish side, though still grandly decorated. The lobby's Esplanade lounge is fine for winding down after a hard night of jazz and zydeco, and the Rib Room (see Dining) is a favored place for power breakfasting and dining. There's a pool at the rooftop La Riviera Club.... *Tel 504/529–5333, 800/843–6664, fax 504/522–7016. 621 St. Louis St. 70140. 330 rms., 16 suites. $$$$$*

Parkview Guest House. Adjacent to Audubon Park, this is a rather funky guest house that nevertheless occupies a grand Victorian house that was built in 1884 for the city's first World's Fair. Some rooms have a lovely view of the park, others have antique furnishings. There's no restaurant and no pool.... *Tel 504/861–7564, fax 504/861–1225. 7004 St. Charles Ave. 70118. 23 rms. D, DC not accepted. $$*

Pelham Hotel. Located in the CBD, and a good choice for those who want to avoid the big convention hotels, the little Pelham has average-sized rooms (inside rooms have no windows), but each has the de rigueur hairdryer and amenity packets in a marble bath. Graham's, one of the city's trendy restaurants, is just off the cozy lobby (see Dining).... *Tel 504/522–4444, 800/659–5621, fax 504/539–9010. 444 Common St. 70130. 60 rms., 2 suites. $$$*

Pontchartrain Hotel. This venerable Garden District hotel is too sedate for newfangled frills like a pool and health club, but it does have one of the city's top-notch (and pricey) restaurants, the Caribbean Room (see Dining). The friendly staff is accustomed to catering to the whims of celebrity guests, and elegant suites are named for stellar personages who have occupied them (Anne Rice, Richard Burton, and Tennessee Williams, among them). But no one fails to turn down your bed if you opt for the less luxurious and far-less-expensive pension rooms in the rear, which have shower baths and nary a grand piano or solarium.... *Tel 504/524–0581, 800/777–6193, fax 504/529–1165. 2031 St. Charles Ave. 70140. 67 rms., 35 suites. $$$$*

Riverside Hills Farm. In an idyllic wooded setting laced with nature trails, the three-bedroom guest cottage (only rented to people traveling together) has warm wood paneling, hardwood floors, colorful patchwork quilts, lots of books, and rocking chairs and a swing on the porch overlooking the

Tchefuncte River. Croissants, muffins, and juice arrive quietly; creature comforts in the big Early American kitchen include a dishwasher and coffeemaker.... *Tel 504/892–1794, fax 504/626–5849. 96 Gardenia Dr., Covington, 70433. 1 cottage. Cash only. $*

Royal Sonesta Hotel. The front doors open onto Bourbon Street, but the Sonesta staff works hard to preserve a sense of peace and serenity. Rooms are average-sized; avoid those with balconies on the front and sides. Those with balconies on the courtyard overlook the pool and orange trees. There are ground-floor shops purveying luxury items, a well-equipped business center, and sundry bars, lounges, and an overpriced restaurant.... *Tel 504/586–0300, 800/766–3782, fax 504/586–0335. 300 Bourbon St. 70140. 465 rms., 35 suites. $$$$*

Rue Royal Inn. Built sometime in the 1830s as a town house, this little guest house is easy to bypass, so unobtrusive is its entry. There is a tiny registration area, usually with cats lounging here and there. Wooden balconies ramble around a central courtyard. Rooms are largish—and also somewhat darkish—and there are sundry four-posters and big sturdy armoires. The biggest room has a Jacuzzi. No restaurant, but a complimentary continental breakfast is offered on Sunday (go figure).... *Tel 504/524–3900, 800/776–3901, fax 504/947–7454. 1006 Royal St. 70116. 17 rms., $$$*

St. Charles Guest House. A lovely entranceway with a small crystal chandelier and attractive wallpaper ushers you into Joanne and Dennis Hilton's unpretentious guest house in the lower Garden District. It ambles all over the place, with simple, functional rooms—some even without air-conditioning (a major negative in summer). A low-key buffet breakfast is served.... *Tel 504/523–6556. 1748 Prytania St. 70130. 36 rms. D, DC not accepted. $*

Saint Louis Hotel. The location is excellent—in the Quarter, and 2 blocks from the CBD—but the 1960s hotel hasn't much in the way of character. Its main attractions are the stunning courtyard and the fine French restaurant, Louis XVI (see Dining).... *Tel 504/581–7300, 800/535–9706, fax 504/524–8925. 730 Bienville St. 70130. 71 rms., 4 suites. $$$$*

Soniat House & Maisonettes. In the quiet lower Quarter, this fine small hotel occupies two adjoining early 19th-century town houses with a flower-filled courtyard. Across the street are seven Jacuzzi suites, and on nearby Esplanade Avenue, Girod House has another six apartments. All are expensively dressed in antiques, Oriental rugs, and framed contemporary prints. There's no pool or restaurant, but there is a 24-hour concierge; continental breakfast (not included in the rate) is café au lait and plump biscuits with homemade strawberry jam.... *Tel 504/522–0570, 800/544–8808, fax 504/522–7208. 1133 Chartres St. 70116. 18 rms., 13 suites. $$$$$*

Sully Mansion. In the Garden District, a block from the St. Charles streetcar, this bed-and-breakfast is in a handsome Queen Anne mansion. The house dates from the 1890s, and has the original stained-glass windows. The whimsical assortment of rooms ranges from large suites with four-posters to a tiny room you can hardly turn around in. The staff is friendly and helpful.... *Tel 504/891–0457, fax 504/891–0457. 2631 Prytania St. 70130. 5 rms., 2 suites. $$$$*

Westin Canal Place. The large and luxurious Westin soars to 30 floors above the tony Canal Place mall, with an 11th-floor lobby, where arched 26-foot-high windows frame the river and the French Quarter. Each room and suite has a marble foyer, pristine white millwork, and soothing-on-the-eyes shades of peach, rose, or green. There's a rooftop pool; a good restaurant, Le Jardin (see Dining); and some 40 or so shops beneath your feet.... *Tel 504/566–7006, 800/228–3000, fax 505/553–5120. 100 Iberville St. 70130. 397 rms., 38 suites. $$$$*

Windsor Court. The city's best luxury hotel has something in the neighborhood of $7 million worth of British artworks and antiques displayed in public rooms throughout; the theme, as the name suggests, is the "House of Windsor." Most rooms are suites done up with four-poster beds. Dipping is done in an Olympic-size pool, and a health club has plenty of machines for working off all the weight you'll put on in the Grill Room (see Dining). The swells do deals over champagne and scones in Le Salon, where afternoon tea is served each day.... *Tel 504/523–6000, 800/262–2662, fax 504/596–4513. 300 Gravier St. 70130. 58 rms., 266 suites. $$$$$*

Woods Hole Inn. On the north shore of Lake Pontchartrain, this private cottage has a big wood-burning fireplace, hardwood floors, colorful patchwork quilts decorating wood-paneled walls, and a handsome four-poster bed. The bathroom has both a clawfoot tub and a separate glass-paneled shower, plus a small TV set—there's a full-sized one in the living room. The fridge is filled with everything you need for a continental breakfast. The home of proprietors Mike and Bea Connick is a discreet distance from the cottage; they're the uncle and aunt of Harry Connick, Jr.... *Tel 504/796–9077. 78253 Woods Hole Lane, Folsom 70437. 1 cottage. Cash only. $*

YMCA International Hotel. If you're on a budget, and you don't mind gang showers, you'll find clean rooms and a good CBD location, right at Lee Circle. That particular spot happens to be a ringside seat for Mardi Gras parades, but be sure you get a room overlooking either St. Charles Avenue or Lee Circle, otherwise you may as well stay in Dubuque. The health club and pool are good enough to entice locals for working out and lapping.... *Tel 504/568–9622, fax 504/568–9622, ext. 268. 920 St. Charles Ave. 70130. 50 rms. AE, D, DC not accepted. Personal checks accepted. $*

NEW ORLEANS | ACCOMMODATIONS

New Orleans Accommodations

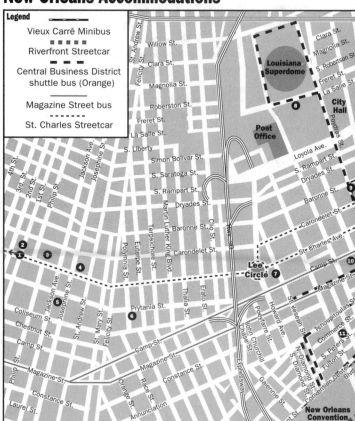

Legend

Vieux Carré Minibus

Riverfront Streetcar

Central Business District shuttle bus (Orange)

Magazine Street bus

St. Charles Streetcar

Biscuit Palace **37**	Hotel Inter-Continental **17**
Chateau Sonesta **23**	Hotel Maison de Ville **29A**
Comfort Suites **14**	Hotel Villa Convento **39**
Dauphine Orleans Hotel **27**	Hyatt Regency Hotel **8**
Doubletree Hotel **20**	ITT Sheraton **18**
Embassy Suites **11**	Josephine Guest House **5**
Fairmont Hotel **13**	Lafayette Hotel **10**
French Quarter Courtyard **41**	Lafitte Guest House **36A**
Hampton Inn **38**	Lanaux House **41**
Holiday Inn Downtown–Superdome **12**	Le Meridien Hotel **16**
Hotel de la Poste **33A**	Le Pavillon Hotel **9**

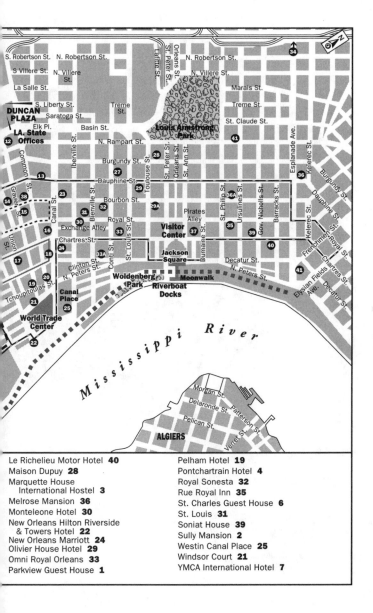

S. Robertson St.   N. Robertson St.

S Villere St.   N. Villere St.

La Salle St.

S. Liberty St.

DUNCAN PLAZA   Saratoga St.

Elk Pl.

LA. State Offices   Basin St.

N. Rampart St.

Burgundy St.

Dauphine St.

Bourbon St.

Royal St.

Exchange Alley

Chartres St.

Clinton St.

N. Peters St.

Woldenberg Park

Canal Place

World Trade Center

Tchoupitoulas St.

Mississippi River

N. Robertson St.

Marals St.

Treme St.

St. Claude St.

Louis Armstrong Park

Treme St.

Lafitte St.

Orleans St.

St. Peter St.

N. Villere St.

Esplanade Ave.

Kerlerec St.

Burgundy St.

Dauphine St.

Royal St.

Chartres St.

Kerlerec St.

Frenchmen St.

Elysian Fields Ave.

Decatur St.

St. Peter St.

Toulouse St.

Orleans St.

St. Ann St.

Pirates Alley

Visitor Center

Jackson Square

St. Philip St.

Ursulines St.

Gov. Nicholls St.

Barracks St.

Dumaine St.

Decatur St.

N. Peters St.

Meonwalk

Riverboat Docks

Morgan St.

Delaronde St.

Pelican St.

Patterson St.

Verret St.

ALGIERS

Common St.

Gravier St.

Union St.

Conti St.

St. Louis St.

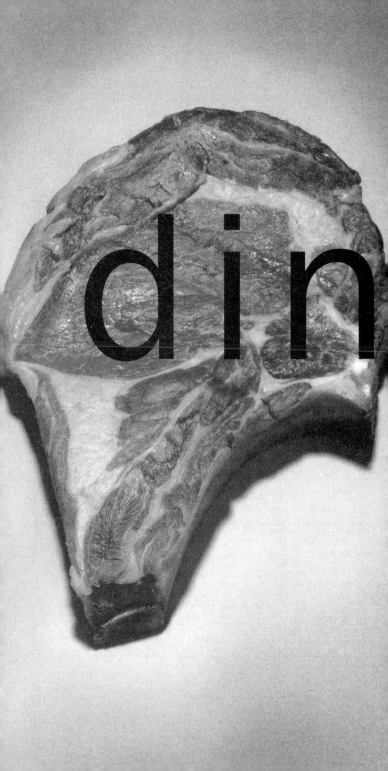

ing

2

Pity the poor soul
who comes to this
city for a week-
end, especially if
it's a first visit. It's
not uncommon
for people to

make themselves sick on a quickie first visit to New Orleans. There are just so many really good restaurants, and the temptation to try as many as possible is almost overwhelming. Fifteen or so years ago there were 10, maybe 15 top contenders, but these days hot new chefs are popping up like dandelions after a spring rain, and the options are almost endless. Rest assured that every restaurant we list serves up great meals—the main variations are location, style of cooking, atmosphere, and price. So, what are you going to do? Well, at least try to pace yourself. If you come waddling out of Galatoire's in mid-afternoon—and of course you will—don't plan to do dinner at Antoine's that night. There's no need to go crazy, as if you're never going to eat another good meal again. Most of the better restaurants will most likely still be here for your next visit—and there will be a next. New Orleans has that kind of effect on you.

No one has ever done a study on why Orleanians are so fixated on food, but they are. Not just eating it, but analyzing it, arguing about it, and especially pontificating about it. And complaining about it. Everybody's a critic here, and whining about the food seems to be a part of the Orleanian psyche, like grousing about politics and the casinos. (Makes you wonder how they'd react if they were ever actually faced with bad food.) Truth to tell, these people are very well satisfied; they love New Orleans's food and New Orleans's restaurants. It wouldn't be wise to chime in and agree with them about the "inedible" food they're carping about.

The opening of a new restaurant gets Orleanians all a-quiver, similar to the way some folks get in anticipation of a new play on Broadway. While openings are rather frequent, closings are rare. New Orleanians eat out a lot, and are far more supportive of eating places than they are, say, of the ballet or the opera. The dining-out mood is usually festive. Again, it's similar to theatergoing in New York, and some spots are almost as splashy and bright as a Broadway musical (well, almost).

The greatest concentration of restaurants lies in the **French Quarter**, where there is at least some kind of food available on virtually every block, even if it's just one of the **Lucky Dog** carts. (The Lucky Dog is a New Orleans fixture, immortalized in John Kennedy Toole's riotous novel *A Confederacy of Dunces*.) Aproned and white-capped Lucky Dog vendors push around enormous fire-engine-red cylinders, shaped like hot dogs and loaded with all the makings for the dogs themselves. The servings here are only slightly smaller than the carts. The **CBD** is likewise bursting with everything from smart hotel dining rooms to skid-row dives. Seafood, of course, is ubiquitous in this port city in the swamps; practically every place serves some manifestation thereof, but the really hard-core fish eaters' havens are out in the **West End** and **Bucktown**, where there are scads of family restaurants and seafood shacks.

Local tastes are wide-ranging. Fancy French Creole restaurants are adored, but the same New Orleanians who eat there also swarm out to ramshackle roadhouses around Lake Pontchartrain, where newspapers are spread on the tables to sop up the juices from boiled crawfish and barbecue shrimp. We're food lovers down here, not food snobs.

Only in New Orleans

First of all, don't get a headache trying to figure out the difference between **Creole** cuisine and **Cajun** cooking. Leave it to locals to sweat the nuances (something they love to do). Suffice it to say that both have French roots, but Creole cuisine evolved in the city kitchens of New Orleans and Cajun cooking developed in the parishes (counties) of Acadian country to the west. There are no pure Cajun restaurants in New Orleans, even though there are several Cajun chefs. Most genuine properly prepared Cajun foods are too time-consum-

Cajun Country

Contrary to what many people seem to think, New Orleans is not a Cajun city. It was French Creoles who colonized New Orleans—the Cajuns were another group of French-speaking folk who migrated down here about 40 years later. They came from Canada and settled in 22 parishes (the Louisiana term for counties) to the west of the New Orleans colony, in an area now known as Cajun Country, or Acadiana, or French Louisiana. These French Catholics were descendants of a group of settlers from northwest France who, in 1603, had colonized a section of present-day Nova Scotia, which they called l'Acadie—or, Acadia. These Acadians were kicked out in the mid-18th century when the English conquered that territory and demanded that the French settlers relinquish their religion and pledge allegiance to the British crown. The Longfellow poem "Evangeline" (a classic that nobody reads anymore) is about this exodus, known as Le Grand Derangement. In 1763, three thousand Acadians were welcomed in Louisiana, then under the rule of Spaniards sympathetic to the Catholics' dilemma. "Acadian" became corrupted into "Cajun."

NEW ORLEANS | DINING

ing for restaurant kitchens—and besides, all that bacon fat, lard, and butter that the authentic dishes call for have, shall we say, fallen out of favor. Paul Prudhomme almost single-handedly kicked off the nationwide Cajun craze of the 1980s, but although he himself is a card-carrying Cajun, the food he serves is an elaborate embellishment of the real thing. "Blackening"—as in blackened redfish—is a Prud-homme invention, not a traditional Cajun preparation. Cajun chefs owe a lot to Chef Paul, however, since he popularized all things Cajun and thus attracted customers to Cajun restaurants. Nowadays people expect—and usually get—at least a few blackened things in any Cajun restaurant. Several local chefs also prepare what they call "South Louisiana cooking," which combines elements of Cajun with Creole and other traditions.

Muffulettas and **po-boys** are the city's two big sandwich happenings. ("Big" may be a bit of an understatement.) The muffuletta comes on a large sesame-seed bun, stuffed with Italian meats and cheese and some very flavorful salad olive salad. You can order quarter, half, and whole sandwiches, and you'd best be hungry if you opt for the last. The Central Grocery Store claims to have invented the muffuletta, and still serves one of the city's best. Po-boys—similar to subs or heroes, only better—are made on whole loaves of French bread, and they come in more varieties than Shirley Mac-Laine could consume in all of her incarnations. Try Johnny's Po-Boys for a mind-boggling variety of these. Locals especially relish fried oyster loaf, roast beef and gravy, and spaghetti and meatballs—these are sandwiches, mind—and the messier they are, the better. When ordering a po-boy, you'll be asked if you want the sandwich "dressed." In these parts, that means with mayonnaise, lettuce, and tomato. Traditionally served on Mondays (after a weekend of gorging on rich, rich foods), **red beans and rice** turn up all over the place, and not just on Monday. Red kidney beans are slow-simmered all day down to a thick, creamy sauce and seasoned with sausage, often andouille.

Pralines are far more prevalent in New Orleans than black-eyed peas—proof, if proof were needed, that New Orleans is not really a southern city. Pralines are sweet candies made of butter, pecans, and sugar, and they, too, come in many different manifestations. (To buy a box, the best spot is the **Old Town Praline Shop** at 627 Royal Street—see Shopping.)

Indigenous Ingredients and Such

Everybody's doing arugula, shiitake, and cilantro—New Orleans chefs see those ingredients and up the ante. Here are some local terms that may not be so familiar:

Andouille: Cajun pork sausage, kin to kielbasa. Emeril Lagasse, of Emeril's and Nola, makes a pretty mean andouille.

Bananas Foster: A rich dessert made of sliced bananas sautéed in butter with brown sugar, cinnamon, and banana liqueur, then flamed with white rum and served over vanilla ice cream. Invented at Brennan's, but possibly even better at Arnaud's.

Barbecue shrimp: Do not be fooled. This is barbecue in name only. It's really peel 'n' eat boiled shrimp in a garlicky sauce.

Beignets: Best known as the sugary crullerlike pastries served at Café du Monde, but appetizers of fried seafood are sometimes also called beignets.

Boudin: Cajun smoked pork sausage.

Bouillabaisse: A stew made of spicy broth and seafood.

Café au lait: Half strong, hot chicory coffee and half hot milk. Get the best at Café du Monde.

Crawfish: Affectionately called mudbugs (they live in the mud of freshwater streams), these tiny crustaceans are known to Yankees as crawdads. Or, worse, crayfish.

Debris: Sounds awful, but it's biscuits soaked in gravy and bits of roast beef, or whatever was cooked.

Étouffée: A spicy, long-simmered stew of shrimp or crawfish, served over rice. French for "smothered." Galatoire's serves a crawfish étouffée that's a classic.

Filé: Ground sassafras leaves used for seasoning.

Gumbo: A thick soup, always made with rice, plus seafood, chicken, sausage, filé. Many variations. The Gumbo Shop is a prime place to sample this.

Jambalaya: Not quite paella, but in that family. Typical Cajun dish, using simple ingredients (yellow rice, tomatoes, bits of shrimp, ham, andouille, and onions) to create (sometimes) a masterpiece.

Mirliton: A squashlike vegetable pear. Yankees call it a chayote; in the Caribbean it's a christophene.

Pain perdu: Literally "lost bread," and what Anglos know as French toast. Here, it's usually made with French bread.

Plantain: Kissing cousin of the banana, but less sweet, often served as a side dish.

Soul Creole: In any other southern city this would be called southern cooking, but, of course, New Orleans is not any

NEW ORLEANS | DINING

other southern city; fried chicken, stewed okra, turnip greens, and cornbread are called…soul Creole. Go to the Praline Connection if you want to learn what this is all about.

Tasso: Smoked, spicy Cajun ham, used for seasoning.

How to Dress

New Orleans is a casual town, and the French Quarter is especially so—in many cafes and restaurants jeans and even shorts are perfectly okay. But New Orleanians also like to get all gussied up on occasion; if you're going to eat in the high-end restaurants, somewhat more formal wear is advised, and sometimes required. Ties are rarely required, but jackets frequently are. (Acts of God notwithstanding. During one deluge, when a group of men dining at Arnaud's saw that the restaurant was in danger of being flooded, they stripped down to their skivvies, put their suits, shirts, and shoes in plastic trash bags, finished eating, and walked out, trash bags in hand.) The listings below tell you which of our recommended restaurants require a jacket and/or tie for men; if you're dining someplace we don't list, the best bet is to ask about the dress code when you call to reserve a table. Or just ask your hotel concierge.

Tips About Tipping

As a general rule, tipping here is not much different from in any other American city, and should always, of course, depend upon the service. Locals tend to tip 15% in low-end eateries and 20% in the most upscale places. If there are six or more in your party (the minimum size of the group varies from place to place), a service charge of 15% to 20% may be added to your bill. It's relatively rare, but some restaurants will tack on a 15% service charge without bothering to mention it. Always check.

Getting the Right Table

Cozy up to your concierge. They are very buddy-buddy with restaurateurs, and always have their fingers placed on the proverbial pulses. If your guest house doesn't have such a critter, call **On the Town** (tel 504/835–7808), which is a free reservation service. If they can't get you into your place of choice, you can rely on them to find you a table someplace where you'll be happy. To be on the safe side, call before you arrive in New Orleans for a reservation at any restaurant you really want to eat at; otherwise, unless Mardi Gras, Jazz Fest, or a huge convention is in town, you should be able to get a table the same day you call. (Except at Galatoire's, which doesn't take reservations.)

At a few top restaurants, there may be certain rooms to which tourists and unfamiliar-looking locals are relegated. A prime example is the front room at Antoine's, which is locally known as Siberia and which Orleanians bypass by using a side door. A concierge's knowledge and pull could really help you. Unfortunately, once you've been shown to a table it's pretty gauche to request another one, unless it's to move to a smoking or no-smoking section.

Where the Chefs Are

Chefs who achieve superstar status in somebody else's restaurant almost always go out and open a place of their own. **Susan Spicer** made her fine reputation with her "New World" cuisine at Le Bistro at the Maison de Ville before opening her own Bayona. **Kevin Graham** turned the Windsor Court's Grill Room into one of the city's premier dining rooms for international cuisine before opening Graham's in the small, chic Pelham Hotel. The Grill Room kitchen is now the domain of the capable **Jeff Tunks**, who continues in Graham's international vein. Native Frenchman **Daniel Bonnot** had a hand in several local French restaurants before opening his Parisian-style bistro, Chez Daniel. His compatriot **Chris Kerageorgiou** has his country-French tavern, La Provence, in the piney woods on the north shore of Lake Pontchartrain. **Paul Prudhomme** needs no introduction; after a long stint as executive chef at Commander's Palace, he then opened K-Paul's Louisiana Kitchen and the rest is history. Prudhomme's protégés include **Emeril Lagasse** and **Frank Brigtsen**, each of whom has a standout restaurant of his own—in the case of Lagasse, two of them, Emeril's and Nola. **Alex Patout** came to the city from New Iberia, in Cajun country, bringing three generations of family recipes to his French Quarter restaurant, Alex Patout's Louisiana Restaurant. **Mike Fennelly** made a name for himself in Santa Fe's Santacafé, then migrated to New Orleans and opened Mike's on the Avenue, serving Continental food with a Southwestern twist. Antoine's executive chef, **Bernard "Randy" Guste**, is a direct descendant of Antoine Alciatore, who founded the French Creole restaurant in 1840. **Jamie Shannon** is now in charge of the kitchen at Commander's Palace, one of several top-notch restaurants established by the highly esteemed Brennan clan, best known for Brennan's, the Royal Street French Creole restaurant famed for "Breakfast at..." Brennan's opened in 1946, and it's still operated by descendants of the founders, but in 1974 four family members left the Royal Street restaurant and opened Commander's Palace in the Garden District. These four family members—known locally as the "Commander's Palace branch," have forged ahead with several other successful restaurants, and the various nieces, nephews, cousins, and other kin may continue on into the next millennium. New Orleanians relish the prospect of any Brennan's opening.

New Orleanians Eat

It's surprising for a 24-hour town, but late-night dining is not really a New Orleans thing. There are only a handful of halfway decent places to eat at 2am (see "Around the clock," below). Most restaurants stop serving around 10:30 or so. Sure, if you're already inside you'll get to eat, but as a rule, don't make reservations for later than 9 or 9:30. Many places have taken to offering prix-fixe "early bird specials"—usually very good buys, but if you want to get the worm, figuratively speaking, you have to be willing to eat around 5:30 or 6. Otherwise, dinner is between about 7 and 10. As for lunch, apart from a few places—notably Galatoire's—that open shortly before noon and stay open through dinner, lunch is generally served from about 11:30 till 2:30 or 3. Lunch prices on the whole are about 20% less than dinner.

The Lowdown

Where the locals go... Longtime **Antoine's** regulars think of the 15-room restaurant as their own private club and their tuxedoed "private waiter" as an old retainer. **Arnaud's**, much less stilted and stratified, has a somewhat gentle ambience, especially for Sunday's jazz brunch, though few locals do the jazz brunch thing. **Galatoire's** is the only restaurant for which folks round here will stand in line—reservations are not accepted. Friday noon and Sunday afternoon the smallish Parisian-style bistro is filled with dressed-up locals (bejeaned people are summarily turned away at the door), with a lot of waving and table-hopping going on. **Tujague's**, the least expensive and most casual of the French Creole restaurants, is particularly popular with Quarterites, for its five-course table d'hote menu and Old New Orleans ambience. The only time you *won't* find locals at **Commander's Palace** is at noon on Saturday and Sunday, when the old-fashioned Victorian house is overrun with tourists for the jazz brunch. (Ignore the local prejudices and go for it; it's great good fun.) Apart from that, this is considered by many Orleanians to be the city's best restaurant. They favor the upstairs Garden Room, which overlooks a lush courtyard. Uptowners especially like the **Caribbean Room** in the Pontchartrain Hotel, with its sophisticated air, Creole cuisine, and superb service. A lot of low-rent roadhouses are also big with locals, who may do the Grill Room one night and the next slip on jeans and go out to **Sid-Mar's** in Bucktown for seafood or **Rocky & Carlo's** in Chalmette for low-rent Italian food. Just off Jackson Square is the **Gumbo Shop**, best known for a combination platter of shrimp creole, red beans and rice, and jambalaya. It's a casual spot in a big high-ceilinged room; though it's a sit-down restaurant, locals have been seen lugging huge containers of gumbo home.

Where locals don't go... Despite the fine blackened dishes, excellent crawfish, and sweet potato–pecan pie at **K-Paul's Louisiana Kitchen**, locals almost never darken the door. They feel that the prices are too high, given that you have to stand in line at lunch and then, after the long wait, you're served martinis in canning jars and may have to share a table with strangers. In 1993, Chef Paul Prudhomme actually ran an ad in the *Times-Picayune* in which he acknowledged that his restaurant was a tourist attraction and said he wanted to encourage his local friends to patronize his place. He opened an upstairs dining room that does take reservations, but only for dinner. That may eventually lure the locals for dinner, but you'll never see an Orleanian in the noontime line. Likewise, no self-respecting New Orleanian would be caught dead at the **Court of Two Sisters** noon jazz buffet. The food is fine, and heaven knows there's plenty of it—a huge spread that includes étouffées, shrimp creole, jambalaya, and other regional

NEW ORLEANS | DINING

specialties—but it's considered merely a tourist attraction by locals .

Where the action is... For New Orleanians, the restaurant scene is a grand stage for socializing, and a number of smart newer restaurants have claimed their share of the action. Since this is a relatively small town, the same folks can be seen one night at **Emeril's**, for chef/owner Emeril Lagasse's homemade everything—from andouille and pasta to Worcestershire sauce and ice cream—and the next at, say, **Cafe Giovanni**. At this elegant Italian trattoria, long stretch limos purr up to the curb and drop the Gucci set off to feast on prosciutto pinwheels, Sicilian grilled pork chops, and cioppino. Emeril Lagasse also attracts the right folks to **Nola**, his French Quarter entry, for huge portions of double-cut pork chops served with pecan-glazed sweet potatoes or a grand and glorious banana-pudding layer cake. JoAnne Clevenger wows them at **Upperline**, a local treasure tucked into a little white frame cottage, where she concocts wonderful fried green tomatoes with shrimp rémoulade, creole white bean soup, jalapeño cornbread, and black-eyed peas. Kevin Graham opened his chic eatery—appropriately called **Graham's**—after leaving as chef at the Windsor Court's Grill Room. Calling his style "curious cuisine," Graham doesn't do traditional Creole cooking on the grounds that others already do it so well; instead, he adds an Asian touch in dishes such as lacquered duck and his versions of pheasant and lobster. Jeff Tunks took over as chef at the **Grill Room** after Graham's departure, no doubt aware that he had a tough act to follow; he has preserved the Grill Room's cachet, even though he changed the menu considerably, offering some lighter dishes and adding more seafood as well as a subtle Asian flavor. Orleanians like the current trend toward blending international styles of cooking, and nobody does it better than Mike Fennelly at **Mike's on the Avenue**—locals love his grilled oysters in a Korean-style barbecue sauce and his Chinese dumplings stuffed with shrimp, ginger, and scallions.

Best places for a quiet tête-à-tête... It must be the thick carpeting on the floors of the **Pelican Club**

and **Alex Patout's Louisiana Restaurant** that tone down the noise; whatever, both of these French Quarter places are minus the clatter found in so many local restaurants, thus making them ideal for quiet chats. At **Sebastian's Little Garden**, a sweetheart of a place just two blocks from Jackson Square, the rear dining room is a quiet, peaceful little garden, romantic as all get-out. Another popular spot for a quiet rendezvous is **Café Degas**, where there's a small, intimate open-air deck topped by a tin roof. It's not far from the house where French Impressionist painter Edgar Degas lived for a while, hence the name.

Worst places for a quiet tête-à-tête... New Orleans abounds with noisy restaurants, largely because of the proliferation of hardwood floors and sky-high ceilings; in those places, the sounds bounce off the walls and make conversation almost impossible. In that category, trendy, popular **Emeril's** immediately springs to mind, as does Ralph and Cindy Brennan's **Bacco**, a fine Italian restaurant. You'll also need a good set of lungs at the **Palace Cafe**—modeled after a grand Parisian bistro, it has stratospheric ceilings and constant clatter. But there are a lot of smaller restaurants, where too-close tables and overflow crowds make talking—rather, hearing—difficult. Small, wildly popular **Gautreau's** looks like it would be a *très intime* spot, but even after the owners installed wall-to-wall carpeting, the noise level failed to lower much. Likewise, the little restored creole cottage that houses Susan Spicer's **Bayona** (pronounced, by the way, buy-ona) would be a wonderful place for a special meeting—if it were only quiet, which it isn't. Even smaller than Bayona, **Gabrielle** is a tiny, triangle-shaped cottage with only 40 seats, so close together you'll be inadvertently eaves-dropping on your next-table neighbors. (It doesn't mat-ter, though—you won't be able to hear them any better than you can your tablemate.) The oil refinery across the street more or less sets the tone for **Rocky & Carlo's**, a working-class Sicilian dive where suits and sweats crowd around the steam tables, the jumble of tables is decorated with plastic bottles of mustard and discarded cafeteria trays, and no one can hear anyone else over the blaring TV set above the bar.

NEW ORLEANS | DINING

Solo dining... If you're by yourself, you won't feel at all conspicuous at **St. Ann's Deli**, a simple coffee shop–cum–deli, where the friendly staff will chat you up or leave you alone—you set the tone—while you wait for your burger, barbecue beef sandwich, or chicken fried steak. The **Quarter Scene** is another friendly, neighborhoody place, where you won't mind being alone while having a wonderful breakfast (waffles are great, and so is the "plantation breakfast" of any-style eggs; sausage, bacon, or ham; home fries; and fist-sized biscuits), hearty and very filling salad, po-boy, or blue-plate special. At **Emeril's**, there is a "food bar"—it's like a sushi bar, but there's no sushi—where you can watch the chefs at work or talk with the other singles who like to hang out there. Chef-watching can help pass the time at **Mr. B's Bistro**, too, a big classy room with potted palms, etched-glass panels behind green vinyl banquettes (much more attractive than it sounds), cafe curtains, and an open kitchen that provides good theater.

Best French Creole... You can almost taste the flavor of old New Orleans in **Antoine's**, where the French Creole menu has changed very little since the doors opened in 1840. You'll have to stomach stuffy service along with your superb oysters Rockefeller, which originated in this kitchen, and waiters kowtow to regulars rather than tourists. But the baked Alaska should sweeten the taste in your mouth. More friendly than Antoine's—and with equally fine fare—**Galatoire's**, with its mirrored walls and white napery, resembles a small Parisian bistro. For the upper-crust Orleanian, it's the place to be for lunch on Friday. The prettiest of the expensive French Creole restaurants is **Arnaud's**, where you can have your shrimp rémoulade and fancy veal in the main dining room (there are 10 other rooms), with its mosaic tile floors, potted palms, and a glass-brick wall. The least formal, and least expensive, of the old French Creole restaurants is atmospheric **Tujague's**, the city's second-oldest eating establishment. Waiters wear black bow ties and big white aprons and the rather closely spaced tables are dressed in neat white cloths.

Best South Louisiana fare... The chef/owner of **Alex Patout's Louisiana Restaurant** is among those who proclaim that Cajun and Creole cuisines have merged into a style called South Louisiana cooking. Maybe so, but Patout, who is an Acadian native, does a mouthwatering version of *cochon de lait*—a classic Cajun dish of sliced pork served in a savory sauce. Patout's roots are reflected in the restaurant's handsome trompe l'oeil ceiling and the framed prints that adorn the wall. Nobody doesn't know of Paul Prudhomme, the PR genius and celebrity chef who put Cajun cooking on the map and set off the "blackened redfish" craze, making redfish an endangered species (literally—there's still a ban on fishing for it). Prudhomme's **K-Paul's Louisiana Kitchen**—a simple cafe with community seating at Formica tables and martinis served in jelly glasses or canning jars—serves outstanding crawfish étouffée, blackened steaks, wonderful jambalaya, and bread pudding. K-Paul's opened in 1979 as an inexpensive cafe, just like scores of them in Cajun country; the downstairs decor is virtually unchanged, but the prices have—it's no longer cheap. (By the way, the "K" in the name is Prudhomme's late wife, whose name was K.) Frank Brigtsen once worked with Prudhomme and got the blackening thing down pat, but the decor is a bit brighter at his **Brigtsen's** (pronounced brite-son) than it is at K-Paul's—cloth-clad tables with small vases of fresh flowers now occupy the erstwhile living room and bedrooms of a little shotgun cottage not far from the river. The **Bon Ton**, which opened its doors in 1953, was Cajun long before Cajun was cool—before it was red-hot, actually (traditional Cajun fare is not as hot-peppery as Prudhomme's version). Red beans and rice, crawfish étouffée, and bread pudding—all traditional Cajun dishes—are served in this upmarket but casual place, with old brick walls, hardwood floors, and red-and-white-checked tablecloths.

Soul Creole... In any other city, what New Orleanians call "soul Creole" is simply down-home southern cooking, but this isn't any other city. **Dooky Chase** exemplifies the genre—the neighborhood is such that you should take a cab there and back, and there isn't much in the way of decoration, but come here for such southern standbys as filé gumbo, stewed okra, and sweet potatoes. The **Praline Connection**, near the French Quarter, is another down-home room serving terrific fried chicken and barbecued ribs, this one with waiters wearing black derbies. (And clothes, of course.) The restaurant is named for the candy store in a separate room at the rear. **Eddie's at Krauss**, a department-store lunch counter, is a CBD haven for luscious fried chicken, pork chops, and po-boys.

Decor to die for... Long as you're paying top dollar, besides getting superb, sophisticated food, you might as well get a beautiful setting as well. Famous for its classic French cuisine, **Louis XVI** is a sedate, understated room with art deco flourishes, such as the polished brass wall sconces. Chairs are upholstered in velvet, carpeting is almost thick enough to sink into, and tall French windows dressed with richly textured drapes overlook a lavish courtyard with a big stone fountain surrounded by tropical greenery. Speaking of which, dreamy scenes of St. Thomas decorate the walls of the **Caribbean Room** at the Pontchartrain Hotel, but this is no funky beach-front shack; it's a small, intimate dining space done up in soft hues of rose and green with luxe upholstered *fauteuils*. A room to swoon over, the lavish **Sazerac** gets you all giddy with its gilded chandeliers, white lace cloths, velvet banquettes, enormous oil paintings, and a trio tuned for cheek-to-chic dancing. And hardly least among the swank eateries is the aforementioned **Grill Room**, where the country-house decor follows the upper-class British theme of the rest of Windsor Court Hotel, and the cooking is routinely divine.

Cheap eats... Locals know that you don't have to spend megabucks in order to find good food. You can get memorable meals in hole-in-the-wall cafes, and there are a couple of plain luncheonettes that Orleanians just love. **Dunbar's**, for example, is an Uptown luncheonette with tables unembellished except for juicy po-boys and big bowls steaming with red beans and rice. And **Eddie's at Krauss** is a department-store lunch counter, where Orleanians love to stop after a morning of shopping. The lunch counter, a separate concession from Krauss Department Store, is the province of Wayne Baquet, whose family has been turning out fried chicken, stewed okra, and heavenly cornbread for ages.

Très French... The spotlight tends to shine on the French Creole kitchens, but there are a handful of classic French kitchens in the city, too. **Chez Daniel** serves classic French bistro fare—great onion soup, thick-textured duck pâté, steamed mussels, and a wonderful steak au poivre. A Belle Epoque mural decorates one wall and cafe curtains dress up the windows of what was once a liquor store. **Crozier's** sits in a concrete shopping mall, but behind a snappy canopy and etched-glass door, you'll find well-turned, if somewhat staid, haute French stand-bys such as entrecôte, coq au vin, tournedos topped with pâté de foie gras, poached pompano topped with hollandaise, and trout meunière. By the time you cross the Causeway to get to **La Provence** you may feel you've traveled all the way to the South of France. It's worth the trip, though, for the authentic escargots, pâté de foie gras, onion soup, and rack of lamb. The **Bistro** doesn't specialize in French cuisine, but it does serve an absolutely marvelous version of steak pommes frites.

A taste of Italy... Andrea Apuzzo, a native of Capri, is the chef/owner of two stellar eateries—**Anacapri**, in the French Quarter, and **Andrea's**, in suburban Metairie, and in both restaurants he uses local ingredients and imports from his homeland to create regional Italian dishes. Go to Andrea's, and you can feast on fine osso buco Milanese as well as dishes with a Continental flair, such as angel hair pasta tossed with salmon and flamed with vodka. At Anacapri, named for the tiny town in which Apuzzo was born, be sure to sample the chef's Italian-style gumbo and risotto New Orleans, made with imported Italian rice and andouille. At **Liuzza's**, Formica tables and a TV set pretty much comprise the decor, but you came for the fried onion rings and fettuccine Alfredo, anyway. The draws at **Bacco** are pizzas baked in a wood-fired oven (you'll find your goat cheese here), homemade pastas, and great garlic mashed potatoes accompanying a thick and juicy rosemary-flavored pork tenderloin. The fine porcelain at **Cafe Giovanni** is as dressed up as the crowd, with regional Italian offerings such as spaghetti alla Bolognese and Italian sausage and peppers. At **Mosca's**, a roadhouse on the West Bank, there is plenty of garlic and olive oil in the restaurant's renditions of spaghetti and meatballs, chicken cacciatore, and Cornish hen.

Best jazz brunches... No one does a jazz brunch better than **Commander's Palace**, which originated the concept. This Garden District outpost of the Brennan's empire is in a marvelous Victorian mansion whose several rooms are done up with pretty wallpaper, curtained windows, and cloth-covered tables; at noon on Saturday and Sunday, balloons festoon the tables, a jazz trio ambles from room to room, and the kitchen turns out superb egg dishes. The venerable Creole **Arnaud's** is a close runner-up for best jazz brunch, and it is, after all, right there in the Quarter, so you don't have to take a cab or streetcar to get there.

Jazziest dining... At the **Palm Court Jazz Cafe**, you can listen to traditional jazz while sampling traditional Creole cooking in an upscale, L-shaped room. Musicians take to the tiny stage and raise the rafters, while the waitstaff tries hard to hear what customers are ordering. Proprietor Nina Buck is always up to speed on local acts and where they're playing, and local musicians often hang out at the bar. But don't come here for inventive cuisine, swift service, or quiet conversation. Dining and dancing... The Hugh Clay trio has been playing for ages in the Fairmont's ritzy **Sazerac** restaurant, where people actually touch while dancing; they even put their cheeks together. The music calls for it. It's a gorgeously romantic room, and the kitchen does a pretty fair version of the Continental standards, which goes down well with the retro mood of the place in general.

Music and meals on paddle wheels... The Steamboat *Natchez* and the *Creole Queen*, both replicas of the old floating palaces, do two-hour nighttime cruises, with traditional jazz, banjos, straw boaters, and tables almost sagging under jambalaya, red beans and rice, shrimp creole, crawfish and shrimp étouffée, and bread pudding. This kind of food translates well into buffets, though, and they don't scale back the spices for unaccustomed palates. It's a very touristy experience, but that said, you do get a lot for your money—food, music, *and* a river cruise. Might as well do it once.

For the literati... When former owner Marc Turk opened the **Bombay Club** in the early 1980s, he cultivated a crowd of local bon vivants and literary types who like to gossip and party together. In 1995, E. J. Maysonave, one of the Bombay's regulars, took over as proprietor, and continues the tradition established by Turk. This isn't the place to gawk at celebrities, but it's a very "in" place for the local literati, and if you strike up a conversation you might pick up on some insider gossip. Tucked away behind the carriageway of the Prince Conti Hotel, the handsome restaurant, with its plush leather booths and captain's chairs, offers boring classics like oysters Rockefeller, escargots, beef tournedos, and New Zealand rack of lamb, but the better deal is the great juicy burgers and the Bombay Club (pun intended, that's a club sandwich). The two-fisted martinis are legendary in these parts—what else would you expect from a writers' hangout?

Best people-watching... Sometimes the food isn't the thing. Opposite Jackson Square, right in the thick of things, **Café du Monde** is an open-air pavilion with a jumble of bare tables adorned only with paper-napkin holders. Sidewalk mimes and musicians vie for loose change while a polyglot crowd chatters over café au lait and beignets. Nearby **Angelo Brocato's**, also right on the square, is a quintessential Italian ice cream parlor with tile floors, old-fashioned ice cream tables and chairs, glass jars, and display cases of cookies and candies. Few tourists brave the all-night **Hummingbird Grill**, but this is where Orleanians go slumming—a Saroyanesque sort of place with crude booths and tables and an assemblage of seedy skid-row types, the cop on the beat, cabdrivers—and, of course, the slummers. There's a novel here waiting to be written.

On the half shell... The **Acme Oyster House** is a funky little spot with red-and-white tablecloths and a long marble bar at which oyster-shuckers shuck to beat the band and locals have been bellying up for ages. Across the street, **Felix's** is only slightly less funky, the main difference being that the oyster bar is rose granite rather than marble. At both raw bars you mix your own cocktail dip of horseradish, hot sauce, and ketchup. Otherwise, almost all of the city's seafood restaurants have an oyster bar, since Orleanians consume freight cars full of the critters. And, of course, oysters appear fashionably dressed as Rockefeller and Bienville at dining rooms all over town.

Something fishy... New Orleans is an island, surrounded by waterways, so it shouldn't come as a surprise that seafood places are very big here. New Orleanians are very democratic in their dining tastes: one night they'll be dressed to the teeth and dining in a most sophisticated manner at Antoine's or Galatoire's, the next they'll be slathering their cut-offs and T-shirts with juices from boiled crabs and barbecue shrimp at some seafood shack out around Lake Pontchartrain. Locals will drive out to the West End and to the nearby little fishing village of Bucktown on the lake and cruise the parking lots to see which one seems to have the fewest cars, and thus a shorter wait to get in. For marvelous seafood, cooked to order—boiled, fried, baked, or étoufféed—head for **Sid-Mar's**, **Deanie's**, **West End Cafe**, or **Bozo's**. All are casual, family-style places, teeming with locals feasting on the catch of the day— atmospheric Sid-Mar's and the boisterous West End Cafe may be the best, but if they're full, you can't go wrong at the other two.

May I get that for you, sir?... The waiters at **Cafe Giovanni** take the time to describe in encyclopedic detail the various Italian specials, and do so with great gusto, though they do have to lean over and speak directly into your ear to be heard over the din. The staff at the homelike **Upperline** are likewise helpful, and they don't have to strain so to make themselves heard; the food is homey, too, with a south Louisiana menu. The friendly waiters at the **Court of Two Sisters** are quite accustomed to patiently explaining how to peel crawfish and cope with other strange delicacies. They get lots of practice, what with all the tourists.

Quirkiest kitchen... Probably the least politically correct place, not just in New Orleans but maybe anywhere, is **Rocky & Carlo's**, a Sicilian blue-collar bastion in Chalmette whose menu—tacked up on the wall for all the world to see—proclaims "wop salad." It's been there for ages, and nobody's ever thought much about it.

Stargazing... A lot of films are shot in New Orleans, so it isn't surprising that celebs turn up in eateries all over town. Julia Roberts, Lyle Lovett, and Kevin Costner have all been spotted at one time or another at the **Napoleon House**, which is also a favorite of Dick Cavett's. Alec Baldwin and Kim Basinger have made the scene at **Emeril's**, and Denzel Washington has been seen at **Nola**. John Lithgow, Tony Goldwyn, and Daryl Hannah have been to **Mike's on the Avenue**. Paul Newman, Joanne Woodward, Ellen Barkin, and Dennis Quaid are on a very long list of movie stars, prime ministers, presidents, and kings who've dined at **Antoine's**—a list that literally fills a booklet: the same restaurant whose waiters so blatantly ignore tourists actually publishes a brochure, filled with factoids and famous names, which is handed out to those very same tourists as they depart! The **Caribbean Room** is in the Pontchartrain Hotel, which is a favorite stopover for celebs. Clint Eastwood, Patrick Swayze, Kathleen Turner, and Shirley MacLaine have dined there, and the chef once spotted famous tenor Pavarotti rolling up his pants legs as he left the restaurant to wade out into a downpour that flooded St. Charles Avenue. The Windsor Court Hotel is another top spot for celebrities, so it's not uncommon to see the likes of Brandon Tartikoff, Francis Ford Coppola, John Goodman, Oliver Stone, Sam Shepard, and Susan Sarandon dining in the hotel's **Grill Room**. The **House of Blues**, part of a chain that began forming in Cambridge, Massachusetts, is a $7-million maze with a 260-seat restaurant and cavernous high-decibel concert hall, both of which are done with an overkill of Louisiana folk art and sculptures. Locals may not darken the door at **Planet Hollywood**, but they do go to HOB, where they might spot buddies of part-owner Dan Aykroyd.

Where to seal a deal... The Royal Orleans's **Rib Room** is big with the business crowd, not only for breakfast but for lunch and dinner as well, where lots of traditional red meat and martinis are served. Afternoons, the movers and shakers move and shake on over to **Le Salon**, the Windsor Court's luxe lobby lounge, where teatime has evolved into primetime business entertaining. Groupings of richly upholstered settees and armchairs are carefully arranged around marble-

NEW ORLEANS | DINING

topped coffee tables—perfect for scoping out who else is there negotiating with whom. Chamber music and trays of pastries help to soothe late-in-the-workday frazzled nerves.

Kid stuff... The booster-seat and peanut-butter-and-jelly crowd zeroes in on the West End and Bucktown seafood places, where the waitresses are pros at mopping up the spilled Cokes and milks. Cruise the parking lots to gauge the wait at **West End Cafe**, **Deanie's**, and the **R&O Pizza Place**. By all means take the youngsters to the Sunday jazz brunch at **Arnaud's** and/or **Commander's Palace**—the musicians play to the little ones, and they love it. They'll also be in hog heaven at **Top of the Dome's** Chocoholic Bar in the Hyatt Regency. Grown-ups are also known to indulge here. Or overindulge.

Between the buns... For many Orleanians, the **Camellia Grill** wins top honors for its thick, juicy burgers on warm toasted buns, but here's a local burger secret: Quarterites love ordering their burgers and fries from plain little **St. Ann's Deli**. (Not a "deli" in the New York sense; somewhere between a coffee shop and a greasy spoon.) The bacon cheeseburgers are out of this world, properly sloppy, with thick rounds of succulent beef and mounds of bacon. There are a few unadorned tables, but phones are always ringing off the hook for deliveries ("free delivery anywhere in the Quarter"). At **Port of Call**, a dark, funky, island-style dive, you halfway expect Fletcher Christian to be manning the ship's wheel; but despite the Polynesian theme (carried out in potent potables with names like Neptune's Monsoon), you can get really good burgers here, big, thick, and delicious, accompanied by a baked potato.

For committed carnivores... Creole and Cajun food get all the press, but New Orleans is also a very good steak town. Among the best for thick juicy cuts is **Ruth's Chris Steakhouse**—the one on North Broad was the first in the chain. (Ruth Fertel purchased a well-known restaurant called Chris Steakhouse and decided to attach her name to it rather than change it.) **Charlie's Steak House** is another functional-looking place serving nothing but standout steaks. If you like your steaks with a French accent, **Antoine's** filet mignon marchand de vin is divine.

Vegging out... Say what? In this city, pure vegetarian restaurants are as rare as a 5-foot snowbank. **Old Dog, New Trick**, only slightly smaller than a phone booth, has a few tables inside and others scattered out on the flagstones, where that which you breathe is less healthful than that which you eat. Even if you don't especially like vegetarian fare, try their take on pizza—it's spicy, succulent, and surprisingly good.

A river runs through it... Perched on the eleventh floor of Canal Place, just off the luxurious lobby of the Westin Hotel, **Le Jardin**'s cushy armchairs are grandstand seats for the great ongoing show on the Mississippi, in front of tall arched windows overlooking the river's great bend. You come here for the views, not the food, but the kitchen puts a Creole spin on Continental food, as if to remind you you're in New Orleans. Don't expect culinary wonders, either, at **Kabby's**, in the New Orleans Hilton Riverside, a large, splashy room whose dominant feature is the 200-foot windows; the big riverboats, freighters, and tugs seem close enough to board. The food is better—at least the pastas—in the romantic second-floor rooms of **Bella Luna**, a French Quarter spot where most dishes are continental, the riverboats glitter like jewels as they glide by in the night.

Best muffulettas... The **Central Grocery Store**, scented with garlic and filled with imported Italian pastas and pans, claims to have originated the muffuletta. The **Progress Grocery Store**, a couple of doors down from Central and hardly distinguishable from it, makes the same claim, and frankly, the sandwich is well made in both places. For a bit more atmosphere, you can also sample muffulettas at the **Napoleon House**, an old bar virtually worshipped by Orleanians. A somewhat wistful-looking portrait of Napoleon gazes out over peeling sepia walls and a clutter of chairs and old wooden tables, carved with initials or merely scarred from ages of elbows. French windows are usually open onto the sidewalk, letting all the sights and considerable sounds of St. Louis and Royal Streets clatter in; it's almost magical at night, when candles flicker on the tables.

Best po-boys... Rest assured that no one at **Mother's** is likely to sidle up to your table and simper, "Hi, I'm Perky, and I'll be your server." Push your way through the jungle of tables to the steam tables and line up with the hordes of CBD office workers who crowd in for cheap eats. The **Napoleon House** does decent po-boys, too, but the most popular French Quarter spot is **Johnny's Po-Boys,** a plain-and-simple place that makes some 35-foot-long varieties of the sandwich.

Just desserts... Many Quarterites consider the little French pastry shop **Croissant d'Or** a national treasure, and patiently stand in line at the glass display cases waiting for unhurried ladies to take their order. French chef Maurice Delechelles turns out mouthwatering chocolate éclairs, strawberry tarts, feathery-light brioches, and scrumptious croissants, rich with fillings of raspberry, apple, almond, or blueberry. The pastries are as American as apple pie at **Miss Jean's Saddlery**. Glass shelves are filled with desserts just like your mother used to make—if she made oh-so-creamy chocolate cream pie, lemon pie topped with mile-high meringue, coconut cream pie, rich layer cakes, and sensational strawberry shortcake. Uptown, on the streetcar line, the **Camellia Grill** is in a little white-columned cottage that looks for all the world as if it were somebody's house; a great place for breakfasts and burgers, it also turns out some of the area's best pies—delicious banana, chocolate, and coconut cream pies, and a wonderful pecan pie topped with whipped cream.

Best bananas Foster... This famous, ungodly rich local dessert originated at **Brennan's**, housed in a 12-room mansion dating from the late 18th century, when it was built for a Spanish nobleman. Waiters are sometimes hard-pressed here to squeeze by all the camera-toting tourists, and the noise level is awesome; you don't always get to watch the preparation of the famous dessert, but hey, if you want to say you ate it at the source, make the pilgrimage here. On the other hand, waiters at **Arnaud's** make great theater out of all the tableside sautéing and flaming that goes into preparing bananas Foster, and some say Arnaud's end result is better, too.

Worth a trek to the West Bank... For reasons unknown, New Orleanians are not very big on restaurants located someplace other than the ground floor. A second-floor restaurant that endures in this city is bound to be good. **Kelsey's** is not only a second-floor walk-up, but it also requires a drive across the Crescent City Connection to the West Bank. Enough said? No? Well, among the lures are chef/owner Randy Barlow's pasta jambalaya, succulent eggplant pirogue, and mirliton stuffed with sausage and shrimp and topped with shrimp-and-cheese hollandaise.

Worth a trek to the north shore... Traditionally, Orleanians don't combine dining out with, say, movie- or theatergoing. They don't normally scarf down a meal to get elsewhere; eating out is usually the evening's entertainment. Expect to make an evening of it when you brave the Lake Pontchartrain Causeway—the world's longest, at 24 miles—to reach casually chic **La Provence**. Reminiscent of a tavern in the French countryside, La Provence has loads of what restaurant critics call ambience, and you won't mind lingering over your wonderful quail gumbo (a house specialty), baked onion soup, escargots, and marinated rack of lamb. In a whole different vein, the North Shore's great Italian entry is **Sal and Judy's**, a run-down place where "chic" is just the first four letters in chicken. You won't mind the drive or the decor, though, when you're feasting on the fine shrimp fettuccine, pastas, and oyster dishes.

Dives worth the drive... Some of the city's best food is served in highly questionable settings. For the best, most succulent macaroni and cheese around, head to **Rocky & Carlo's**, a classic *tavolo caldo* that could have been picked up anywhere in Italy and transported to Chalmette, 5 miles downriver of the city. An outstanding oyster casserole put **Mosca's** on the dining map—a drab, no-frills roadhouse on the West Bank, about a 45-minute drive across the river. Look for the Budweiser sign out front and be prepared to wait, reservations or no. In addition to the oysters, there is a great marinated crab salad, garlicky chicken cacciatore, and spaghetti dishes—served bordelaise or with meatballs. (Mosca's doesn't do "pasta," they do "spaghetti.") **Sal and Judy's** virtually defines the word "funky," but the creamy shrimp fettuccine is well worth the hour's trek across the causeway.

Around the clock... A lunch counter, a few booths and tables, and a couple of flashing neon signs light up the wee hours at **Poppy's Grill**, while nigh towls nostalgic for the sixties wander into **Kaldi's Coffeehouse and Museum**, a high-ceilinged room with big windows, gunny sacks of coffee beans plopped here and there, and the faithful grouped around well-worn tables. Cappuccinos and pastries are top choices here. At **Bailey's**, a split-level coffee shop in the Fairmont Hotel, the food is overpriced and the service is slow, but it's an oasis in the CBD after the music clubs close. **St. Ann's Deli** (great for burgers), **Café du Monde** (best for beignets), and the **Hummingbird Grill** also hum all night long; the Hummingbird's breakfasts are worth waiting up for.

The Index

$$$$$	over $40
$$$$	$30–$40
$$$	$20–$30
$$	$12–$20
$	under $12

Acme Oyster House. At this down-home old-timer with red-and-white tablecloths and a long marble bar, the big draw is salty oysters on the half-shell, knocked back by ice-cold beer. Acme lures legions of loyal Orleanians, which means you'll probably have to line up. By all means, join 'em.... *Tel*

504/522–5973. 724 Iberville St., French Quarter. D, DC, MC not accepted. $$

Alex Patout's Louisiana Restaurant. Chef Patout's roots are deep in Cajun country and his cuisine here is South Louisianian: His white bean with tasso soup is a pleasant alternative to the more common gumbo, although his version of that ubiquitous dish is thick and hearty. Roast duck is served with oyster dressing, and red snapper comes stuffed with shrimp and eggplant. The mashed sweet potatoes are divine. The restaurant is handsomely designed with a trompe l'oeil ceiling and bayou country paintings on the wall.... *Tel 504/525–7788. 221 Royal St., French Quarter. Reservations advised. $$$*

Anacapri. Murals of the Blue Grotto, the *faraglioni*, and other famous landmarks of the romantic isle of Capri adorn the walls of this stylish Italian restaurant. Homemade pasta and imported Italian and local ingredients come together in risotto New Orleans, made with andouille and imported Italian rice, and in buttery capelli d'angelo New Orleans bordelaise, a mélange of angel-hair pasta, onions, garlic, shallots, and fresh parsley.... *Tel 504/522–9056. 320 Decatur St., French Quarter. $$$$*

Andrea's. Inside this ranch-style suburban house, it's a surprise to find crystal chandeliers and fine china and crystal. You'll know it's Italian when you see the huge platters of antipasti and a crowd feasting on osso buco Milanese and angel-hair pasta dressed up with salmon and flamed with brandy; another recommended dish is roast Long Island duckling, with raspberry sauce and rice dressing. Take I-10 West to the Causeway Blvd. North exit and turn right. Drive to 19th Street and turn right again. Andrea's is on the right side of the street.... *Tel 504/834–8583. 3100 19th St., Metairie. Reservations advised. $$$$*

Angelo Brocato's. An old-fashioned ice cream parlor, with ice cream chairs and little round tables, Brocato's has been serving spumoni, cannoli, amaretto ice cream, and Italian cookies and candies for more than 85 years. It's a great place for watching the Jackson Square action.... *Tel 504/525–9676. 537 St. Ann St., French Quarter. No credit cards. $*

Antoine's. This traditional Creole restaurant first opened in 1840. It only recently loosened up enough to add English subtitles to the French menu and to offer a moderately priced lunch menu. The 15 rooms range from a huge main dining room with dimly lit chandeliers and walls lined with celebrity caricatures to the smaller Rex Room, all a-glitter with crowns, scepters, and Carnival memorabilia. Yes, the tuxedoed waiters can be stuffy here, and they do cater to the old-line regulars. But the food is extraordinary. The salty puffed potatoes are better even than Arnaud's. Oysters Rockefeller originated here; so did pompano *en papillote* (fish baked in a paper bag). Save room for the fantastic baked Alaska.... *Tel 504/581–4422. 713 St. Louis St., French Quarter. Reservations advised. $$$$$*

Arnaud's. Dating from 1918, Arnaud's is a large, lovely, rambling restaurant serving justly famous Creole specialties. The light, airy puffed potatoes are addictive, and you can easily wolf down too many before forking into the shrimp Arnaud, served in a very spicy rémoulade sauce. The house veal specialty—surnamed Wohl—is topped with lump crabmeat. You're safe ordering any of the flaming desserts.... *Tel 504/523–5433. 813 Bienville St., French Quarter. Reservations advised. $$$$$*

Bacco. The Brennan family's Italian entry has several swank rooms in which locals chatter noisily beneath handpainted Venetian silk chandeliers and high ceilings studded with ersatz stars. Homemade pastas, designer pizzas from a wood-fired oven, roasted chicken with garlic mashed potatoes, and a unique cinnamon ice-cream sandwich are among the standouts.... *Tel 504/522–2426. 310 Chartres St., French Quarter. Reservations required. $$$$$*

Bailey's. The Fairmont Hotel's all-night coffee shop is a big split-level room with a stained-glass canopy over the front bar and big windows overlooking Baronne Street. The cheeseburgers are scrumptious, served with piles of fries, and there's a selection of regional foods, plus eggs Benedict and such. Not the place to come if you're in a hurry.... *Tel 504/529–7111. 123 Baronne St., CBD. $$*

Bayona. Chef/owner Susan Spicer's followers are almost religious in their devotion. She calls her cuisine "New

World," but it's mostly Mediterranean and all designer-nouvelle. Consistent winners are her cream of garlic soup, grilled duck breast glazed with pepper jelly, and shrimp in coriander sauce. The setting is a restored Creole cottage, decorated with elaborate floral arrangements, photographs of New Orleans, and a trompe l'oeil painting of the Mediterranean.... *Tel 504/525–4455. 430 Dauphine St., French Quarter. Reservations required. D, DC not accepted. $$$*

Bella Luna. Here, you get an eclectic selection of eats (including Northern Italian) and ringside seats (courtesy of big windows) for the nightly show of lit-up riverboats. An elegant, romantic setting for alligator soup, good pasta dishes, osso buco, and fancy desserts.... *Tel 504/529–1583. 914 N. Peters St., French Quarter. $$$$*

Bistro. The Palace Cafe, designed along the lines of a big Parisian bistro, is in a historic Italianate/Baroque building that once housed the Werlein Music Co. One of the Brennan family's restaurants, it's a big clattery place with a grand spiral stairway, tile floors, and splashy murals of homegrown musicians. The word "seafood" is prominently displayed at the top of the menu. Seafood is king, but the kitchen turns out a mean filet too. The white chocolate bread pudding became a legend about 10 minutes after it was first served.... *Tel 504/523–1661. 605 Canal St., French Quarter. Reservations advised. D not accepted. $$$$*

Bombay Club. An elegant, clubby place with leather captain's chairs, objets d'art, and rich draperies, the Bombay has for years been treasured by local literary types. You can go the oversized-burger-and-fries route or opt for Continental fare—escargot en croûte or grilled New Zealand rack of lamb accompanied by batter-fried eggplant. Among the regional specialties are good crawfish étouffée. Chef Jeff Hilgenberg also offers suppers of club sandwiches and crêpes.... *Tel 504/586–0972. 830 Conti St., French Quarter. $$$*

Bon Ton. Since 1953, this cozy, down-home place with its red-and-white-checked cloths has been serving Pierce family Cajun recipes for jambalaya, crawfish étouffée, hearty gumbo, butter-drenched broiled seafood, and warm, spicy bread pudding. Jammed at lunch with CBD office types, and closed weekends.... *Tel 504/524–3386. 401 Magazine St., CBD. Reservations required. D, DC not accepted. $$$*

Bozo's. The setting isn't great—a concrete mall—yet Bozo's is a very New Orleans place where seafood comes cooked to order: fried, broiled, boiled, stuffed, or, in the case of oysters, raw. Great for the whole family, including Grandma and the kids. Take I-10 West to Causeway Blvd. North exit and turn right. Cross Veterans Blvd., go to 21st St., and turn right.... *Tel 504/831–8666. 3117 31st St., Metairie. AE, D, DC not accepted. $$*

Brennan's. Not overly popular with locals—prices are sky-high and there are almost always throngs of tourists—Brennan's is nevertheless worth a trip for its classic French Creole breakfasts (brunch, really), sherry-spiked turtle soup, apples in double cream, and poached eggs drenched in superb hollandaise sauce. The signature dessert is bananas Foster, which originated here. At night things are somewhat more subdued. Brennan's is set in an 18th-century mansion, with a gorgeous courtyard and fountain; flocked wallpaper and crystal chandeliers sum up the decor.... *Tel 504/525–9711. 417 Royal St., French Quarter, Reservations advised. No jeans. $$$$$*

Brigtsen's. Frank Brigtsen, an erstwhile protégé of Paul Prudhomme, serves creative South Louisiana dishes in a little shotgun house near the Mississippi River. The menu changes daily, but you can usually bank on blackened prime rib, fresh fish (expertly sautéed and served with a light sauce), Brigtsen's signature cream of oysters Rockefeller soup, and homemade ice cream.... *Tel 504/861–7610. 723 Dante St., Riverbend. Reservations advised. D, DC not accepted. $$$$*

Café Degas. French Impressionist painter Edgar Degas lived and worked not far from this restaurant, which has a postage-stamp-sized covered pavilion. A limited menu leans toward omelets and crêpes (ham and asparagus is great), but there are also good steaks, salade niçoise, and several superb desserts.... *Tel 504/945–5635. 3127 Esplanade Ave., Mid-City. D, DC not accepted. $$*

NEW ORLEANS | DINING

Café du Monde. It would be hard to figure out how many paper napkins have wiped how many fingers and faces in this open-air pavilion over the last century or so. Every T-shirt and dashiki, every miniskirt and Mardi Gras getup rises from the bare tables wearing a liberal dusting of powdered sugar, thanks to the irresistible beignets; café au lait, orange juice, and chocolate milk make up the rest of the menu. Much of the world comes here, 24 hours a day. On the edge of Jackson Square.... *Tel 504/525–4544. 800 Decatur St., French Quarter. No reservations. No credit cards. $*

Cafe Giovanni. The beautiful people turn up fashionably late, sweeping into this small, chic, wood-paneled room. Highly favored is the hot prosciutto pinwheel, an elaborate concoction featuring puff pastry stuffed with goat cheese and fresh basil. The saffron-flavored cioppino of clams, mussels, shrimp, and scallops is also a crowd pleaser, and there is a lengthy list of classic Italian specialties.... *Tel 504/529–2154. 117 Decatur St., French Quarter. Reservations advised. $$$$*

Camellia Grill. Sooner or later everybody in town eats at this counter-only diner, with its tuxedoed waiters, maitre d', and occasional long lines. The main attractions are some of the city's best burgers and fries, substantial breakfasts (especially good waffles), and heavenly banana cream pie.... *Tel 504/866–9573. 626 S. Carrollton Ave., Uptown. No reservations. No credit cards. $*

Caribbean Room. Uptowners and the Pontchartrain Hotel's celebrity guests frequent this understated room, all done up with Louis XIV–style armchairs, soft lighting, and murals of Caribbean scenes. They come for the turtle soup, snapper Eugene (broiled and lemon-buttery, topped with shrimp and lump crabmeat), and the signature "mile high" ice cream pie drizzled with chocolate sauce.... *Tel 504/524–0581. 2031 St. Charles Ave., Garden District. Reservations advised. $$$$$*

Central Grocery Store. Belly up to the rear counter and have the Sicilian grocer wrap you up a plate-sized muffuletta—a half or quarter order can fill you up. Fresh whole rounds of Italian bread are stuffed to bursting with imported Italian

NEW ORLEANS | DINING

meats and cheese and spicy olive salad. Get a Barq's root beer and then go munch your lunch on a park bench on the Moonwalk, watching the Mississippi's parade of tugs and riverboats.... *Tel 504/523–1620. 923 Decatur St., French Quarter. No reservations. No credit cards. $*

Charlie's Steak House. Beyond the security guard out on the sleazy street and up one flight, Charlie's is a no-decor, no-nonsense place for platter-sized steaks and great fries. Vegetarians need not apply.... *Tel 504/895–8323. 4510 Dryades St., Uptown. D, DC not accepted. $$$*

Chez Daniel. Over the years French-born Daniel Bonnot has been involved with some of the city's top French restaurants. His own place, dolled up with a Belle Epoque mural, is a romantic spot with a strolling guitarist, serving French bistro fare: cold duck pâté, onion soup, steak au poivre. Bonnot's specials are shrimp Madelyn, named for his wife, which comes in a light cognac-spiked cream sauce, and steamed mussels accompanied by a wine-flavored cream sauce that you can eat like soup. Take I-10 West to the Causeway Blvd. South exit, turn left and go to Metairie Rd. and make another left.... *Tel 504/837–6900. 2037 Metairie Rd., Metairie. Reservations required. Jackets preferred. $$$$*

Commander's Palace. This distinguished restaurant, whose menu blends Creole and American traditions, is simply one of the country's best. It's housed in a marvelous Victorian mansion in the Garden District; try for a window table in the second-floor Garden Room, overlooking the attractive courtyard, but you'll be vying with a host of locals, and they get top priority. Top menu choices are turtle soup laced with sherry, trout wrapped in a crispy pecan crust, and a sinful Creole bread pudding soufflé served with crème anglaise. Commander's originated the now-ubiquitous jazz brunch, and they do a fun one, with festive balloons and a trio.... *Tel 504/899–8221. 1402 Washington Ave., Garden District. Reservations required. Jacket required for dinner and brunch. $$$$$*

Court of Two Sisters. Before you start filling your plate at the noon jazz lunch (tourists galore), stroll around the 60-odd dishes and consider your options: In addition to the usual suspects—jambalaya, boiled crawfish, shrimp creole, étouf-fées, and every other imaginable regional special—there are carving boards of roast beef and ham, fried chicken, barbe-cued ribs, mashed potatoes and gravy, and several different kinds of desserts. The mind boggles. Dinner is more sedate, with candlelight, escargots in mushroom caps, roasted duck, and interesting trout Picasso, which comes with bananas, grapes, and peaches.... *Tel 504/522–7261. 613 Royal St., French Quarter. $$$*

Creole Queen. A sleek replica of a 19th-century riverboat, replete with a big red paddle churning up the Big Muddy, the *Queen* does nightly two-hour cruises with traditional jazz (and gangs of tourists) aboard. She begins boarding at 7pm and departs about an hour later. Dinner is a buffet of jam-balaya, shrimp creole, red beans and rice, étouffées, gumbo, and bread pudding.... *Tel 504/529–4567, 800/ 445–4109, fax 504/524–6265. Canal St. Wharf. Reservations required. D, DC not accepted. $$$$*

Croissant d'Or. In this wildly popular little patisserie with tiny marble-topped tables, choose fresh-from-the-oven raspber-ry, almond, apple, and blueberry croissants from the display case, along with plump brioches, chocolaty eclairs, and var-ious other cream-filled and fattening French pastries. Good cappuccino, too. For lunch you can get croissant sandwich-es and sundry salads.... *Tel 504/524–4663. 617 Ursulines St., French Quarter. No credit cards. $*

Crozier's. Hidden in a concrete shopping mall, you'll find a romantic setting—soft lighting, dark wood paneling, pol-ished brass trim. Gerard Crozier's classic French cuisine (uninfluenced by Creole) has been attracting locals for ages. Leading the list are coq au vin, steak au poivre, entrecôte, tournedos topped with pâté de foie gras, shrimp, and light cream sauce, trout meunière, and lemony veal sweetbreads. Take I-10 West to Causeway Blvd. North, then turn left on West Esplanade Ave.... *Tel 504/833–8108. 3216 W. Esplanade N., Metairie. Reservations required. Jacket advised. $$$$*

Deanie's Seafood Restaurant. Bowls of seasoned boiled new potatoes start things off, and your fingers will already be sticky before your barbecue shrimp arrives, served in a hot cauldron with butter-and-garlic sauce—a typical New Orleans peel 'n' eat dish. There's a prodigious listing of other fried, boiled, and broiled seafoods in a cavernous, unpretentious space. Take I-10 West to West End Blvd., drive north on West End Blvd. for about 1.5 miles to Robert E. Lee Blvd.; drive west on R. E. Lee Blvd. across the 17th St. Canal Bridge, where R. E. Lee Blvd. becomes Old Hammond Hwy. Across the bridge, go one block and turn left. Deanie's is at Lake Ave. and Plaquemine St.... *Tel 504/831–4141. 1713 Lake Ave., Metairie. D, DC not accepted. $$*

Dooky Chase. A down-home place where the main attractions are chicken breast stuffed with oyster dressing and baked in marchand de vin sauce (called Chicken à la Dooky), filé gumbo, stewed okra, sweet potatoes, and pork chops smothered in onions. The dining room is decorated with paintings by local African-American artists. Take a cab to and from Dooky's—it's in a questionable neighborhood.... *Tel 504/832–2294. 2301 Orleans Ave., Treme. Reservations advised. D, DC not accepted. $$*

Dunbar's. This is an unadorned luncheonette in a questionable neighborhood, but the crunchy fried chicken comes three pieces per plate, the cornbread is sweet and fluffy, and there are terrific po-boys, smoked sausage, and red beans and rice.... *Tel 504/899–0734. 4927 Freret St., Uptown. AE, D, DC not accepted. $*

Eddie's at Krauss. At Krauss Department Store, Eddie Baquet's lunch-only counter is on the second floor; there are also a few tables. Enjoy generous portions of crisp and spicy fried chicken, pork chops, potato salad, and red beans and rice. Baquet's take on the roast beef po-boy is made with boiled beef brisket.... *Tel 504/523–3311. 1201 Canal St., CBD. No reservations. No credit cards. $*

Emeril's. Housed in a restored warehouse, Emeril's showcases splashy Expressionist art on plain adobe walls. Chef/owner Emeril Lagasse is renowned for his homemade everything: andouille, pasta, Worcestershire sauce, ice cream, you name it. His signature salad is warm wilted spinach dressed with homemade goat cheese and andouille sausage vinaigrette. Cornbread-andouille dressing accompanies the roulade of chicken, and Louisiana caviar tops the fresh corn crêpe.... *Tel 504/528–9393. 800 Tchoupitoulas St., Warehouse District. Jackets advised. D not accepted. $$$$*

Felix's Restaurant and Oyster Bar. A casual seafood place across the street from the Acme Oyster House, and with a somewhat lengthier menu, Felix's has a good oyster bar and cooked-to-order fresh seafoods.... *Tel 504/522–4440. 739 Iberville St., French Quarter. $$*

Gabrielle. Shaped like a triangle, this tiny 40-seat restaurant is the bastion of Greg Sonnier, whose wife, Mary, makes those fiendishly delicious carrot cakes and cobblers. Sautéed veal and fried oysters are served with tasso-mustard sauce, and panéed rabbit comes with crawfish and wild mushroom pasta.... *Tel 504/948–6233. 3201 Esplanade Ave., Mid-City. Reservations advised. D, DC not accepted. $$$$*

Galatoire's. Open since 1905, this is a classic French Creole bistro with polished brass rails, mirrored walls, white cloths, tuxedoed waiters, and hordes of old-line Orleanians patiently lined up on the littered Bourbon St. sidewalk outside. Fried oysters and bacon en brochette, broiled pompano, trout amandine, and excellent chicken dishes are all winners on the 5-page menu. Crawfish étouffée is a popular off-the-menu special.... *Tel 504/525–2021. 209 Bourbon St., French Quarter. No reservations. Jackets required for dinner and all day Sun., no jeans. AE, D, DC not accepted. $$$$*

Gautreau's. This local favorite is housed in an erstwhile pharmacy, with polished wood, a pressed-tin ceiling, and wonderful photographs of old New Orleans. Lobster bisque, curried butternut-squash soup, and a marvelous duck confit are top appetizers; then try roasted quail, stuffed with pecan and sun-dried cherry dressing, on a bed of mascarpone risotto; there's also a wonderful lineup of filets mignon. Leave room for any of the desserts that involve chocolate.... *Tel 504/899–7397. 1728 Soniat St., Uptown. Reservations required. D, DC not accepted. $$$$$*

Gold Room. One of the city's best bargains is the lunch buffet in the main dining room of Le Pavillon Hotel. In a room decorated with crystal chandeliers and oil paintings, the hotel puts out a gigantic spread of salads, meats, vegetables, and desserts—all you can eat at a very modest price.... *Tel 504/581–3111. 833 Poydras St., CBD. Reservations advised. $$*

Graham's. In late 1994, Kevin Graham left the Grill Room kitchen to open his own place, the small, almost spartan dining room with unadorned, gray granite–top tables in the Pelham Hotel. He changes the menu twice weekly, but expect creations such as lacquered duck, wild mushroom and tomato bisque, and seared yellowfin tuna served with Tuscan bean salad.... *Tel 504/524–9678. 200 Magazine St., CBD. Reservations required. $$$$$*

Grill Room. The sumptuous dining room of the Windsor Court, with its British artworks and antiques, maintains its luster under chef Jeff Tunks. The menu changes every two or three weeks, but you can expect the likes of Hudson River Valley foie gras done up with apricots and port wine; heavenly Chapman Cove oysters on the half-shell; or seafood cake liberally speckled with chunks of lobster and crawfish in spicy rémoulade sauce. Desserts are works of art. Superb service, plus a 23-page tome of wines.... *Tel 504/522–1992. 300 Gravier St., CBD. Reservations and jacket advised for dinner. $$$$$*

Gumbo Shop. Stroll down the narrow alley at the side to reach this easygoing neighborhood eatery. Best known, of course, for gumbo, and for the sampler of New Orleans specialties: shrimp creole, jambalaya, and red beans and rice.... *Tel 504/525–1486. 630 St. Peter St., French Quarter. $$*

House of Blues. The kitchen is surprisingly good, considering that this is first and foremost a live music venue. Southern-style cooking dominates, with the star attraction being baby-back ribs slow-smoked over mesquite and hickory, served with au gratin potatoes spiked with Southern Comfort and turnip greens. Crusty fried catfish fillets come with sides of turnip greens, mashed sweet potatoes, and hush puppies. Gospel music makes the Sunday brunch a soulful affair.... *Tel 504/529–2583. 225 Decatur St., French Quarter. Dinner reservations accepted only for concert ticket–holders and groups of 10 of more. DC not accepted. $$$*

Hummingbird Grill. Cops, cabbies, skid-row characters, and even the occasional tuxedoed dandy turn up in this quintessential 24-hour greasy spoon. Cheap eats include big platters of meatloaf and mashed potatoes, liver and onions, heavenly cornbread, and great breakfasts of fluffy biscuits, ham 'n' eggs, and grits.... *Tel 504/523–9165. 804 St. Charles Ave., CBD. No reservations. No credit cards. $*

Johnny's Po-Boys. Not much in the way of decor, but the roast beef and gravy, oyster, and other po-boys are popular with Quarterites, and breakfast is served all day.... *Tel 504/524– 8429. 511 St. Louis St., French Quarter. No credit cards. $*

K-Paul's Louisiana Kitchen. Cajun celebrity chef Paul Prudhomme no longer presides over the kitchen at this famous down-home cafe, but it's still his'n, and his inter- pretation of Acadian cooking is the star attraction. The menu includes good gumbo, crawfish étouffée, blackened yel- lowfin tuna, corn-flour biscuits, and sweet potato–pecan pie. Skip lunch, when the downstairs room has only community seating, and reserve a table for dinner.... *Tel 504/524– 7394. 416 Chartres St., French Quarter. Reservations accepted and required for dinner only. DC, MC, V not accepted. $$$$*

Kabby's. The floor show is on the river, with a splendid view cour- tesy of 200-foot windows. Watch the riverboats and tugs while forking into your catfish or duck breast accompanied by andouille dressing. Things seem to taste even better dur- ing Sunday's jazz brunch, to the tunes of Tim Laughlin's trio.... *Tel 504/584–3884. New Orleans Riverside Hilton, 2 Poydras St., CBD. Reservations advised for dinner. $$$*

Kaldi's Coffeehouse and Museum. Gourmet coffees, includ- ing wonderful iced cappuccino, lots of sweet, sticky pastries and cakes, and sixties-era ambience, plus occasional evening entertainment.... *Tel 504/586–8989. 940 Decatur St., French Quarter. No reservations. No credit cards. $*

Kelsey's. This sunny L-shaped room, filled with pretty plants, is on the second floor of an office building. Randy Barlow's renditions of South Louisiana cooking include good étouf- fées and gumbo, and a rich, spicy jambalaya that by itself is worth the trip to the West Bank. Take the Crescent City Connection (bridge) to the West Bank and turn left at the first exit, General de Gaulle Blvd. The restaurant is about a mile and a half from the bridge.... *Tel 504/366–6722.*

3920 General de Gaulle Dr., West Bank. Dinner reservations advised. $$$

La Provence. In a casual country-French tavern, with an open hearth and waitresses in the native dress of Provence (birthplace of chef Chris Kerageorgiou), gorge on fresh-baked country bread, a wonderful pâté, duck à l'orange, and rack of lamb, all superbly prepared. Desserts are really wicked. Cross the Lake Pontchartrain causeway and turn right on U.S. 190. The restaurant is 7 miles from the causeway, on the right side of the road, just past Fountainbleau State Park..... *Tel 504/626–7662. U.S. 190, Mandeville, North Shore. Reservations advised. Jacket advised. D, DC not accepted. $$$*

Le Jardin. From its eleventh-floor vantage point, the Westin's dining room overlooks a lush courtyard, and beyond it, the great bend in the Mississippi. Continental meets Creole here, with offerings of turtle soup, thick bisque liberally flecked with lump crabmeat and wild mushrooms, lamb chops flavored with rosemary, and an assortment of seafood. Sunday brunch buffet offers a stunning display of dishes and traditional jazz.... *Tel 504/566–7006. Westin Canal Place Hotel, 100 Iberville St., French Quarter. $$$$*

Le Salon. The ritzy lobby lounge of the very British Windsor Court Hotel has cushy settees, armchairs, and chamber music. Your choice of tea (and/or champagne) is served each afternoon, accompanied by plump scones, dainty little finger sandwiches, cookies, and chocolate truffles.... *Tel 504/523–6000. 300 Gravier St., CBD. Reservations advised. $$*

Liuzza's. Settle down at one of the Formica tables next to the bar, ignore the TV set, order one of the trademark 18-ounce beers, and prepare to enjoy out-of-this-world fried onion rings. Deep frying is a way of life here—fried eggplant sticks, fried shrimp, and fried oyster po-boys compete with fettuccine Alfredo, spaghetti, and calf's liver smothered with onions.... *Tel 504/482–9120. 3636 Bienville St., Mid-City. No credit cards. $*

Louis XVI. The design is art deco, the mood subdued, and the cuisine classic French, with expert tableside service. Onion soup gratinée, roasted breast of duckling in Escoffier sauce, tournedos with wild mushrooms and Madeira sauce, exceptional veggies, and flaming desserts are all presented with great panache.... *Tel 504/581–7000. St. Louis Hotel, 730 Bienville St., French Quarter. Reservations advised. Jackets required for dinner. $$$$*

Mike's on the Avenue. In chef Mike Fennelly's hot-ticket eatery, whitewashed walls are decorated with his paintings, and big plate-glass windows overlook St. Charles Ave. and Lafayette Square. A trendsetter if ever there was one, he weds Southwestern with Asian, to mixed reviews from locals—some swear by grilled oysters on the half-shell with tart Korean barbecue sauce, others rave about Chinese dumplings stuffed with shrimp and scallions, but still others find the food too avant-garde and recommend buying Fennelly's handpainted ties instead.... *Tel 504/523–1709. 628 St. Charles Ave., CBD. Reservations advised. $$$$$*

Miss Jean's Saddlery. This sunny little cafe, with its long wooden bar, glass-topped tables, and bentwood chairs, is one of the few places in town where you can get American-style home cooking, like chicken and dumplings and calf's liver and onions. Miss Jean comes in at 4am to begin making those mouthwatering pies, cakes, and cobblers.... *Tel 504/522–5172. 240 Decatur St., French Quarter. No reservations. $*

Mr. B's Bistro. Noted for its hickory grill, Ralph and Cindy Brennan's sleek bistro is all done up with etched glass, white cloths, potted palms, and an open kitchen. Pasta primavera and barbecue shrimp are excellent; jambalaya here is made with pasta, andouille, and shrimp. Warm bread pudding, soaked in Irish whiskey sauce, is a standout, but there are also some chocolate desserts that will knock your socks off.... *Tel 504/523–2078. 201 Royal St., French Quarter. Reservations and jackets advised for dinner. $$$$*

Mosca's. Garlic is king here, and the kitchen turns out splendid renditions of chicken, spaghetti and meatballs, and Cornish hen. There's a great crab salad, with lumps of white crabmeat, served in a bracing vinaigrette. Rather than oysters on the half-shell, oysters Mosca are baked en casserole, with breadcrumbs, artichokes, olive oil, and

NEW ORLEANS | DINING

herbs, a succulent reason why locals make the 45-minute drive here. From downtown, U.S. 90 crosses the Crescent City connection; cross the bridge and head west on U.S. 90. After passing the town of Waggaman, keep an eye peeled on the left side of the road.... *Tel 504/436–9942. 4137 U.S. 90 W., West Bank. Reservations advised. No credit cards.* $$$$

Mother's. The ladies behind the steam tables stay busy cooking the roast beef, baked ham, and turkey po-boys for which this blue-collar spot is famous. Stake out a table before lining up at the cafeteria for plates of spicy jambalaya, red beans and rice, po-boys, and bread pudding. Great for cheap, hearty breakfasts, too.... *Tel 504/523–9656. 401 Poydras St., CBD. No credit cards.* $

Napoleon House. This beloved institution defines old New Orleans atmosphere—worn wooden tables, peeling sepia walls hung with pictures of Napoleon, and canned classical music. Some amount of time will be frittered away waiting for a waiter, but no one—patrons or staff—is in a hurry here. Pimm's cup, served with a garnish of cucumber, is the featured beverage; po-boys and warm muffulettas are the main fare; and there is a salad bar in a cozy adjacent room.... *Tel 504/524–9752. 500 Chartres St., French Quarter.* $

Nola. Some people think Emeril Lagasse's split-level French Quarter entry is even better than his Warehouse District restaurant—witness the crowds and clatter. Among the popular entrees is crowder peas and heavenly southern-style greens flavored with homemade Worcestershire sauce accompanying a very spicy mixed grill of boudin, andouille, rabbit, and chicken. The wood-fueled oven turns out roasted lamb shank crusted with sun-dried tomatoes and goat cheese. Emeril's tuber standouts are pecan-glazed sweet potatoes and roasted garlic creamed potatoes.... *Tel 504/522–6652. 534 St. Louis St., French Quarter. Reservations advised for dinner. D not accepted.* $$$$

Old Dog, New Trick. Only slightly smaller than a phone booth, this vegetarian eatery has a few tables jammed inside and others scattered out on the flagstones. Good vegetarian burgers and pizzas.... *Tel 504/522–4569. 307 Exchange Alley, French Quarter. Reservations not accepted. D, DC, AE not accepted. $*

Palm Court Jazz Cafe. Tile floors, pretty cafe curtains, ceiling fans, and white-clothed tables are the setting for the only place in town where you can have dinner while listening to traditional jazz. Dig into oysters bordelaise, steak and mushroom pie, jambalaya, and red beans and rice. And bread pudding, of course.... *Tel 504/525–0200. 1204 Decatur St., French Quarter. Reservations advised. D, DC not accepted. $$*

Pelican Club. In a restored 19th-century town house with carpeted floors, handsome wall sconces, and soft lighting, dressed-up legal eagles and politicos do deals over roasted rack of lamb in a garlic-herb crust, platters of seafood (grilled Maine lobster, crab cakes, steamed mussels, and shrimp), and spicy curried chicken and linguine, served with sides of crushed peanuts, yogurt, and mango and peach chutney. The chef also does a great paella-style jambalaya.... *Tel 504/523–1504. 312 Exchange Place, French Quarter. Reservations and jackets advised. D not accepted. $$$$*

Poppy's Grill. If you stagger out of Pat O'Brien's at 3am in search of a burger and fries, cross the street to this 24-hour grill. No decor except for some neon and a jukebox. Cheap breakfast specials begin at 5am.... *Tel 504/524–3287. 717 St. Peter St., French Quarter. D, DC not accepted. $*

Port of Call. At this funky dive with a nautical motif, the juicy two-fisted burger—a half-pound of freshly ground chuck served with a huge two-fisted baked potato—is among the best of the genre. No-nonsense pizzas, New York strip, filet mignon, rib-eye, and mushrooms sautéed in red-wine sauce are other attractions.... *Tel 504/523–0120. 838 Esplanade Ave., French Quarter. No credit cards. $*

Praline Connection. All of the waiters wear black derbies at this small, crowded neighborhood joint. Smothered pork chops, stewed or fried chicken, mustard greens, barbecued ribs, cornbread, and pecan pie are among the terrific soulful offerings.... *Tel 504/943–3934. 542 Frenchmen St., Faubourg Marigny. $*

Progress Grocery Store. At this unpretentious Italian grocery store, they make wonderful take-out muffulettas.... *Tel 504/525–6627. 915 Decatur St., French Quarter. No credit cards. $*

Quarter Scene. This place does great salads, burgers, blue-plate specials, and breakfasts. It's a friendly neighborhood cafe, with two tiny rooms, cloth-covered tables, and big windows overlooking—well, the Quarter scene.... *Tel 504/ 522–6533. 900 Dumaine St., French Quarter. $$*

R&O Pizza Place. Plain and noisy, R&O churns out pizzas, spaghetti and meatballs, and appropriately messy po-boys. There's a busy takeout line, as well as a lineup of folks waiting for a table. Take I-10 West to West End Blvd., drive north on West End Blvd. for about 1.5 miles to Robert E. Lee Blvd., then drive west on R. E. Lee Blvd. across the 17th St. Canal Bridge, where R. E. Lee Blvd. becomes Old Hammond Hwy. Continue straight ahead; R&O is 2 blocks from the bridge, at Old Hammond Hwy. and Carrollton Ave.... *Tel 504/831–1248. 216 Old Hammond Hwy., Metairie. No reservations. No credit cards. $*

Rib Room. Power-dining is the game local politicians play in the swank Royal Orleans Hotel's brick-walled main dining room, with deals cut over "wash-bucket" martinis, spit-roasted prime ribs, rack of lamb flavored with garlic and rosemary, or the thyme-tested veal tenderloin.... *Tel 504/529–7045. 621 St. Louis St., French Quarter. Reservations advised for dinner. $$$$*

Rocky & Carlo's. At this rustic *tavolo caldo* that would be at home in Palermo, po-boys are as messy as they should be, and the fried seafood is great. But baked macaroni and cheese is the real reason people make the 5-mile trek downriver. From downtown, go east on N. Rampart St. which becomes St. Claude Ave., then becomes St. Bernard Hwy. The restaurant is about 5 miles from downtown, on the left side of the road across from a Mobil Oil Refinery.... *Tel 504/279–8323. 613 W. St. Bernard Hwy., Chalmette. No reservations. No credit cards. $*

Ruth's Chris Steakhouse. In a big unadorned room, aged prime beef, thick-cut fries, and green salad all arrive in prodigious portions. Excellent food, pricy but popular with

NEW ORLEANS | DINING

politicos and Saints players.... *Tel 504/486–0810. 711 N. Broad St., Mid-City. $$$$$*

St. Ann's Deli. This plain coffee house–cum–deli has burgers and fries, good American-style sandwiches, po-boys and muffulettas, daily specials, and breakfast anytime, plus great desserts such as pineapple upside-down cake, banana pudding, and carrot cake.... *Tel 504/529–4421. 800 Dauphine St., French Quarter. D, DC not accepted. $*

Sal and Judy's. Let's be charitable and call it "rustic." But don't worry when you clap eyes on this joint: You're here for the homemade Italian sausage, chicken cacciatore, and shrimp fettuccine, and it'll be worth it. Take the Lake Pontchartrain Causeway to the North Shore, turn right on U.S. 190, and drive about 10 miles into the town of Lacombe. The restaurant is on the left side of the street.... *Tel 504/882–9443. U.S. Hwy 190, Lacombe. D, DC not accepted. $$$*

Sazerac Restaurant. A room to swoon over, with white lace tablecloths, huge oil paintings, and plush velvet banquettes. The cognac-spiced lobster bisque, steak tartare, Dover sole meunière, and cherries jubilee are recommended; the pièce de résistance is the almost life-sized swan ice sculpture wheeled out to serve the sorbet. Skip the dessert soufflés.... *Tel 504/529–4733. Fairmont Hotel, 123 Baronne St., CBD. Reservations and jackets advised for dinner. $$$$$*

Sebastian's Little Garden. A tiny little place with a romantic rear garden, Sebastian's has a menu listing that's almost bigger than the restaurant, ranging from stir-fried veggies to veal marsala. Pork slices duded out in apricots and rum sauce is a winner; the praline sweet potatoes are great; and there are several chicken, pasta, meat, and seafood offerings.... *Tel 504/524–3041. 538 St. Philip St., French Quarter. D, DC not accepted. $$*

Sid-Mar's. The screened porch of this ramshackle roadhouse is a favorite place for boiled crawfish and the fresh seafood caught almost at the front door. Take I-10 West to West End Blvd., go north on West End Blvd. about 1.5 miles to Robert E. Lee Blvd. and turn left onto R. E. Lee. Go straight on R. E. Lee Blvd. until you get to the red light at the 17th St. Canal, then turn right—don't cross the bridge—onto Orpheum Ave. You'll see fishing boats on the right along the canal, and Sid-Mar's on the left.... *Tel 504/831–9541. 1824 Orpheum Ave., Bucktown. $$*

Steamboat *Natchez*. A floating palace in the 19th-century riverboat tradition, the 1,500-passenger *Natchez* is a steam-powered beauty decked out—so to speak—in gingerbread trim, wood paneling, brass wall sconces, and crystal chandeliers. At 7pm she begins boarding to the tune of a shrill calliope, and departs at 8 for a two-hour harbor cruise with Dixieland bands and a huge buffet of Creole and Cajun specialties—jambalaya, red beans and rice, étouffées, gumbo, and bread pudding.... *Tel 504/586–8777, 800/233–BOAT, fax 504/587–8708. Toulouse St. Wharf behind the Jax Brewery, French Quarter. Reservations required. DC not accepted. $$$$$*

Top of the Dome. All dressed up in nighttime twinkling lights, the city looks splendid from the only revolving restaurant in town (Top of the Mart spins, too, but only for cocktails). Starters include barbecued duck breast basted with cane syrup and served with fruit and nut couscous, and gnocchi made with andouille, fresh basil, Creole tomatoes, and shredded Parmesan. For the main event, try roasted prime rib au jus or rack of lamb with roasted garlic, braised rosemary lentils, and marinated artichoke hearts.... *Tel 504/561–1234. 500 Poydras Plaza, CBD. $$$*

Tujague's. "Two jacks," as it's pronounced, opened in 1856, and is the city's second-oldest restaurant (after Antoine's). It has black-and-white tile floors, crisp white napery, and photos of old New Orleans lining the walls. The menu is French Creole; a five-course table d'hôte meal features soup, shrimp rémoulade, boiled brisket of beef in Creole sauce, a choice of three entrees, and dessert—with bread pudding the top seller. A classic New Orleans experience.... *Tel 504/525–8676. 823 Decatur St., French Quarter. Dinner reservations advised. $$$*

Upperline. Dining in this white-frame cottage is almost like eating at someone's home; paintings from owner JoAnne Clevenger's private collection of works by regional artists line the walls. "A Taste of New Orleans" is the restaurant's best-seller, with samples of seafood gumbo, Creole white bean soup, fried green tomatoes with shrimp, andouille, and crawfish étouffée. A favorite dessert is coconut layer cake.... *Tel 504/891–9822. 1413 Upperline St., Uptown. Reservations advised. D, DC not accepted. $$$*

West End Cafe. A family place, boisterous with kids and folks singing along with the blaring jukebox, the West End has homey daily specials like baked chicken served with macaroni and cheese, crispy fried catfish fillets, and meatballs and spaghetti. You can always get mountains of great fried onion rings, seafood platters, and for the kids, peanut-butter-and-jelly sandwiches. Don't miss the good hearty breakfasts. Take I-10 West to West End Blvd., go north on West End Blvd. about 1.5 miles to Robert E. Lee Blvd. Stay in the left lane; look for a Regions bank on the left. Just past the bank turn left on 21st St. and go one block. The restaurant is on the left.... *Tel 504/288–0711. 8536 Pontchartrain Blvd., West End. No reservations. D not accepted. $*

New Orleans Dining

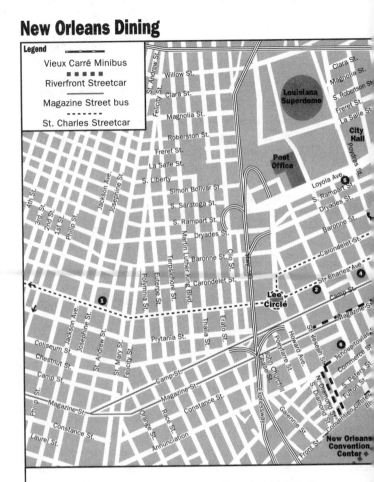

Legend

━━━━━ Vieux Carré Minibus

■ ■ ■ ■ Riverfront Streetcar

Magazine Street bus

- - - - - St. Charles Streetcar

Bailey's **13**
Bon Ton **12**
Carribbean Room **1**
Creole Queen Riverboat **8**
Eddie's at Krauss **14**
Emeril's **6**
Gold Room **3**
Graham's **7**
Grill Room **10**

Hummingbird Grill **2**
Kabby's **9**
Mike's on the Avenue **4**
Mother's **11**
Sazerac **13**
Top of the Dome **5**

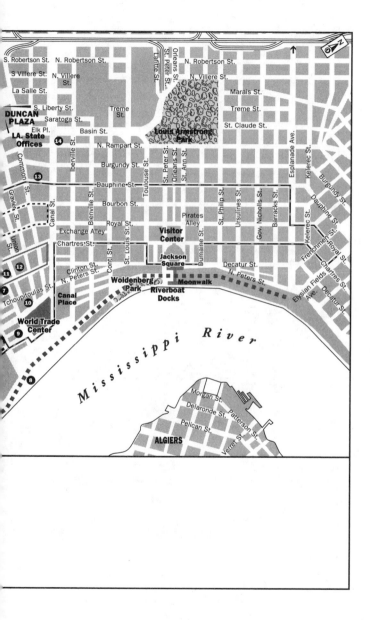

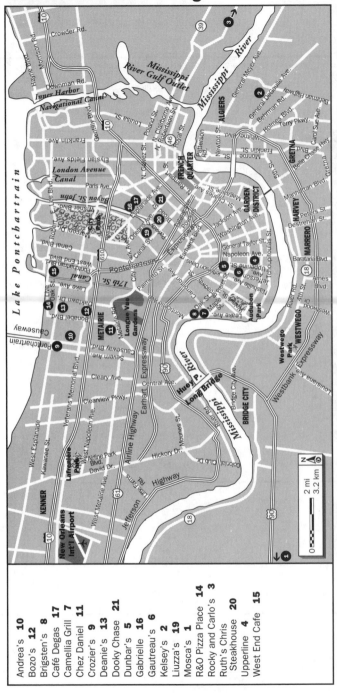

Andrea's 10
Bozo's 12
Brigsten's 8
Café Degas 17
Camellia Grill 11
Chez Daniel 7
Crozier's 9
Deanie's 13
Dooky Chase 21
Dunbar's 5
Gabrielle 16
Gautreau's 6
Kelsey's 2
Liuzza's 19
Mosca's 1
R&O Pizza Place 14
Rocky and Carlo's 3
Ruth's Chris Steakhouse 20
Upperline 4
West End Cafe 15

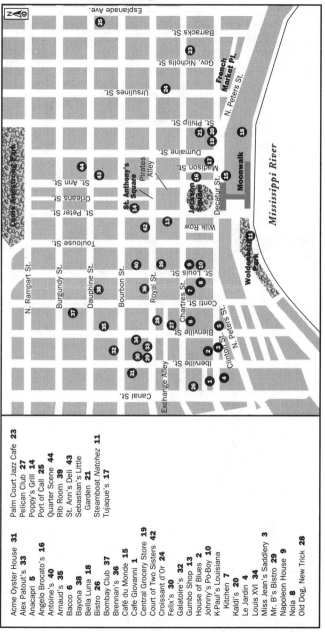

Acme Oyster House **31**
Alex Patout's **33**
Anacapri **5**
Angelo Brocato's **16**
Antoine's **40**
Arnaud's **35**
Bacco **6**
Bayona **38**
Bella Luna **18**
Bistro **26**
Bombay Club **37**
Brennan's **36**
Café du Monde **15**
Cafe Giovanni **1**
Central Grocery Store **19**
Court of Two Sisters **42**
Croissant d'Or **24**
Felix's **30**
Galatoire's **32**
Gumbo Shop **13**
House of Blues **2**
Johnny's Po-Boy **10**
K-Paul's Louisiana Kitchen **7**
Kaldi's **20**
Le Jardin **4**
Louis XVI **34**
Miss Jean's Saddlery **3**
Mr. B's Bistro **29**
Napoleon House **9**
Nola **8**
Old Dog, New Trick **28**

Palm Court Jazz Cafe **23**
Pelican Club **27**
Poppy's Grill **14**
Port of Call **25**
Quarter Scene **44**
Rib Room **39**
St. Ann's Deli **43**
Sebastian's Little Garden **21**
Steamboat *Natchez* **11**
Tujague's **17**

3

sions

Food, music, and
celebration—these
are the main
reasons why
travelers come to
New Orleans.
Most special

events in town, especially the big blasts of Mardi Gras and Jazz Fest, happily combine these three elements. But otherwise things here are pretty low-key, despite the city's rowdy reputation. There is no Taj Mahal, no Parthenon, no Great Wall. The city has just enough attractions to keep you from feeling you've blown the airfare, but nothing to get so lathered up about that you feel guilty if you just hang out at the Napoleon House or Kaldi's, gearing up for another night of gorging and easygoing debauchery. The main attraction is the sui generis French Quarter, and there's no need to crack out of bed in a rush to get there—it's been where it is for going on 300 years, and chances are good it'll still be there at noon. Besides, if you're like most people, your hotel is probably in the Quarter already. Just ease out the door and enjoy it on unhurried strolls.

Unless you need a vacation from them, don't hesitate to bring the kids. Despite its carefully cultivated reputation as a sin-loving city, New Orleans has plenty of activities for the little ones. (There are, after all, little ones who live here, and they don't all grow up inside a Bourbon Street bar.) The Monday edition of the *Times-Picayune* carries a full page of "Parents and Children" happenings, and the Friday edition's "Lagniappe" section runs a calendar of kids' activities. There's a top-notch zoo, an excellent aquarium, a couple of fun streetcars to clang around on, and great parks for relaxing or exploring. All very laid-back. Just don't expect the Taj Mahal.

Getting Your Bearings

You probably will not get your bearings in New Orleans—at least, not if you depend upon mundane directions like north, south, east, and west. Nobody in town knows which way is up, if you ask directions by compass points. The Mississippi River, which carved out this crescent-shaped land mass in the first place, cuts an S-shaped swath through the city and creates chaos with such conventional directions. The sun rises in the east here, just like it does anywhere else, but in New Orleans it appears first over the West Bank. Which is east of the East Bank. You'll make yourself crazy if you try to outsmart the river. Creative Orleanians go with the river's flow: Uptown is upriver, Downtown is downriver, "lakeside" is toward Lake Pontchartrain, and "riverside" is toward the Ol' Man.

The **French Quarter** is riverside, nestling up against a great bend in the Mississippi. The Quarter's downriver border is Esplanade Avenue, Rampart Street lies lakeside, and

Iberville Street is the Uptown border. (By some accounts, Canal Street is the Uptown border, but not according to the Vieux Carré Commission, a body set up in 1936 by the state legislature to oversee the preservation of the Quarter. The blocks between Iberville and Canal Streets are not under the jurisdiction of the VCC, and tend to be on the raunchy side.) The French Quarter's streets—laid out by French engineers in 1721, back when the French Quarter was called "La Nouvelle Orleans"—are designed in a regimental grid, covering about one square mile. The Vieux Carré, as the Quarter is also called, means Old Square, but this term is misleading—it's more a parallelogram than a square. The centerpiece is Jackson Square, neatly hemmed in by Decatur, St. Ann, St. Peter, and Chartres Streets.

The **Central Business District (CBD)** is adjacent to the French Quarter, the great divide between the two being Canal Street. Canal separates not only the Quarter and the CBD but also Uptown from Downtown. Everything above, or upriver, of Canal Street is Uptown; everything below it, or downriver, is Downtown. The foot of Canal Street stands smack at the Mississippi; when you stroll on Canal with your back toward the river, you're headed lakeside. The somewhat loosely defined boundaries of the CBD are Canal Street, Loyola Avenue, Howard Avenue, and the river. Within the CBD lies the **Warehouse District**, a pocket of abandoned 19th-century warehouses now renovated as restaurants, nightclubs, art galleries, and apartments.

Just uptown of the CBD is the **Lower Garden District**, a residential area struggling to restore and repair itself, and beyond it lies the **Garden District**, the ritzy residential area that the Lower Garden District aspires to catch up with. Continuing uptown beyond the Garden District you come to **Audubon Park**, with its terrific zoo, and the **university section**, home to Loyola and Tulane Universities. With its proliferation of kinetic college kids, the university section has some of the best and grungiest bars and music clubs. New Orleans proper, which is all of Orleans Parish, extends across the river to include **Algiers**, an old neighborhood on the West Bank, as well as up to Lake Pontchartrain; the big soup bowl called **Mid-City** stretches between Downtown and Lake Pontchartrain. Much of New Orleans lies 5 to 8 feet below sea level, and much of New Orleans is Mid-City. This is where the first French settlers camped, along Bayou St. John, before moving along a Native American portage (now called Bayou

Road) toward the river to stake out the colony that is now the French Quarter. Mid-City is predominantly residential, but within it are the 1,500 green acres of City Park, a slew of cemeteries, and the Fair Grounds, main stomping grounds not only of Thoroughbred racehorses but of the Jazz Fest.

Normal directions get a little easier once you get away from the serpentine river. Lake Pontchartrain forms the northern border of the city proper; on its north shore lies **St. Tammany Parish**, with its homes and pretty parks and pine trees. On the south shore, Lakeshore Drive laces alongside the lake, running about 5 miles from Lakefront Airport to the **West End**. (The lake is big with locals for fishing, boating, and picnicking; swimming, however, is officially banned in its polluted waters.) The West End is awash with seafood restaurants, some of the city's best; Orleanians will drive out to the West End and just cruise the parking lots, checking to see which seafood shack they can get into with the least amount of waiting time.

If you fly into town, as most people do, you'll land at New Orleans International Airport, a.k.a. Moisant Field, which occupies a good chunk of **Kenner**, a Jefferson Parish town about 15 miles west of downtown New Orleans. The greater New Orleans metropolitan area includes Jefferson Parish— where predominantly residential **Metairie** has a host of great eating and drinking establishments—and, to the east, **St. Bernard Parish**, which is of vital interest to people who live there but has almost nothing of interest to visitors.

A Madness Called Mardi Gras

It's the biggest party thrown on the North American continent. Thousands of people flock into town for the big event—and a host of Orleanians leave town to avoid them. In the final throes of the Carnival season a million or more people jam the streets of the French Quarter and the CBD. Shrieking, screaming throngs line the parade routes, cheering on the big, gaudy floats that lumber through the streets, juking to the music of the marching bands, and scrambling like animals for the trinkets tossed out into the crowd by the float riders. Those in the know know that "Carnival" and "Mardi Gras" are not interchangeable. Carnival is the season, beginning on January 6 (the twelfth night of Christmas) and continuing for roughly a month until it ends abruptly at midnight before Ash Wednesday, when Lent begins. Literally speaking, "Mardi Gras" is one day, Fat Tuesday, but Orleanians usually refer to the final frenzied two weeks of the

Carnival season as Mardi Gras. Fat Tuesday is a legal holiday in New Orleans; it may as well be, seeing as how you can scarcely manage to cross the streets for the throngs, let alone get to an office.

If you haven't actually been in the city during the celebration you haven't seen Mardi Gras, because much of it is X-rated. Camerafolk catching the live action on Bourbon and Canal Streets have to exercise extreme caution—otherwise the kiddies are liable to get a big surprise. New Orleans families head for the neutral ground Uptown or in the 'burbs, where the scene is a little less raunchy.

Carnival is famously celebrated in other places—notably Venice, Rio, and Trinidad, to name but three—but the specialty of the house in New Orleans is the "throws." Float riders toss souvenirs to the crowds, in the form of colored plastic beads, "doubloons" (aluminum coins), bikinis, mini-footballs, candies, or whatever. The most coveted of all souvenirs are the gilded coconuts of the Zulu Social Aid & Pleasure Club, which the riders hand out mostly to pals they see along the parade route. (The grass-skirted Zulus also throw spears, so it's kind of a good idea to keep an eye out.) People will

Mardi Gras Roots

Mardi Gras came to Louisiana from France. On March 3, 1699, when French-Canadian Pierre LeMoyne, Sieur d'Iberville, the founder of Louisiana, made camp south of the present city, he noted in his diary that the day was Mardi Gras, and christened the site Pointe du Mardi Gras. By most accounts, the early celebrations of the occasion were little more than rowdy street brawls. The modern tradition of Mardi Gras began in 1857, when six Englishmen joined with 13 Creoles to form a secret men's society—the Mystick Krewe of Comus (note the Olde English spelling)— and staged the first Mardi Gras parade. The first Rex parade was hastily thrown together in 1872, to entertain a royal visitor, the Grand Duke Alexei Alexandrovich Romanov. Rex began some of the enduring customs—the Mardi Gras colors of purple, gold, and green, and the "theme" song, "If Ever I Cease to Love," which blares all over town. A silly song for a ridiculously silly season.

NEW ORLEANS | DIVERSIONS

do almost anything to snag souvenirs, and what with the float riders hollering "Show me your tits, babe," anything is what goes. To reach up to riders heaving beads on the double- and triple-decker floats, you'll need a pair of shoulders to ride on, and they don't necessarily have to belong to someone you know. Things get right friendly on Canal Street. Over on Bourbon Street, the scene is even more, um, colorful. Balconies nearly sag under the weight of all those revelers, many of whom are under the impression that a local ordinance requires baring the anatomy for Fat Tuesday. Down on the street, otherwise sane people howl for more baring and bead-slinging.

Costumes, on those folks who aren't bared, range from the tacky to the wildly extravagant; for the most outrageous, check out the annual gay competition at St. Ann and Burgundy Streets. All of the local television stations have roving reporters on Bourbon, down on the street and up on balconies, interviewing Howdy Doodies, Napoleons, Marilyn Monroes, and walking lipsticks, crawfish, raisins, and trash cans.

Things get moving pretty early on Mardi Gras morn, with the appearances around town of the Mardi Gras Indians. The "Indians" are blacks whose "tribes" meet and do ritualistic calls and responses, usually around Orleans and Claiborne Avenues—not in the Quarter. They wear Carnival's most elaborate costumes, with huge feathered, beaded, and sequined headdresses—the costumes are all handmade, and they usually take a year to make. Other early risers are the various walking clubs, most famously Pete Fountain's Half-Fast Walking Club and the Jefferson City Buzzards. They amble around in costumes, accompanied by marching bands, and manage to hit all the bars along the route. The first major parade of the day is the Zulu Social Aid & Pleasure Club, which lurches onto Canal Street somewhere around 10am (their scheduled arrival is 8:30am). The almost all-black krewe, decked out in grass skirts and blackface, was begun in 1909 as a spoof on the Rex parade.

Code Words

If you're in town more than 10 or 15 minutes you'll probably hear the word krewe bandied about. Krewes (pronounced like crews) are the social and civic clubs that mastermind, pay for, and "put on" Mardi Gras. All of the krewes host elaborate Carnival balls, and some 60 or so of them stage the parades for which this city is so famous. Members pay annual dues—in some cases, they're pretty stiff—which go toward the cost of the floats, the costumes they wear on the floats, and the souvenirs they toss to the crowds along the parade routes.

Sometime after noon, the spoofed krewe itself—Rex, King of Carnival—heads down St. Charles Avenue, the king's appearance heralded by his captain on a splendid white stallion and 33 lieutenants, all of them in masks and elegant costumes, with helmets and high white plumes. Rex himself, a middle-aged businessman wearing tights, wig, and theatrical makeup, rides on a glittering white float shaped like a crown, regally waving his silvered scepter. The parade stops at Gallier

Hall for the ritual toast from the mayor and then lumbers onto Canal Street. There, the king toasts his queen (who is always a debutante), speechifies, and presents her with a big bouquet of roses. Hard on the heels of the Rex parade come the truck parades, dearly beloved by the crowds because they are very generous with their throws. The partying is flat-out up until midnight, when mounted police with bullhorns enter the Quarter at Canal Street and move slowly along Bourbon, announcing in stentorian tones that Mardi Gras is over. And on Ash Wednesday, the beginning of Lent, the faithful head for the altars and the ashes.

To get suitably costumed to join the hordes, see "You Probably Didn't Know." Do as locals do and pick up Arthur Hardy's *Mardi Gras Guide,* a glossy magazine that'll give you updates on krewes, balls you can buy tickets to (though locals wouldn't be caught dead doing that), and, most important, parade routes and schedules. A Mardi Gras bible.

Jazz Fest

The city's second-biggest blow-out is the ten-day-long **New Orleans Jazz and Heritage Festival**, which everyone calls the Jazz Fest. The Jazz Fest crowd is much more subdued than the Mardi Gras celebrants—they are dedicated, let us say devout, music lovers who come to hear the likes of B. B. King, Ray Charles, Gladys Knight, and Chuck Berry, not to mention homegrowns like the Neville Brothers, the Marsalis family, Harry Connick, Jr., Ernie K-Doe, Irma Thomas, Wanda Rouzan, and Marva Wright. Some 4,000 musicians perform during the Fest, which begins the last weekend in April and continues through the first weekend of May.

The main venue on weekends is the infield at the Fair Grounds. Tents and stages are set up, and about 70,000 jukin' and jivin' fans show up daily, dancing in the dirt, second-lining, licking jambalaya off their fingers, and just generally having a fine old time. Craftspeople bring their handiwork to hawk (don't expect museum-quality artworks), and there is plenty of good regional food. Non-Orleanian Fest fans return year after year; some people have even moved to the city permanently as a result of it. For information, call 504/522–4786, or write to the New Orleans Jazz and Heritage Festival, 1205 N. Rampart St. 70116. Jazz Fest admission is a one-time charge at the gate; once you're inside the Fair Grounds, you don't pay for any of the music events. As for purchasing advance tickets: you can avoid long lines at the gate by purchasing tickets through Ticketmaster (tel 504/522–5555), but there are no reserved seats (no seats at all) at the Fair Grounds. However, during the Fest there are various events in auditoriums and on riverboats, and tickets for those should be purchased as soon as they go on sale. Best bet is to call or write to the New Orleans Jazz and Heritage Festival to ask for a schedule and to find out when tickets go on sale. Reserving a hotel room a full year in advance is not unheard of. This is a very, very popular event. You should reserve as soon as you decide you'd like to be in New Orleans during the Jazz Fest because rooms are very tight.

The Lowdown

Must-sees for first-time visitors from Peoria...

There's only one thing in town that a traveler really can't go home without seeing: the **French Quarter**. One of the nation's favorite partying places, the Quarter is an ongoing show, with a cast of characters right out of a Fellini flick. Pay no mind to the spooky-looking woman with the iron-gray hair, silver-colored crash helmet, and long black clothes—she's but one of the French Quarter fixtures, along with flamboyant transvestites, white-robed priests, gritty skinheads, tattooed bikers in battered jeans, grungy street musicians, and park rangers in their Smoky-the-Bear hats. Oceans of badge-wearing tourists pour through every day, mixing in with some 5,000 or so Quarterites, who have grown inured to living in this unsanitized equivalent of Disneyland. This movielike setting was, for the most part, designed by the Spanish, not the French—almost all of the original French colony La Nouvelle Orleans burned in the 18th century and was rebuilt by the ruling power at the time, which just happened to be the Spaniards. Narrow, straight-as-an-arrow streets run in front of small, colorful structures that hunker right down flush with the sidewalks, all done up with an overkill of fancy ironwork, galleries, dormers, courtyards, and gingerbread trim. These 19th-century town houses, carriage houses, slave quarters, and stables now house apartments and hotels, restaurants, guest houses, creaky old bookstores, shabby jazz joints, museums, markets, and newsstands.

Perhaps the Quarter's most notorious street is **Bourbon Street**, at least the stretch between Bienville and St. Ann Streets. It has all the flavor of a carnival midway, including tourists gawking along down the middle of the street with a go-cup of booze, craning their necks to peer indoors at a male strip show or a ladies' mud-wrestling competition. Carny-type barkers bark outside many of the joints, spieling the X-rated marvels inside. Doors of music clubs are flung wide to let the sounds out and lure the customers in. Bourbon is actually relatively harmless, as long as you stay aware of where your wallet is, don't volunteer for the mud-wrestling, and take care not to trip over all the discarded go-cups. (A tourist once wrote to the *Times-Picayune* suggesting that a ban on go-cups would go far toward cleaning up all that litter on Bourbon. The letter drew shrieks of laughter from Orleanians: Yeah, sure—why not just board up all the bars while you're at it? Close the street altogether. Besides, locals don't drive two blocks without a go-cup of something, even if it's just iced tea.)

Special moments... As you walk along the streets of the Quarter, peering into the pretty **courtyards** tucked away behind the streetfront buildings, don't be surprised if someone—an apartment dweller, the building owner, someone—appears behind the iron gate and asks if you'd like to come in and take your picture among the banana trees and petunias. Residents of this neighborhood may be used to having their home turf overrun with tourists, but that doesn't mean that they're blasé about the Quarter's charms—many of them actually get a kick out of sharing the place with appreciative strangers. The Quarter is generally a ripe place for serendipitous encounters; keep your ears open and eventually you'll hear an *a capella* rendition of "Amazing Grace" or some other inspiring number, sung by some grungy **street musician** who just happens to have an awesome voice. For some reason, in New Orleans even the most touristy experiences can seem magical. While strolling in the Quarter, you'll suddenly hear a wheezy, off-key calliope belting out the tune to "If You Knew Susie..."—and you'll know it's the **Steamboat *Natchez***, warbling away at the Toulouse Street Wharf. The calliope is deliberately tuned wrong, to attract attention and to sound charmingly small-time. The boat itself is a totally slick commercial operation, but somehow that old-timey riverboat song gets you every time. Another corny tourist fixture is those **fringed surreys** prowling the Quarter, drawn by poor mules wearing dumb straw hats. Thanks to them, Quarter streets smell more like mule-doo than magnolias, but the sharp *clip-clop* of their hooves echoing off the walls of the quiet narrow streets does make your heart flip-flop. If you're someone who doesn't embarrass easily, go ahead and take a ride—the Quarter really does look especially romantic from inside a fringed surrey.

Only in New Orleans... For obvious reasons, nowhere else can you tour the **Historic New Orleans Collection**, an incredible private archive housed in the beautifully restored 18th-century Merieult House. This Spanish Colonial house survived the fire of 1794 almost intact, and clichéd as it may sound, touring it truly gives you the feeling of stepping back in time. You'll see just enough to marvel at the persistence (some might say obsessiveness) of the late Kemper and Leila Williams, who basically devoted their lives to gathering precious documents and memorabilia pertinent to New Orleans's past, eventually amassing one of the nation's largest such collections. The Williams Gallery on the ground floor mounts changing exhibits of regional interest, and a gift shop sells some uniquely New Orleans items—the miniature carousel flying horses are precious.

A total tourist trap, but one you'd find nowhere else, the **New Orleans Historic Voodoo Museum** cultivates a spooky atmosphere as it documents the history of this weird animistic religion imported with slaves from Africa, via the West Indies, in the 19th century. Real voodoo worshippers would never come near this place, but it's kind of a hoot, if you take it with a grain of salt. Another aspect of New Orleans's eccentric dark side is its above-ground **cemeteries** (see "Cities of the Dead," below), included on every bus tour and a fair number of postcards, but well worth a look-see.

For local color, try the **Old Farmers' Market**, where farmers have been bringing their products for almost 200 years. Less overrun with tourists than the shops and eateries of French Market (also on N. Peters Street, but a couple of blocks closer to Jackson Square), this produce market is open around the clock. Early in the morning, the chefs compete with one another for the freshest veggies and fruit. From dawn until dusk, more or less, a flea market also sprawls around the rear of the sheds around

Barracks Street. Locals love browsing through the array of old records, paperbacks, jewelry, knickknacks, doodads, and gadgets. (If you hate crowds, this is not the place to be.) **Lafitte's Blacksmith Shop** is a crumbling old cottage in the lower Quarter, with wood floors, brick walls, candlelight (at night, anyway), and atmosphere oozing out of every crack. The house was built around 1772 and according to legend was a blacksmith shop operated by Jean and Pierre Lafitte as a front for their nefarious smuggling and slave-trading activities. Despite all this colorful history, it's not a tourist hangout but a great favorite of locals.

Best people-watching... The hub of the Quarter is **Jackson Square**, where a flagstone pedestrian mall surrounds a small green park—Place d'Armes to the French, Plaza de Armas to the Spanish, and later Public Square to the Americans. In the early days, the militia trained on their parade grounds here, and the square was the site of various public hangings and lashings, slave auctions, and numerous grisly happenings. These days, the square is alive with clowns, mimes, Dixieland bands, bongo players, tarot-card readers, sidewalk artists, and sundry vendors, as well as crowds of locals and tourists strolling around enjoying the mad whirl.

Lazing alongside the Mississippi, **Woldenberg Riverfront Park** is a 13-acre landscaped park where you can stretch out on the grass, catch the breeze, and watch the ever-changing river scenes. Quarterites like to flop down on the green grass under a shade tree and read or watch the play of river traffic.

Cities of the Dead... Ghoulish as it may sound, New Orleans's graveyards are a perennial tourist draw. These so-called Cities of the Dead really do look like minicities, with their surrounding walls, network of sidewalks, and above-ground tombs trimmed with fancy ironwork and surrounded by little iron picket fences. There are little white cottagelike tombs, but also wildly elaborate temples, mausoleums, and statuary. Why are the tombs above ground? Well, back in the early days, before all the drainage canals and pumps were installed, below-ground burials were pretty gruesome affairs—with much of the city below sea level, a grave dug six feet under what passed for ground soon filled up with water, and coffins bearing the dear departed had an unsettling way of bobbing right up to the surface. Long poles were used to push the coffins back down; sometimes holes were bored in the coffin bottoms, so they would fill with water and sink. A great deal of hideous gurgling ensued, adding considerably to the grief of the bereaved. It probably didn't take much of that before the Creoles began "burying" folks above ground. The oldest of the city's cemeteries still on its feet is **St. Louis Cemetery No. 1**, established in 1789 beyond the ramparts of Rampart Street. Among the city's early notables interred here, the most famous may be 19th-century voodoo queen Marie Laveau. Look for a whitewashed tomb in St. Louis No. 1, engraved "Glapion" (Laveau's married name) and usually decked with flowers, voodoo charms, and crosses scratched with redbrick dust. In the Garden District's **Lafayette Cemetery**, laid out in the early 1800s as the burial ground for Lafayette, at least one wedding has taken place and scenes from the movie *Interview with the Vampire* were shot. The most famous tomb here is the mass tomb of the Jefferson Fire Company No. 22, erected in 1852 and featuring a huge bas-relief of a fire engine. **Lakelawn Metairie Cemetery**, the city's largest, was once a racetrack, which accounts for its oval shape; it's the only cemetery you can drive through, and has capitalized on this advantage by offering cassette tapes at the entrance to help you on your touring. Bring your camera along for close-ups of the elaborate statuary. Except for Lakelawn Metairie, which you can view from the protection of your car, it is not safe to wander through these graveyards by yourself. Muggers know that naive tourists may be exploring these cemeteries, and it's too good an opportunity for them to pass up. The three St. Louis Cemeteries are in crime-ridden, drug-friendly neighborhoods; even Lafayette Cemetery, in the upscale Garden District, can be risky (that's why its gate is generally kept locked). Cemetery tours led by groups like **Save Our Cemeteries** or **Magic Walking Tours** offer safety in numbers, as well as having tour guides who can tell you fascinating stories. Orleanians themselves visit the cemeteries on All Saints Day, November 1, which is a legal holiday here, and practically a minifestival—folks drive to the graveyards to clean the tombs of their loved ones and lay fresh flowers on them. Families often bring picnics and spend the entire day.

A streetcar named St. Charles... One of the best ways to get an overview of the Garden District, Uptown, and the University sections is to take a round-trip ride aboard the streetcar (New Orleanians never say trolley), the city's moving National Historic Landmark. The St. Charles Streetcar line is one of the world's oldest street railway systems; it began as a mule-and-carriage line in 1835, linking New Orleans with the little towns of Lafayette and Carrollton, both incorporated into the city in the 1850s. The old-fashioned green cars, with their wooden seats and plank floors, start their clanking, rumbling in the CBD at Canal and Carondelet Streets. Once you cross Jackson Avenue, you'll be rolling through the **Garden District**, the city's ritziest residential district, bounded by Magazine Street and St. Charles, Louisiana, and Jackson Avenues. Settled by the Americans who came barging downriver following the 1803 Louisiana Purchase, the Garden District was developed from an area of former sugar plantations; while the Creoles in the French Quarter hid their courtyards from the streets, notice how the Americans surrounded their palatial homes with magnificent gardens. The most prevalent architectural style here is Greek Revival, but there are also lovely Queen Anne houses, replete with turrets, verandas, and stained-glass windows. Upriver of the Garden District lies 400-acre **Audubon Park**, notable for its live oak trees and the Audubon Zoo. Upriver of St. Charles near Audubon Park lies **Tulane University**, founded by a group of doctors in 1834 as the Medical College of Louisiana and still noted for its medical school as well as its law school. Tulane is Louisiana's largest private university, with a student body of more than 12,000. **Loyola University**, adjacent to Tulane, is somewhat smaller, with a student body of around 6,000. Louisiana native Edward Douglas White, chief justice of the U.S. Supreme Court from 1910 until 1921, was a Loyola alum. At the great upriver bend in the Mississippi, where St. Charles Avenue deadends, the streetcar hangs a right onto Carrollton Avenue, and eventually pulls to a stop at Palmer Park—the end of the line. There, if you're round-tripping, you pay an additional fare and reverse the wooden seat so that you face forward for the trip downtown. A round-trip takes about 90 minutes. Mind, this is a commuter line for many Orleanians, and you'd be wise to avoid the crowds during morning and afternoon rush hours, and along about 3pm when school lets out.

Save it for a rainy day... Those lacy cast-iron galleries and balconies in the Quarter are utilitarian as well as decorative, extending over the banquettes (a.k.a. sidewalks) to provide some protection from the elements. Unless there's a downpour—not unusual here in the subtropics—you can generally keep on browsing through the Quarter, sprinting from the shelter of one overhang to the next. But if the rain comes down in buckets, you might want to take to the great indoors. Zip up to City Park to the **New Orleans Museum of Art** (NOMA), in a pretty white neoclassical building built mid-century or so. It's actually a place worth visiting even when it's not raining—the permanent collection is truly impressive, covering 17th-century to 19th-century European art. Traveling shows here tend to be of high quality too, but make a beeline for the fabulous Fabergé eggs. You can while away a fair amount of time in the gift shop alone. It might take a rainstorm to drive you into the offbeat **New Orleans Pharmacy Museum**, but once here you'll be fascinated—though you'll also thank your lucky whatevers you didn't live in the 19th century when you see the lineup of terrifying medical implements on display. America's first licensed pharmacist, Louis J. Dufilho, had this house built in 1823 as his apothecary shop and home; he lived upstairs, grew things of a medicinal nature in the rear courtyard, and worked in the ground-floor shop.

If the sight of more water doesn't depress you, drop into the **Aquarium of the Americas**, a big, modern facility, opened in 1990, that just keeps growing. Several thousand species swim and slither about in the various exhibits, representing the Caribbean, Gulf of Mexico, Mississippi River, and Amazon rain forest; the Amazon one is the best of the lot. In October 1995, a new $25-million wing opened, with a 354-seat theater featuring a giant IMAX 3-D screen.

If you're not in the mood for cultural pursuits, head for **Keuffer's** (pronounced kway-fers) or **Checkpoint Charlie's** and join the locals shooting pool. Both are favorite hanging-out joints. Aslosh with slots and gaming tables, the **Treasure Chest Casino**—an old-style riverboat docked not far from the airport—does a land-office business out in Kenner. Or if you're in the mood for more dainty pursuits, try romancing the scones in **Le Salon**, the lobby lounge of the ever-so-British Windsor Court hotel. This tea salon is an eminently cushy affair, with chamber music (often played just a bit too loud) and trays of fancy scones, finger sandwiches, and chocolate truffles. Orleanians love to come late in the afternoon, after a hard day at the law firm or the ad agency. But the most time-honored hall for whiling away a rainy day is the **Napoleon House**, so named because its owner in the early 1800s, New Orleans mayor Nicholas Girod, spearheaded a failed attempt to rescue exiled Napoleon Bonaparte from St. Helena and bring him to New Orleans (the third floor was added as the emperor's new home, though he died—in 1821—before the rescue could be carried out). Pull up a chair at a weathered table next to the open French doors, nurse a Pimm's cup or a cappuccino, order a muffuletta if you like—they're wonderful here—and just watch the rain splattering on the pavement.

Home sweet historic home... The **Gallier House**, one of three house museums in the French Quarter, is the one you should make the most effort to see. The private home of architect James Gallier, Jr. (whose father was known for St. Patrick's Church and Gallier Hall, see below), who designed and built it in 1857, it's a stately place, with wrought-iron galleries outside and Corinthian columns inside. The house is decorated in 19th-century Creole style, meaning very grand: velvet and brocaded antique furnishings, an etched-glass skylight over the stairs, handsome gas chandeliers hanging from 12-foot ceilings, and rich displays of silver and porcelain. Docents walk and talk you through it, which is good, because you wouldn't want to miss a single gorgeous detail.

Just a block away, look for the Greek Revival portico of the **Beauregard-Keyes House**, built in 1826. Though it's pretty and has lovely English gardens, this house is most worthwhile for its relics of two famous former occupants. After the Civil War, Confederate General Pierre Gustav Toutant Beauregard—a native Orleanian (called in these parts "the Great Creole") and the commander who ordered the first shot fired at Fort Sumter—lived for a short time in the house. It was bought in the 1940s and restored by Frances Parkinson Keyes, the novelist who wrote *Dinner at Antoine's, Steamboat Gothic*, and other tales of the region. (Her books are sold in the gift shop.) And while you're at it, continue on to the third house museum in the neighborhood, the **Hermann-Grima House**, an American-style town house dolled up with green shutters and lacy balconies. It was built in 1831 for a rich Philadelphia merchant named Samuel Hermann; in 1844 it was purchased by Judge Felix Grima. The most memorable thing about this house is the way its curators dress it up for each season, changing the upholstery covers and adding various holiday touches —all the historic houses do Creole Christmas decorations, but only Hermann-Grima sets up a funeral tableau for Halloween. Pay special note to the formal dining room, laid out with fine crystal, china, and silver. In the rear outbuildings, off the landscaped parterre gardens, Creole cooking demonstrations (and tastings) take place from October through May.

Well worth the $8 cab fare from the Quarter, **Longue Vue House & Gardens** is a bit of an oddity in New Orleans, designed after a grand English manor rather than a plantation house. This mansion once was home to New Orleans's philanthropist Edgar Stern and his wife, Sears heiress Edith Rosenwald Stern; it's not so much an architectural landmark as a museum of decorative arts. Of all New Orleans's house museums, this one has the best grounds, with eight acres of manicured theme gardens and a stunning formal Spanish court inspired by the Generalife Gardens of Alhambra, Spain.

If you liked the Louisiana furnishings displayed at the New Orleans Museum of Art, you may want to swing on over to the **Pitot House** nearby, a marvelous old relic that dates from about 1799. Now headquarters of the Louisiana Landmarks Society, which moved the house to its present site in 1962, the creaky old place is filled with some knockout Federal antiques. It's also a fine example of a West Indies–style house, of brick-between-posts construction. New Orleans mayor James Pitot bought it in 1810 as a quiet retreat for himself and his family. The most unusual houses in the city, though, are the **Doullut Houses**, built right by the levee, downriver of the French Quarter. Also called the Steamboat Houses, these are two identical homes designed by steamboat captain M. Paul Doullut—one for him and his wife (also a riverboat captain), the other across the street for their son. Set by the levee where they could be as close as possible to the Doulluts' beloved river, the houses look like two steamboats run aground, right down to their pilothouses and the big wooden beads strung between the posts on the galleries. The very quirkiness of these houses is what's most appealing about them; they're a ways off the beaten track, though, and you have to make an appointment to tour them.

Scarlett O'Hara doesn't live here anymore...

Drive about an hour west of New Orleans and you'll be smack-dab in plantation country, where many 19th-century homes along the river and the bayous have been restored and filled with lovely antiques. **Tours by Isabelle** runs half-day minivan trips to the area (also known as the River Road), but while this will save you driving, it isn't necessary to hook up with a tour—docents walk you through nearly all of these houses, cueing you to ooh and aah over the *garconnières*, *pigeonnières*, petticoat mirrors, armoires, and testers carved by the top cabinetmaker of the day, Prudent Mallard, and sideboards nearly sagging from the weight of all that silver. If you have time for only one, make it **Madewood Plantation**, down on the West Bank near Bayou Lafourche. Currently operated as a B&B, it's also open for touring, but it's the least blatantly commercial of the pack—and probably the most perfectly restored. The 21-room Greek Revival mansion was designed by Irish architect Henry Howard and "made of wood" (hence the name) in 1846 for Colonel Thomas Pugh. Before you leave, wander out to take a look at the old gravestones in the Pugh family cemetery.

The better-known **Houmas House** is indeed a gem—a well-preserved Greek Revival mansion famous in these parts for its spiral staircase, and for having been the setting for the gothic movie thriller *Hush... Hush, Sweet Charlotte.* The main problem here is that so many tourists pass through it that the hoop-skirted young docents look glassy-eyed and bored as they recite their canned spiel. (Interrupt them to ask an unscripted question and you'll get a blank stare in reply.) Still, the house is worth the trip, the grounds are gorgeous, and the river looks splendid from atop the levee. And while you're in the neighborood, you can also head a short way west to drive past **Ashland Belle-Hélène**, a magnificent but unrestored Greek Revival that unfortunately is no longer open to the public. (A years-long dispute among family members about what to do with the house finally ended when they stopped arguing long enough to sell it to an oil company, which has announced plans to stabilize if not restore it.) You can only see it from a distance, a ghostly beauty snoozing beneath tall, moss-draped oaks, but it's a classic example of what went with the wind—you can almost imagine Yankee soldiers pillaging it.

Also along River Road, but quite different from the fully restored plantation houses, **Laura Plantation**—a complex of 12 Creole structures built in 1805—is fascinating to visit as a restoration-in-progress, which should eventually be opened as a bed-and-breakfast. The restoration work is based on 100 pages from the diary of Laura Locoul, great-granddaughter of the Spanish commandant who built the house in 1805. Laura was born on the sugar plantation in 1861, inherited the whole shebang when she was 19, and was still alive when JFK was elected president. Lifesized cutouts of family members stand throughout the house and tour guides take on the characters of the people who inhabited the house, telling family secrets and talking about the displays—everything from false teeth to dancing slippers. Historical documents show that Senegalese slaves here first told the folk tales that were later adapted by Joel Chandler Harris as the Brer Rabbit stories.

Blasts from the past... Of the four buildings that comprise the **Louisiana State Museum** complex—the Cabildo, the Presbytère, the 1850 House, and the Old U.S. Mint—the most interesting is The Cabildo. It is the most famous building in the complex, built on Jackson Square in 1795 as a home for the *cabildo*, or Spanish governing council, replacing an earlier wooden structure that went up in flames in 1788; another fire swept through the building almost exactly 200 years later, in 1988, causing enough damage to require six years and several million dollars in restoration. Some people think the end result looks far too new and spiffy for so venerable a building—it may be much safer, but it doesn't creak and groan anymore. It's a historic site—transfer papers for the 1803 Louisiana Purchase were signed here in the second-floor *sala capitular*, and the Marquis de Lafayette stayed here while on a triumphal tour in 1825—and the artifacts and artworks displayed give a very politically correct version of history. The nearby Presbytère, almost an identical twin of the Cabildo (it was originally built as a residence for the priests who served in the adjacent St. Louis Cathedral, but never was used as such), presently offers changing exhibits of varying interest. The museum's fourth building is a bit farther off, on the fringe of the Quarter—the Old U.S. Mint, which was built in 1835 as a branch of the federal mint and churned out about $300 million in coins during its career. When Louisiana seceded from the Union in 1861, the Yankees shut it down; it reopened in 1879, following Reconstruction, and went out of the coin-minting business for good in 1909. It now houses two exhibits paying tribute to modern New Orleans's two top attractions: Jazz and Mardi Gras. The jazz exhibit does a pretty good job of tracing the music's history, but the Mardi Gras exhibit is more show than substance. The 1850 House is a restored apartment that demonstrates how mid-19th-century Creole city folk lived.

If you want history to leap to life, better try the "Louisiana Legends" exhibits at the **Musée Conti Wax Museum**. No kidding. Not at all a schlocky wax museum, New Orleans's answer to Madame Tussaud's displays more than a hundred colorful tableaux of the city's history. All of the legends are here—Lafitte the pirate, Marie Laveau and her voodoo dancers, Madame Delphine Lalaurie—and wax effigies of more modern figures such as Governor Edwin Edwards and clarinetist and native son Pete Fountain.

If you're into "old," the **Old Ursuline Convent** on Chartres Street will satisfy your quest for the wonderfully ancient. This is actually the second convent to occupy this site; a magnificent masonry building, with pitched roof and dormer windows, it was begun on orders of Louis XV in 1745 and completed in 1752. (The sisters of Ursula arrived from Rouen in 1727, shortly after la Nouvelle Orleans got on its feet, to try to straighten out the sundry convicts, prostitutes, and miscreants who were emptied out of French jails to settle the colony. The sisters operated the first school for Indians and the first school for blacks, and taught the young ladies of the colony how to behave in an appropriately aristocratic manner.) It's the oldest building in the lower Mississippi valley, the only structure known for certain to have survived the 18th-century conflagrations that destroyed the colony, and thus the only extant example of pure French Creole architecture. Andrew Jackson came to St. Mary's Chapel, a part of the complex, to personally thank the sisters for their prayers for victory in the Battle of New Orleans.

Civil War relics... During the War Between the States, New Orleans fell to Union troops in 1862 and was occupied longer than any other southern city. The occupying commander, General Benjamin "Beast" Butler, was so locally hated that ladies lined their chamberpots with pictures of him. There's surprisingly little evidence of that grim time in history down here, but if you sat through that whole PBS series and got hooked on Civil War history, check out the **Confederate Museum**, hunkered in a forbidding-looking Romanesque Revival building near Lee Circle. Dedicated in 1891, it's a dank and musty place, full of glass cases containing bloody old battle flags, letters and documents, oil paintings, and weapons—including the first hand grenade ever used on a battlefield. Jefferson Davis's widow donated many of her husband's personal effects to the museum, and parts of Robert E. Lee's silver campaign service are displayed. Some 2,000 Confederate prisoners of war were held during the war in the **Old U.S. Customhouse**, a huge Egyptianesque gray granite building begun before the war, in 1845, but not completed until 1881, well after the war ended. It's still a working customhouse today; there's no sign of its wartime role left, but walk inside anyway to see the Great Marble Hall, a splendid Greek Revival room that stretches 95 feet by 125 feet and soars 54 feet high.

Dueling churches... When the Americans came barging down the river in the early 1800s, it seemed to them that in **St. Louis Cathedral**, "God spoke only in French." Sitting placidly between the Cabildo and the Presbytère, St. Louis Cathedral, named for the French saint-king Louis IX, is the third church to occupy this site (the first was a small wooden church, built in 1724 and blown away by a hurricane; the second burned in the fire of Good Friday, 1788, when the colony burned because, for fear of disturbing the peace, priests would not allow the church bells to be rung in warning). The present church was dedicated in Christmas Eve services in 1794. Small as it is, it's America's oldest active cathedral, designated a minor basilica by Pope Paul VI in 1964; Pope John Paul II visited in 1987, when the plaza in front was named Place Jean Paul Deux. Inside, it's airy and light, with pastel-colored ceiling frescoes and a large mural over the high altar depicting the saint-king Louis IX announcing the seventh crusade. Notorious 19th-century voodoo queen Marie Laveau was said to have worshipped here, maybe even have married here, and after Napoleon's death his Orleanian fans staged a huge mock funeral for him here.

Snubbed by the Creoles, the Americans built their own house of worship in their own sector (the area that's now the CBD). On Lafayette Square, which was the Americans' answer to the Place d'Armes, arose **St. Patrick's Church**, a vastly different house of worship from the French Quarter cathedral. This stark, narrow, gray Gothic church was designed in 1833 by Irishmen James and Charles Dakin, who patterned it after the York Minster Cathedral in England. Most of the interior was the work of James Gallier, Sr., another Irishman (christened "Gallagher" in Dublin, he changed his name to Gallier so as to blend in with the Creoles). Much more ornate inside than St. Louis Cathedral, it's also darker and more brooding, whatever that tells you about the difference between the French and American styles of worship: check out the handsome stained-glass windows and the dramatic murals over the altar, painted in 1841 by Leon Pomerade for a fee of $1,000. While you're here on Lafayette Square, look over at **Gallier Hall**, a Greek Revival masterpiece (not open to the public) across the square, also designed by James Gallier. Ionic columns support a pediment with sculptured figures of Justice, Liberty, and Commerce. Built around 1850, this served as City Hall when the three rival municipalities were united in 1852, dealing a bitter blow to the Creoles, who'd expected the city's administration to be run from their former headquarters, the Cabildo on Jackson Square. In the 1950s, City Hall moved to its present location on Loyola Avenue.

Views to ooh and ahh at... The star attractions, viewwise, are the Mississippi River and Lake Pontchartrain. At **Top of the Mart**, on the 33rd floor of the World Trade Center, you can settle in a comfy chair and nurse a drink while gazing out at the river writhing down toward the Gulf of Mexico. Give yourself about 90 minutes to complete one lazy spin around the compass. If you've got kids with you, though, you won't be allowed in the lounge; you'll be exiled to the 31st-floor Viewpoint, where the surroundings are less plush but you can gaze at the landscape through huge pay telescopes. Provided the notorious New Orleans haze isn't too thick, you might be able to see for 30 miles or so, upriver and down. To enjoy riverside views with fresh air, try landscaped **Woldenberg Riverfront Park** or, a bit farther downriver, near the French Market, **Moonwalk**, an open-air wooden promenade lined with park benches and lollygaggers. It's quite spellbinding after dark, with the lights of the floating palaces and the Crescent City Connection (the bridge connecting the East and West Banks) glitter on the water, though this isn't the safest place to be when the crowd thins out very late at night. On the other side of town—lakeside—**Lakeshore Drive** offers some knockout views as it skirts alongside Lake Pontchartrain, where spiffy white sailboats decorate the water and fisherfolk line up on the flood wall.

Where to read a book... Crack open a book at **Kaldi's** and settle down with an iced cappuccino. Billing itself as a "Coffeehouse and Museum," this relaxed joint in a turn-of-the-century bank building backs up its claim with displays of antique coffee machines, with gunnysacks of coffee at their feet. The back room at **La Marquise** and the rear courtyard of **Croissant d'Or**, two sister patisseries, are both fit places for relaxing and reading over wonderful French pastries made by French chef Maurice Delechelles.

Wheels of fortune... Casinos are to New Orleans in the 1990s what the oil business was in the 1980s—touted as an economic cure-all, at least by those who stand to make big bucks out of the whole thing. A host of Orleanians, in particular preservationists, fought long and hard to prevent the encroachment of casino gambling into the Crescent City; most locals fear that the city will lose its special character and become "another Atlantic City." But the casino crowd, comfortably cozied up to the governor and other elected officials, won the day. Well, the streets ain't paved with gold yet, but real estate values in the Quarter have escalated, driving out the kinds of folks who've always made the place authentically charming. A number of casinos have already opened for business, and they do everything in their power to entice you to stay indoors all day, all night. The only one with its feet firmly planted on dry land is **Harrah's Casino New Orleans**, in Armstrong Park adjacent to the French Quarter. The

76,000-square-foot Mardi Gras–themed gambling den is in the old Municipal Auditorium, within which Jolson, Sinatra, and Elvis once sang (though not together), Baryshnikov danced, and kings and queens of Carnival glittered. Hot controversy attended the conversion of the auditorium into a den of iniquity; Quarterites were in a tizzy about the month-long laser show for Harrah's May 1995 opening. The announced game plan is for Harrah's to turn the keys to the building back to the city once Harrah's opens "the world's largest casino" on Canal Street in May 1996. (Shudder.) Few local observers really think that will happen; Harrah's spent $6 million in high-tech crime-prevention gadgets alone, not counting the megabucks spent on renovations to the building. So far, New Orleans's other casinos are all on boats: The four-decker *Flamingo* floats on the river at the Poydras Street Wharf adjacent to the Hilton Hotel; country-western is the theme at the three-decker *Boomtown Belle*, docked on Harvey Canal on the West Bank in Jefferson Parish; and on Lake Pontchartrain, *Belle of Orleans* is the city's newest floating casino, opened in the summer of 1995 as part of Bally's Casino Lakeshore Resort; it has more or less the same complement of slots and gaming tables as the others.

Can't make it to Mardi Gras?... If you aren't here during Carnival season, you can still get a taste of Mardi Gras—a pretty touristy taste—by visiting the world's largest float builder, headquartered in New Orleans, a ferry ride across the river from the CBD. Blaine Kern designs and builds floats for an international clientele—including some whoppers for Macy's big Thanksgiving Day parade—but locally he's more famous for his rolling Carnival extravaganzas, which are built and stored in the "dens," or warehouses, of **Blaine Kern's Mardi Gras World**. Stop in to watch the artists and craftspeople making fantastic Mardi Gras trappings. Take your camera along—and your kids—for snaps of critters like the gigantic Kong family of the Bacchus parade: King, Queen, and Baby Kong. There's also a film to watch and a souvenir shop for picking up Carnival souvenirs.

Green spaces... Walt Whitman may have been daydreaming about **City Park** and **Audubon Park** when he wrote "I Saw in Louisiana a Live Oak Growing"—the trees in both these parks are simply splendid. By virtue of its being the larger of the two parks, 1,500-acre City Park, up near Lake Pontchartrain (about a ten-minute drive up Esplanade Avenue from the French Quarter), has the lion's share of trees—more than 30,000 of them, the world's largest stand of mature live oaks—but Audubon Park, which is near the Garden District and on the St. Charles Streetcar route, has 3,600 oaks that are no less grand, making perhaps an even more impressive show in the smaller space. Giant exposed roots form natural, if gnarled, park benches, for reading, rendezvousing, and daydreaming. From late November until early January, the trees in City Park are decorated with millions of lights, and Orleanians line their cars up for blocks and blocks waiting to cruise slowly through. (This display is somewhat mysteriously called "A Celebration in the Oaks"; these used to be called "Christmas lights," just as the "celebration" was until recently called "Christmas in the Oaks." Secularism triumphs.)

Besides the natural wonders, both parks offer diversions for those who prefer action to idling (see Getting Outside). Along with plenty of sports stuff, City Park has the New Orleans Museum of Arts (see below) and the Peristyle, where outdoor plays and concerts are sometimes held. There's an amusement park here, with a beautiful antique carousel that locals call the "flying horses" and the P.G.T. Beauregard miniature tram scooting around. Eight miles of lagoons lace dreamily beneath the trees, where swans, ducks, and geese seem pretty much oblivious to the canoers and pedal-boaters out on the water. Audubon Park's main attraction is the zoo (see "Kid-Pleasers," below), but that's a pretty significant attraction. If you want some peace and quiet, head for City Park, where there's room enough to get away from the crowds; lively Audubon Park is better for people-watching and mingling with locals.

Out on the water... In a lot of ways, New Orleans is an "inland island," and it's always easy to get out on the water. (Note, that's "on," not "in." There's water, water everywhere, and not a place to swim, except in manufactured pools. Only the suicidal leap into the river, the lake, or—heaven forbid—the outlying swamps.) The steamboat *Natchez*, the little *John James Audubon*, the

Cajun Queen, and the *Creole Queen* all ply the river. Mark Twain, who knew a thing or two about riverboats, called them "wedding cakes without the complications," which pretty much sums up the look of these replica paddlewheelers: gingerbread trim, gangplanks, railed decks, and interiors with wood paneling, chandeliers, and brass sconces. (Of the four, the *John James Audubon* is the smallest and the least interesting to look at.) Both the *Natchez* and the *Creole Queen* do dinner-with-jazz evening cruises, and there isn't a dime's worth of difference between the two: The *Natchez* is bigger, and ton for ton probably has more frills and geegaws, but the food and music on the boats is about the same—thoroughly competent Dixieland jazz bands and huge buffets of quite good food, served with plastic plates and cutlery (elegant it's not). The *Cajun Queen* and the *John James Audubon* cruise between the aquarium and the zoo; the *Natchez* and the *Creole Queen* do two-hour harbor cruises; and the *Creole Queen* also goes down to the Chalmette Battlefield, where Andrew Jackson fit the Brits during the 1815 Battle of New Orleans, celebrated in song, legend, and souvenirs. Kids may enjoy the food and Dixieland music on the evening cruises, but they're almost guaranteed to get tired and cranky if you haul them off on a two-hour harbor cruise, let alone for the trip to Chalmette. And once you're aboard, there's no getting off. Think about it.

The same goes for the swamp tours. Typically, points of embarkation are an hour or two outside of town by car or minivan, and a tool out on the swamp waters lasts about 90 minutes. So you're looking at around four to six hours total, which may be a bit much for little ones (or even some grown-ups). That being said, Louisiana swamplands are eerily beautiful, and tours through them are enormously popular. Independent-minded travelers enjoy going to the Barataria Unit of the Jean Lafitte National Historical Park Service (see Getting Outside) and renting a canoe at **Bayou Barn** to paddle through the wetlands (guided or unguided). You'll need a car, and it entails an hour's drive down to the West Bank. If you'd rather not go it alone, hook up with **Honey Island Swamp Tours** and let wetland ecologist Dr. Paul Wagner point out the blue herons and tell you about the swamp monster. He's accustomed to people asking him what the difference is between an alligator and a crocodile.

Conveniently, they'll pick you up at your hotel in a mini-van, feed you some red beans and rice after the tour, and then take you back.

Life on the Mississippi... For the ultimate inland-water outing, consider a trip on one of the three overnight paddle wheelers of the **Delta Queen Steamboat Company**, whose home port is in New Orleans: The cozy little 188-passenger *Delta Queen* and her larger, grander sisters, the 420-passenger *Mississippi Queen* and the 436-passenger *American Queen* (launched in 1995 and christened by Mrs. Paul Harvey, wife of the radio commentator, with a giant bottle of Tabasco sauce). All authentically steam-powered, with huge red paddle wheels kicking up froth, gingerbread trim, etched glass, wood paneling, and stained-glass trim, they paddle along at a snail-paced 7 knots or so. The *Delta Queen* is a National Historic Landmark—because of her wooden rather than all-steel superstructure, she sails under a special dispensation from the U.S. Congress; the *Mississippi Queen* and the *American Queen* are essentially luxury cruise ships disguised as 19th-century floating palaces, with whirlpools, exercise room, and movie theater (in which the film *Showboat* is often the feature). These floating bed-and-breakfasts make 3- to 12-night trips that feature Southern cooking, banjos, Dixieland, hoopskirted hostesses, warbling calliopes—the whole moonlight-and-magnolias bit—calling almost every day at a riverport city (among the many, Natchez, Memphis, Cincinnati, St. Louis, and St. Paul), where passengers may debark for a shore excursion at an additional, though modest, charge. With an occupancy rate among the three boats of 97 percent, the steamboat company must be doing something right. For one thing, they know their market: the average voyager's age is 64, and the overwhelming majority of them are well-heeled retirees. Evening entertainment leans heavily toward the 1940s, with Stage Door Canteen and USO-type shows, and the audience loves 'em. The food is good if not grand, and tends to be rather bland; the staff is so perky, at times you feel you're on a floating Disney World. Life on board is pretty laid-back; these boats are not for Type A's. There are various theme cruises throughout the year, including the annual New Orleans–to–St. Louis Great Steamboat Race, during which the *Delta Queen* and the *Mississippi Queen* replicate a famous 1870 race between the original *Natchez* and *Robert E. Lee* steamboats.

Kid-pleasers... By all means, take the kids to City Park's **Carousel Gardens** and set them astride one of the wonderful "flying horses." They won't care that the carousel on which they giggle is on the National Register of Historic Places—but it is. The carved-wood carousel was built in 1906, and its giraffes and horses and other critters have all been beautifully restored. Near the carousel, **Storyland** is a children's playground with Mother Goose characters made for scrambling over and into, and a castle for storytelling and puppet shows. There's even more for them to do at the **Louisiana Children's Museum**, in the heart of the Warehouse District. The kid-sized port has a tugboat to be captained and a cargo net to be loaded with sacks of coffee, and there's also a "Body Shop," where "Mr. Bones" helps little ones bone up on health and fitness. The **Louisiana Nature and Science Center**, spread over 86 acres of bottomland hardwood forest in eastern New Orleans, is another place where kids can learn by doing, with nature trails, a children's Discovery Loft with hands-on exhibits, and a planetarium that has weekend laser shows. Riverside of Audubon Park, the 58-acre **Audubon Zoo** is home to 1,800 critters who roam in habitats such as the Louisiana Swamp exhibit, the Asian Domain, and the African Savannah. The local story goes that Monkey Hill, in the back of the zoo, was built in the 1930s so schoolchildren in these flatlands could understand what was meant by the word "hill." The zoo's sister attraction, the **Aquarium of the Americas**, takes the natural history lesson underwater; lots of kids have fun here, especially if they're the types who like touching wet and slimy things.

Older kids may well get a kick out of the **New Orleans Historic Voodoo Museum**, especially if they're savvy enough to take it for the kitsch it is. Doll-lovers should not miss Frances Parkinson Keyes's outstanding doll collection, on display at the **Beauregard-Keyes House**. The **St. Charles Streetcar** and **Riverfront Streetcar** are New Orleans's real-life, working equivalents of a theme-park ride, and the **Canal Street Ferry** is a quick way to get kids out on a boat on the river (though they may get restless during the loading and unloading,

NEW ORLEANS | DIVERSIONS

which takes up most of the 25-minute ride time). Otherwise, try the *Cajun Queen* or *John James Audubon* cruises between the zoo and the aquarium.

For free—or almost... There's almost always a show of some sort in Jackson Square, where the clowns, mimes, and musicians compete for the attention of passersby. Pop into **St. Louis Cathedral**, which takes a serene view of the earthly goings-on just outside its front door. This three-steepled white-stone 18th-century church is surprisingly small and unfussy for a cathedral; it's on Chartres Street, but don't expect the Chartres cathedral.

Park on a bench on **Moonwalk** and watch the world go by on the water. Your only expense may be a quarter to toss into the hat of the occasional saxophonist, trumpet player, or other street musician; beware of panhandlers, though, who may hassle you. Or walk on to the foot of Canal Street and take the **Canal Street ferry** (free to pedestrians) for a brief and breezy ride across the river to the West Bank and back. It boards at the Canal Street Landing, taking on both pedestrians and vehicles, and churns leisurely from East Bank to West Bank and back. There are no food concessions on board and no frills except the scenes of the river, the riverboats, and the skyline. The view is especially romantic at night, when the Crescent City Connection, the bridge connecting the East and West Bank, is all lit up and excursion boats are all a-glitter.

On dry land, board the **St. Charles streetcar** for a ramble up St. Charles Avenue through the Garden District and Uptown. A round trip all the way from Canal and Carondelet to the end of the line at Palmer Park takes 90 minutes and only costs $1; or buy a one-day VisiTour Pass for $4 (see Hotlines and Other Basics) and you can get on and off as many times as you like, hopping off to see the palatial Garden District mansions and, farther along, Audubon Park and its zoo. The **Riverfront Streetcar**, which runs near but not exactly on the riverfront, makes a breezy run from Esplanade Avenue all the way up to the Warehouse District, making strategic stops at attractions in the French Quarter and the CBD; it only costs $1.25.

Stop in **Dutch Alley** in the French Market for the early-afternoon jazz concerts and for people-watching

French Quarter characters (of which there are legions). And on Bourbon Street you can loll against a lamppost and hear music galore without so much as turning loose a penny. From the **Folklife Center**, park rangers of the Jean Lafitte National Historical Park lead free daily walking tours of the French Quarter, the Garden District (you only have to pay your streetcar fare), and a "Tour du Jour," which is a sort of potluck tour. Tours are conducted rain or shine, so take your umbrella.

Gallery hopping... Royal Street in the Quarter has for ages been the place to head for art galleries and antique stores. The gallery of Cajun artist **George Rodrigue**, internationally famous for his Blue Dog, is a Royal Street fixture; thousands of pictures of this mournful-looking royal-blue dog with staring yellow eyes have been sold worldwide, and several of them stare wistfully through the windows of this gallery. The Blue Dog, modeled after Rodrigue's late terrier, made her first appearance as an illustration in a book of ghost stories, and the rest, as they say, is herstory. Other fixtures are the **Hall-Barnett Gallery**, where you can see hot up-and-coming regional artists, and **Nahan Galleries**, for graphic design and sculpture. But in recent years, the scene—most notably, the contemporary arts scene—has shifted to the Warehouse/Arts District, which the local arts crowd likes to refer to as the "SoHo of the South." Old abandoned warehouses have been, and continue to be, renovated to hold restaurants, nightclubs, museums, and galleries. The most conspicuous of the galleries is the **Contemporary Arts Center**. The big, airy center has 10,000 square feet of space, with several galleries, changing exhibits, and two theaters showcasing the experimental and the avant-garde (see Entertainment). Each year the first Saturday in October is devoted to Art for Art's Sake—a series of gallery openings and parties that draws hundreds of exuberant artists and dilettantes. The big bash that closes the event is held at the CAC, with revelers pouring out into the streets. The city's oldest contemporary art gallery, **Galerie Simonne Stern**, one of the first to move from the French Quarter to the Warehouse District, displays the paintings and sculptures of a tricoastal roster of artists (as in the East Coast, the West Coast, and the Gulf Coast). Abstract paintings and contemporary drawings and sculptures—including the often offensive but locally admired work of George Dureau—are shown at the **Arthur Rogers Gallery**, and small decorative crafts in contemporary designs can be seen at **Ariodante**. **LeMieux Galleries** shows off its avant-garde credentials with multimedia installations; photographs, abstract paintings, and ceramics are shown at **Marguerite Oestreicher Fine Arts**. Handblown vases and decorative pieces are created and shown at the **New Orleans School of Glassworks**, a marvelous place with a glassblowing workshop in the rear- and front-room displays of glass sculptures by Mignon Faget, John Bullard, and Jim Blanchard, among others. Call to ask about the daily demonstrations, done in front of the 550-pound furnace.

Great walks... **Royal Street** in the Quarter is row after row of galleries and antique stores and upscale poke-around places. At night the street is lit by antique street lanterns, and buskers, mellowed out after a hard day's busking, hunker down in doorways and on street corners to softly strum guitars or coax the last few songs from a saxophone. The blocks between Bienville and St. Ann Streets are well trafficked and safe after dark. Tawdry **Bourbon Street** is a blast, always, at any hour of the day or night, even if you don't go inside any of its tourist-trap bars or burlesque shows. When you take the **St. Charles streetcar** up to the zoo, you can catch the free shuttle that runs from the streetcar stop to the zoo, but you can also opt to saunter through the park. Get off the streetcar in front of Tulane University, cross St. Charles Avenue, and take the macadam path that leads alongside the park golf course, beneath great gnarled live oak trees overdressed in Spanish moss. During the day—but never at night—the levees beckon strollers and joggers: Upriver of the Quarter, where St. Charles Avenue dead-ends at Carrollton Avenue and the Mississippi takes a great bend, the man-made **Riverbend levee** is a favorite place for strolling and watching kite-fliers catching the breeze.

Tours for Lestat lovers and others... Are you curious about vampire chronicler Anne Rice? Want to get the dish on Tennessee Williams? Or hear gruesome tales of below-ground burials in these swamplands? Hook up with a guided tour and you'll learn some of the secrets tucked away in those courtyards and carriage houses. Dr.

Kenneth Holditch, a research professor at the University of New Orleans, conducts walking tours of the French Quarter, and if you think "research" and "professor" sound dull, think again—his **Heritage Tours** zero in on the city's rich literary heritage, with quirky and colorful anecdotes about Tennessee Williams, William Faulkner, Sherwood Anderson, Lillian Hellman, and some very ditzy literati who lived, worked, and hung out in the Quarter. The **Magic Walking Tours** are a kick, especially for the tales told during the Haunted House, Vampire, and Ghost Hunt outings. Their cemetery tours walk you through St. Louis Cemetery No. 1, and Garden District tours run you by for a streetwalker's view, so to speak, of novelist Anne Rice's houses (she owns more than one). The **Preservation Resource Center**, whose staff is deeply involved in preserving the city's architectural treasures, organizes occasional tours; if you're in town during one of their "Stained Glass in Sacred Places" tours, go along to ooh and aah over the city's church windows. **Hidden Treasures Tours** emphasize influential New Orleans women during van tours of the Garden District, and **Le'Ob's Tours** focus on African American contributions to the city. John McCusker, staff photographer for the *Times-Picayune*, gives well-researched **Cradle of Jazz** tours where you can learn about pioneers of the genre like Buddy Bolden, Kid Ory, and King Oliver. And if you've a hankering to see plantation country to the west of the city, hook up with **Tours by Isabelle**, which conducts half-day minivan trips to that area, with a lunch stop at Madewood Plantation. For a one-shot overview, nationwide stalwart **Gray Line** offers a more standard city bus tour, in addition to orientation, plantation, and swamp tours; the Loop Tour handily loops around to a dozen different attractions and shopping centers, making stops every hour, with unlimited all-day boarding (admission to sightseeing attractions not included). This is a very good idea.

The Index

Aquarium of the Americas. A lot of fishy business goes on in the Gulf of Mexico, Caribbean Reefs, Amazon Rain Forest, and Mississippi River/Gulf Shores exhibits in this watery place beside the Big Muddy. A giant IMAX theater opened here in 1995.... *Tel 504/861–2537. Canal St. at the river, Woldenberg Riverfront Park. Open Sun–Thur 9:30–6, Fri–Sat until 7. Admission charged.*

Ariodante. This small, chic gallery of contemporary crafts lies in the heart of Gallery Row in the Warehouse/Arts District. Most of the Warehouse District galleries show paintings, but Ariodante shows decorative pieces, such as pottery, small sculptures, lamps, and the like.... *Tel 504/524–3233. 535 Julia St., Warehouse/Arts District. Open Mon–Sat 11–5. Admission free.*

Arthur Rogers Gallery. One of the city's most respected gallery owners, Arthur Rogers often showcases the work of well-known Orleanian George Dureau—jarring paintings, drawings, and sculptures, many of them depicting disabled children.... *Tel 504/522–1999. 432 Julia St. Warehouse/Arts District. Open 10–5. Closed Sun. Admission free.*

Ashland Belle-Hélène. Beloved by filmmakers, this handsome plantation house is no longer open for tours, but if you're going to Houmas House anyway, drive 15 miles farther west to see this. A good example of what the exterior of these old places looked like post-Yankee and pre-restoration, it's worth a look, even if you don't get out of the car. From Houmas House (see below), continue on Rte. 942 to the town of Darrow, turn left on Rte. 75, and drive toward the town of Geismar.... *No phone. Rte. 75, between the towns of Darrow and Geismar.*

Audubon Park. This 400-acre park features gnarled, moss-draped oaks, a jogging path, tennis courts, a golf course, a riding stable, and the Audubon Zoo (see below).... *Tel 504/861–2537. 6800 St. Charles Ave., Uptown.*

Audubon Zoo. On the riverside of Audubon Park, the sister of the aquarium (see above) is a world-class zoo, where more than 1,800 creatures great and small laze around in simulated natural habitats. Friends of the Zoo operate a free shuttle from the St. Charles streetcar stop in front of Tulane University; you can also walk from the streetcar through Audubon Park, or take the Magazine St. bus to the front entrance.... *Tel 504/861–2537. 6500 Magazine St., Uptown. Open 9–5. Admission charged.*

Bayou Barn. At this funky little place—part Cajun dance hall, part souvenir shop, part cafe—you can rent canoes and hire a guide for paddling out on the ghostly beautiful wetlands. Be sure to ask them about the schedule for moonlight tours. Follow Decatur St. across Canal St., where it becomes Magazine St.; cross the Crescent City Connection and follow the West Bank Expressway (U.S. 90) to Barataria Blvd. (Rte. 45), where you turn left on Rte. 45 and watch for signs for the Barataria Unit, Jean Lafitte National Historical Park. Bayou Barn is across the street from it.... *Tel 504/689–2663, 800/TO–BAYOU. Intersection of Rtes 31, 34, and 45, near Crown Point. Open 9–5, later when tours or dances are scheduled. Fee charged.*

Beauregard-Keyes House. Across the street from the Old Ursuline Convent in the lower Quarter, this hyphenated house with a Greek Revival portico was built in 1826 as a private home. Once home to Confederate General P .G. T. Beauregard, in the 1940s it was bought by novelist Frances Parkinson Keyes, whose studio in the rear slave quarters is preserved.... *Tel 504/523–7257. 1113 Chartres St., French Quarter. Open Mon–Sat 10–3, tours on the hour. Admission charged.*

Belle of Orleans. This floating casino within Bally's Casino Lakeshore Resort has the usual 800 or so slot machines and tables for roulette, big six, craps. It docks on Lake Pontchartrain.... *Tel 800/57–BALLY. 1 Stars and Stripes Blvd., Lake Pontchartrain. Open 24 hours.*

NEW ORLEANS | DIVERSIONS

Blaine Kern's Mardi Gras World. Where the fabulous floats for Carnival are created and stored. You can wander through on your own or take a guided tour to watch artisans sculpting and painting the giant papier-mâché figures. Take the Canal St. ferry across to Algiers and board the free Mardi Gras World shuttle.... *Tel 504/361–7821. 223 Newton St., Algiers. Open 9:30–4:30. Closed 2 weeks prior to Mardi Gras. Admission free.*

***Boomtown Belle* Casino.** Everybody's gotta have a gimmick, and the one on this riverboat gambling den is a country-western theme—there's a dance hall and a saloon to which you can repair and regroup between attacks on the one-armed bandits and other gambling devices.... *Tel 504/366–7711. 4132 Peters St., Harvey, West Bank. Open 24 hours.*

Cajun Queen. Although she's a bit less glamorous than either the *Creole Queen* or the *Steamboat Natchez*, the *Cajun Queen* nevertheless does her dead-level best to imitate the old-fashioned 19th-century sternwheelers that once plied the waters of the Mississippi. The boat ferries passengers up to the zoo and back; the return trip is especially refreshing after a summer day with the animals.... *Tel 504/529–4567, 800/445–4109. Departs from the aquarium. Operates daily. Admission charged.*

Canal Street Ferry. The ferry takes on foot passengers and cars at the bottom of Canal St. for the run across to Algiers on the West Bank. The round trip takes about 25 minutes, with about 20 minutes of that time devoted to loading and unloading. If you ride at night, don't forget that the ferry makes its last trip to Algiers at 9:30pm, where it spends the night.... *Tel 504/364–8114. Canal St. at the river. Operates 5:45am–9:30pm. Free for pedestrians, toll charged for vehicles.*

Carousel Gardens. In City Park, adjacent to Storyland, you'll find a restored 1906 carousel, with delightful "Flying Horses," as the carved-wood critters are called by locals. Adults can ride too.... *Tel 504/483–9356. Victory Ave., City Park. Open Tue–Sun 10–4:30. Admission charged.*

Checkpoint Charlie's. A late-night blues joint, this favorite local hangout has pool tables, and even a Laundromat where you can do your dirty clothes.... *Tel 504/947–0979. 501 Esplanade Ave., on the fringe of the French Quarter. Open 24 hours.*

City Park. Within this urban oasis's 1,500 acres, you'll find 4 golf courses, a 39-court tennis center, children's playgrounds, a delightful antique carousel (see above), softball diamonds, lagoons for pedal-boating and canoeing, the New Orleans Museum of Art (see below)—all sprawled beneath hundreds of moss-draped live oak trees.... *Tel 504/482–4888. 1 Palm Dr., Mid-City. Admission free to park.*

Confederate Museum. Opened in 1891, the museum displays arms and artifacts pertaining to the War of Northern Aggression. Personal effects of President Jefferson Davis and campaign paraphernalia used by General Robert E. Lee are among the exhibits.... *Tel 504/523–4522. 929 Camp St., CBD. Open Mon–Sat 10–4. Admission charged.*

Contemporary Arts Center. This renovated warehouse holds several galleries and two theaters devoted to the avant-garde and the experimental. It's ground zero for the annual October Art for Art's Sake openings and parties.... *Tel 504/523–1216. 900 Camp St., Warehouse District. Galleries open Mon–Sat 10–5, Sun 11–5. Admission charged.*

Cradle of Jazz Tours. If you're curious about the origins of jazz, hook up with these tours and learn about Buddy Bolden and other early luminaries.... *Tel 504/282–3583. By appointment. Admission charged.*

Creole Queen Riverboat. One of the boats sans casino at play on the Mississippi, the replica *Creole Queen* has all the requisite fittings of a 19th-century riverboat. During the day she heads downriver for tours of the Chalmette Battlefield, and after the sun goes down she takes on food and a Dixieland band for an evening outing.... *Tel 504/529–4567, 800/445–4109. Departs from the Poydras St. Wharf, Riverwalk. Operates daily. Reservations required for dinner cruise. Admission charged.*

Croissant d'Or. Dearly loved by Quarterites and virtually every visitor who comes to town, this little patisserie is a great place for breakfast and light lunches.... *Tel 504/524–*

4663. 617 Ursulines St., French Quarter. Open 7am–5pm. Closed Wed.

Delta Queen Steamboat Company. More than a century old, the company operates the nation's only remaining overnight riverboat cruises, lasting 3 to 12 days and calling at port cities like Natchez, Memphis, Cincinnati, St. Louis, and St. Paul.... *Tel 504/586–0631, 800/543–1949. 30 Robin St. Wharf. Admission charged.*

Doullut Houses. The two "Steamboat Gothic" houses beside the levee downriver of the Quarter were designed and built in 1905 by Captain M. P. Doullut, the first for him and his river-pilot wife, the second for their son. With their fanciful beadwork, spindles, and galleries, the twin houses look like riverboats run aground.... *Tel 504/949–1422. 400 Egania St., Bywater. Open 10–4 by appointment. Admission charged.*

Dutch Alley. At this open-air plaza in French Market Place, where Dumaine Street dead-ends at North Peters St., free jazz concerts are frequently held—usually from noon until about 3pm. Schedules available at the adjacent visitors' center.... *Tel 504/596–3424. 900 Decatur St. (Visitors' Center). Concert schedule varies, Visitors' Center open 9–5:30. Admission free.*

Flamingo Casino. Hundreds of slot and video poker machines, plus 32 gaming tables including blackjack, craps, and roulette; live Dixieland jazz in the evening; smoking and nonsmoking gaming areas—the whole shooting match.... *Tel 504/587–7777, outside New Orleans 800/587–LUCK. Poydras St. Wharf, behind the Hilton. Open 24 hours.*

Folklife Center, Jean Lafitte National Historical Park. Exhibits pertaining to the state's and city's rich ethnic mix are displayed here, and a very good film about Acadiana is shown. This is the kickoff place for free walking tours conducted daily by park rangers of the French Quarter and Garden District. Gather up information about the Chalmette Battlefield and the Barataria Unit, both administered by the park service. This is an excellent facility.... *Tel 504/589–2636. 916–18 N. Peters St., French Market, French Quarter. Open 9–5. Admission free.*

Galerie Simonne Stern. The oldest contemporary art gallery in the city, founded in 1965. Monthly changing exhibits of modern and contemporary art.... *Tel 504/529–1118. 518 Julia St., Warehouse/Arts District. Open Mon–Sat 10–6. Admission free.*

Gallier Hall. Designed by New Orleans architect James Gallier, Sr., and completed about 1850, this handsome building has been hailed by the American Institute of Architects as the city's most brilliant extant example of Greek Revival architecture. Now used for private functions, it is not open to the public.... *Tel 504/565–7457. 545 St. Charles Ave.*

Gallier House. This was the home of architect James Gallier, Jr., who designed and built it in 1857. A stunnng restoration; be sure to look at the antique carriage in the carriageway.... *Tel 504/523–6722. 1118–32 Royal St., French Quarter. Open Mon–Sat 10:30–4:30, Sun 12:30–4:30. Admission charged.*

Gray Line. The old familiar bus tour, but with a local twist—or loop, anyway: the Loop Tour ticket lets you visit a dozen different attractions and shopping centers with unlimited boarding and reboarding. Buses board behind the Jax Brewery on the Toulouse St. Wharf.... *Tel 504/587–0861, 800/535–7786. Loop Tour operates 9–5:45. Admission charged.*

Hall-Barnett Gallery. Howard Barnett's highly regarded gallery is devoted to showcasing up-and-coming regional artists. The focus is on contemporary, expressionist works in several media.... *Tel 504/525–5656. 320 Exchange Alley, French Quarter. Open Mon–Sat 10–6, Sun 11–5. Admission free.*

Harrah's Casino New Orleans. The controversial 76,000-sq-ft casino occupies the old Municipal Auditorium, built in 1930 and formerly used for Carnival balls and concerts. There are plenty of slots and tables at which you may lose your shirt, plus food and music aimed at keeping you inside and out of the clutches of the French Quarter across the street. The only thing that sets this casino apart from any other garish gambling den is the Mardi Gras theme: the lavish decorations were designed by Blaine Kern (see Blaine Kern's Mardi Gras World above).... *Tel 504/533–6000, 800/427–7247. 1201 St. Peter St., Treme. Open 24 hours.*

NEW ORLEANS | DIVERSIONS

Heritage Tours. This group offers a Tennessee Williams walk that is rich with anecdotes pertaining to *A Streetcar Named Desire*; a general literary walk recounts tales of Williams, Lillian Hellman, Truman Capote, William Faulkner, and other literati who lived and hung out in New Orleans.... *Tel 504/949–9805. By appointment only. Admission charged, 3-person minimum.*

Hermann-Grima House. One of three house museums in the Quarter, this one is an American-style town house built in about 1831. Of particular interest are the formal dining room and the rear parterre gardens and outbuildings, where Creole cooking demonstrations take place on Thursdays from October until May.... *Tel 504/525–5661. 820 St. Louis St., French Quarter. Open Mon–Sat 10–4. Admission charged.*

Hidden Treasures Tours. Minivans tool around the Garden District, while guides focus on women who have been influential in New Orleans.... *Tel 504/529–4507. By appointment only. Admission charged.*

Historic New Orleans Collection. Changing exhibits in the ground-floor Williams Gallery focus on the city and its environs. The private collection of lithographs, drawings, maps, sketches, and historical documents may be seen on a guided tour of the historic Merieult House. Local writers know to plant themselves in the research library, where the helpful staff can produce material on anything from floor plans to Marie Laveau to famous floods.... *Tel 504/523–4662. 533 Royal St., French Quarter. Open Tue–Sat 10–4:15. Gallery free; admission charged for house tour.*

Honey Island Swamp Tours. Operated by wetland ecologist Dr. Paul Wagner, these intriguing tours take you through backwater bayous and secret sloughs.... *Tel 504/242–5877 (in New Orleans), 504/641–1769 (in Slidell). 106 Holly Ridge Dr., Slidell. Open daily, hotel pick-up available. Admission charged.*

Houmas House. The oldest section of this River Rd. plantation dates from the late 1700s and connects by covered carriageway to an 1840s Greek Revival mansion filled with period antiques. Costumed docents lead tours. Take I-10 west to Rte. 44 and head south toward Burnside, where signs point the way to the house.... *Tel 504/522–2262. 40136 Rte. 942, near Burnside. Open Feb–Oct 10–5, Nov–June 10–4. Admission charged.*

John James Audubon Riverboat. The least interesting architecturally of the sightseeing boats, the *JJA* paddles back and forth between the aquarium and the zoo. Unless there's a downpour, sit on the upper deck where you can at least enjoy the river views and breezes.... *Tel 504/586–8777, 800/ 233–BOAT. Daily departures from the aquarium at 10, noon, 2, and 4; from the zoo at 11, 1, 3, and 5. Admission charged.*

Kaldi's. This coffee house, in a turn-of-the-century bank building, rivals the Napoleon House as a favored hanging-out place. Gourmet coffees and pastries are the only items served; there is no menu. You just belly up to the counter and point to the goodies in the glass case. An occasional trio entertains in the evening.... *Tel 504/586–8989. 940 Decatur St., French Quarter. Open 24 hours.*

Keuffer's. Pronounced kway-fers, this neighborhood bar is a popular spot for shooting pool, chatting up the friendly bartender, and just generally hanging loose. It's at the corner of Chartres and Toulouse Sts.... *Tel 504/523–8705. 540 Chartres St., French Quarter. Open 11am until the place empties.*

La Marquise. This little patisserie, just off Jackson Square, is a sister to Croissant d'Or on Ursulines St.... *Tel 504/524– 0420. 625 Chartres St., French Quarter. Open 7am–5pm.*

Lafayette Cemetery. This ancient walled City of the Dead is in the heart of the Garden District, across the street from Commander's Palace Restaurant. "Decorated" with elaborate above-ground tombs, this cemetery appeared in *Interview with the Vampire*.... *No phone. Bounded by Washington Ave. and Coliseum, Prytania, and Sixth Sts.*

Lafitte's Blacksmith Shop. Tattered and tumbledown though it may appear, this ancient bar is a much-loved local hangout. Legend hath it that the Lafitte brothers, Jean and Pierre, used this cottage as a front for their illegal deeds. There is sometimes a pianist, but for the most part this place is for relaxing and knocking back Dixies.... *Tel 504/523–0066. 941 Bourbon St., French Quarter. Open 11am–1 or 2am, depending upon traffic.*

Lakelawn Metairie Cemetery. The only one of the city's graveyards safe enough to explore unguided is this huge one in Mid-City. Established in 1872, it has more than 2,200 tombs, temples, and mausoleums, many of them featuring elaborate statuary. At the entrance, you can pick up cassette tapes.... *Tel 504/486–6331. 5100 Pontchartrain Blvd. Open 8:30–5:30. Admission free.*

Laura Plantation. Different from the dressed-up antebellum mansions along River Rd., Laura is a restoration-in-progress, with ample evidence remaining to show the changes that have taken place over the past 200 years. The Creole plantation and its 12 outbuildings date from 1805. Take I-10 west, turn south on I-310, cross the Mississippi River Bridge to Rte. 3127, and head toward Donaldsonville. Turn right on Rte. 20 and drive into Vacherie. When you come to Rte. 18 (River Rd.), turn right. The plantation is a few hundred yards away on the right.... *Tel 504/265–7690 (in Vacherie); 504/488–8709 (in New Orleans). 2247 LA 18, Vacherie. Open 9–5. Closed Christmas Day, Thanksgiving Day, Easter, and New Year's Day. Admission charged.*

Le'Ob's Tours. Knowledgeable guides conduct tours that take in sites and sights pertaining to the contributions African Americans have made to the city's culture and history.... *Tel 504/288–3478. 4635 Touro St., Uptown. Office hours Mon–Sat 9–5. Admission charged for tours.*

LeMieux Galleries. A restored warehouse is the setting for some exciting changing exhibits of contemporary art in multimedia.... *Tel 504/522–5988. 332 Julia St., Warehouse/Arts District. Open Tue–Fri 10–5, Sat 11–4, closed Sun and Mon. Admission free.*

Le Salon. Afternoon tea in the lobby lounge of the Windsor Court is a very British affair. Sip tea or champagne, snack on scones, dainty finger sandwiches, and bonbons.... *Tel 504/523–6000. Windsor Court Hotel, 300 Gravier St., CBD. Open daily 2–6. Reservations advised.*

NEW ORLEANS | DIVERSIONS

Longue Vue House & Gardens. This grand English-style manor is now a museum of decorative arts, with especially notable china collections. It sits in 8 acres of manicured theme gardens.... *Tel 504/488–5488. 7 Bamboo Rd., Mid-City. Open Mon–Sat 10–4:30, Sun 1–5 (last house tour, 4:15). Admission charged.*

Louisiana Children's Museum. Kids can play at being a stevedore, telecasting the news, and running a streetcar, and they can also keep busy with sundry other learn-by-doing hands-on exhibits.... *Tel 504/523–1357. 420 Julia St., Warehouse District. Open Mon–Sat 9:30–4:30. Admission charged.*

Louisiana Nature and Science Center. A planetarium, laser rock shows, and exhibits pertaining to the natural and the scientific are among the attractions here. The center also conducts occasional nature walks and swamp tours.... *Tel 504/246–5672. Joe Brown Park (enter at Read Blvd. and Nature Center Dr.), East New Orleans. Open Tue–Fri 9–5, Sat 10–5, Sun noon–5. Admission charged.*

Louisiana State Museum. The state museum is a complex of buildings, three of them on Jackson Square and one on the fringe of the French Quarter. The most important among them is the 18th-century **Cabildo**, where the Louisiana Purchase transfer papers were signed in 1803. The nearby **Presbytère**, from the same period, was built as a home for priests who served in the adjacent St. Louis Cathedral. Both buildings now house changing exhibits. The **1850 House,** in the lower Pontalba Apartments, is done up in the style of a 19th-century Creole cliff dweller. The **Old U.S. Mint** on Esplanade Ave., which once minted tons of coins, is home to both jazz and Mardi Gras exhibits.... *Tel 504/568–6972, 504/568–6968. 731 Chartres St., Jackson Square; Old U.S. Mint, 400 Esplanade Ave. Open Tues–Sun 10–5. Closed Mardi Gras, Thanksgiving Day, Christmas Day, and New Year's Day. Admission charged for each building.*

Loyola University. Across from Audubon Park and adjacent to Tulane University, Loyola University was incorporated in 1912.... *Tel 504/865–2011. 6363 St. Charles Ave.*

Madewood Plantation. On the banks of Bayou Lafourche, this 21-room Greek Revival mansion welcomes overnighters to sleep in canopied beds and four-posters. Overnight stays include a wine-and-cheese cocktail hour, Southern meals in the candlelit dining rooms, coffee and liqueurs in the formal drawing room, and full breakfast. Don't expect gourmet food; chat up the friendly staff, breathe deeply of the fresh country air, and remember that you were looking for a quiet retreat. The plantation is 74 miles from downtown New Orleans. Take I-10 west, turn south on Rte. 70, cross the Sunshine Bridge, and follow the Bayou Plantation sign. Turn left on Spur 70 and left again on Rte. 308.... *Tel 504/ 369–7151, 800/749–7151. 4250 Rte. 308, near Napoleonville. Open 10–5 for tours. Closed Thanksgiving Day, Christmas Eve, and Christmas Day. Admission charged.*

Magic Walking Tours. Guided tours walk you through St. Louis Cemetery No. 1, the French Quarter, and the Garden District; the Haunted House, Vampire, and Voodoo tours take a ghostly look at the Quarter. Check at the Dead Mozell Cafe, or phone for where to meet for the tour of your choice.... *Tel 504/593–9693. 1015 Iberville St., French Quarter. Admission charged.*

Marguerite Oestreicher Fine Arts. Regional and national artists are represented in Oestreicher's gallery of contemporary sculpture, abstract paintings, and photography.... *Tel 504/581–9253. 626 Julia St., Warehouse District. Open Tues–Sat 10–5. Admission free.*

Moonwalk. An open-air wooden promenade, lined with park benches, that stretches right alongside the Mississippi River, Moonwalk is a favorite Quarterite and tourist place for relaxing and watching the riverboats, tugs, and other traffic parading on the water.... *No phone. Alongside the Mississippi River, between St. Ann and Toulouse Sts., French Quarter.*

Musée Conti Wax Museum. A painless and fun way to brush up on Louisiana's and New Orleans's histories, the wax figures in "Louisiana Legends" illustrate events from the late 17th century, with new "people" added from time to time.... *Tel 504/525–2605. 917 Conti St., French Quarter. Open 10–5:30. Closed Mardi Gras and Christmas Day. Admission charged.*

Nahan Galleries. Original graphic designs and sculptures are sold in this venerable French Quarter gallery. Among the internationally known artists displayed are Rolland Golden, Theo Tobiasse, and Mayeu Passa.... *Tel 504/524–8696. 540 Royal St., French Quarter. Open Mon–Sat 9:30–6, Sun 11–6. Admission free.*

Napoleon House. One of the city's most popular bars, decorated with memorabilia pertaining to Napoleon. The warm muffulettas are terrific, but the main attraction is the decadent ambience.... *Tel 504/524–9752. 500 Chartres St., French Quarter. Open Mon–Sat 11am–1am, Sun 11–7.*

New Orleans Fair Grounds. The fairgrounds does double duty as a Thoroughbred racetrack—the nation's third oldest—and as the main hootin' and hollerin' place for the Jazz Fest. The racing season begins on Thanksgiving Day and runs, so to speak, until late March or early April. Hard on the heels of the horses, the Jazz Fest stomps off the last weekend in April and roars through the first weekend in May. (See Jazz Fest sidebar.).... *Tel 504/944–5515, 800/262–7983. 1751 Gentilly Blvd., Mid-City. Open Wed–Sun, mid-Nov–Mar, post time 1:30. Jackets for men (no jeans or shorts). Reservations required for the clubhouse. Admission charged.*

New Orleans Historic Voodoo Museum. A creaky old place determined to spook you, the museum displays gris-gris (voodoo charms), an altar, potions, artifacts, and such, a whole raft of it pertaining to Voodoo queen Marie Laveau, a 19th-century voodoo priestess and one of New Orleans's favorite legendary figures. They'll also run you around on guided tours to various haunts. Take it all with a grain of gris-gris.... *Tel 504/523–7685. 724 Dumaine St., French Quarter. Open 10–7. Admission charged.*

New Orleans Museum of Art. A white neoclassical building set in lush City Park, NOMA displays European paintings from the 17th to the 19th century, Asian artworks and African tribal art, antique Louisiana furnishings, and a collection of Fabergé eggs, made by jeweler Peter Carl Fabergé for the royal Romanovs of czarist Russia.... *Tel 504/488–2631. 1 Collins Diboll Circle, off Lelong Ave., City Park. Open Tues–Sun 10–5:30. Admission charged (Louisiana residents with proper ID admitted free Thurs 10–noon).*

New Orleans Pharmacy Museum. The apothecary shop of the nation's first licensed pharmacist, Louis J. Dufilho, Jr., has been converted into a museum of medical artifacts. Gruesome but fun.... *Tel 504/565–8027. 514 Chartres St., French Quarter. Open Tues–Sun 10–5. Admission charged.*

New Orleans School of Glassworks. This combination glass-blowing workshop and art glass gallery holds daily demonstrations.... *Tel 504/529–7277. 727 Magazine St., Warehouse District. Open Mon–Sat 10–5. Admission free.*

Old Farmers' Market. Area farmers have been bringing their fresh produce to these open-air sheds for going on 200 years. It's open 24 hours a day, and crowded with locals (including famous New Orleans chefs) and visitors picking through the bins of fresh foodstuffs.... *Tel 504/596–3420. 1235 N. Peters St., French Quarter.*

Old U.S. Customhouse. A gray chunk of granite occupying the entire 400 block of Canal Street, the customhouse was begun in 1845, but construction was interrupted several times, most notably by the War for Southern Independence. During The War, the incomplete structure was headquarters for Union officers, and at one time held more than 2,000 Confederate prisoners of war. Normal customs activities are carried out in the second-floor Great Marble Hall, a stunning Greek Revival room.... *Tel 504/589–2976. 423 Canal St., CBD. Open Mon–Fri 9–5. Admission free.*

Old Ursuline Convent. Guided tours take you through the oldest structure in the lower Mississippi Valley, where you can see the ancient cypress spiral staircase, from an even earlier 18th-century convent on this site, and displays of 18th-century furniture, religious iconography, and documents pertaining to the building's history.... *Tel 504/529–3040. 1100 Chartres St., French Quarter. Tours Tue–Fri at 10, 11, 1, 2, 3; Sat–Sun at 11:15, 1, 2. Admission charged.*

Pitot House. Dating from about 1799, this West Indies–style house, all decked out with galleries and jalousies, is a great place to get a glimpse of how the early planters lived.... *Tel 504/482–0312. 1440 Moss St., Mid-City. Open Wed–Sun 10–3; last tour at 2:15. Admission charged.*

Preservation Resource Center. Just as the name may suggest, this is the administrative office for the city's strong preservationist movement. The PRC spearheaded the drive to renovate the Warehouse District, in which its offices are located, and works diligently on programs such as Operation Comeback in the Lower Garden District. From time to time, PRC does worthwhile architectural tours.... *Tel 504/581–7032. 604 Julia St., Warehouse District. Office hours Mon–Fri 10–5. Admission charge for tours.*

Riverfront Streetcar. Called by the tourist brochures the "Ladies in Red," for the brightly colored cars on the line, the Riverfront streetcar runs between Esplanade Ave. on the lower border of the French Quarter, all the way up to Julia St. in the Warehouse District. Among its scheduled stops are the Jackson Brewery, Woldenberg Riverfront Park, the Aquarium of the Americas, Riverwalk, and the Convention Center. The St. Charles and Riverfront streetcars, as well as the city's buses, are operated by the Regional Transit Authority.... *Tel 504/248–3900 (24-hour RideLine information). 101 Dauphine St. Operates Mon–Sat 6am–midnight, Sat–Sun 8am–midnight. Fare $1.25.*

Rodrigue Gallery. George Rodrigue's claim to great fame and immense fortune is his late terrier, immortalized by the Acadian painter as a mournful-looking royal-blue dog with staring yellow eyes. Thousands of Blue Dogs have been sold worldwide, and several of them stare wistfully through the windows of this gallery. The Blue Dog made her first appearance as an illustration in a book of ghost stories, and the rest, as they say, is herstory.... *Tel 504/581–4244. 721 Royal St., French Quarter. Open 10–6. Admission free.*

St. Charles Streetcar. The St. Charles Streetcar line, one of the world's oldest street-railway systems, run from the CBD at Canal and Carondelet Sts., up past the grand mansions of St. Charles Ave., Audubon Park, and Tulane and Loyola Universities, ending at Palmer Park. The St. Charles and Riverfront streetcars, as well as the city's buses, are operated by the Regional Transit Authority.... *Tel 504/248–3900 (24-hour RideLine information). 101 Dauphine St. Operates 24 hours. Fare $1.*

St. Louis Cathedral. Relatively small, as cathedrals go, this white-stone church, with its three steeples and shingled roof, dates from 1794; it's the third church to occupy this site. The large mural over the high altar, depicting Louis IX announcing the Seventh Crusade, and the ceiling frescoes were painted in 1872 by Eraste Humbrecht. Mass is conducted daily, and guided tours of the cathedral are conducted irregularly during the day, except during church services.... *Tel 504/525–9525. 615 Pere Antoine's Alley. Tours Mon–Sat 9–5, Sun 1:30–5. Admission free.*

St. Louis Cemeteries. Haunted though they are—not so much, perhaps, by the other-worldly beings as by very earthly muggers—these three above-ground cemeteries are often near the top of visitors' must-see lists. The oldest of the city's cemeteries is St. Louis Cemetery No. 1, established in 1789 (Basin St. at St. Louis St.); St. Louis No. 2 is at North Claiborne Ave. and Bienville St.; St. Louis No. 3, the largest of the three and the youngest, is at 3421 Esplanade Ave., not far from City Park.... *Tel 504/482–5065. Administrative office 3421 Esplanade Ave. Guided tours conducted by Save Our Cemeteries (tel 504/588–9357) or Magic Walking Tours (tel 504/593–9693).*

St. Patrick's Church. Built as a house of worship for the Irish Catholics who settled in the American sector, this gray Gothic church was designed in 1833 by Irishmen James and Charles Dakin; the interior was the work of James Gallier, Sr. The church is famous for the dramatic murals over the altar, painted in 1841 by Leon Pomerade.... *Tel 504/525–4413. 724 Camp St., Warehouse District. Open Mon–Fri 11–12:30, Sat. 3:30–5:30, Sun 8am–1pm. Admission free.*

Save Our Cemeteries. Tours conducted by this group walk you through Lafayette Cemetery and St. Louis Cemetery No. I, and all proceeds go toward preservation of the "cities of the dead." Tours begin Sunday mornings at Coffee Blend in the Quarter, where you can have your croissants and coffee before ambling to the graveyards.... *Tel 504/588–9357. Tours meet at Coffee Blend, 623 Royal St., French Quarter. Sun only, 10am. Admission charged.*

Steamboat *Natchez*. This gingerbready replica of a 19th-century paddlewheeler does two-hour harbor cruises, evening dinner-with-jazz outings, and a midnight cruise designed for the moonlight-and-magnolias crowd.... *Tel 504/586–8777, 800/233–BOAT. Board at the Toulouse St. Wharf, behind* the Jax Brewery. Reservations required for evening and mid-night cruises. Admission charged.

Storyland. A pint-sized amusement park in City Park, best for the very young.... *Tel 504/483–9382. Victory Ave., City Park. Open 10–4:30. Admission charged.*

Top of the Mart. A great place to get an overview of the city and the river, this revolving cocktail lounge sits on the 33rd floor of the World Trade Center at the foot of Canal St. On a clear day you can see about 30 miles—but good luck with the New Orleans haze.... *Tel 504/522–9795. 2 Canal St., World Trade Center, CBD. Open Mon–Fri 10am–midnight, Sat 11am–midnight, Sun 2pm–midnight. 1-drink minimum.*

Tours by Isabelle. Orientation tours of the city, plus outings to plantation country (with lunch at Madewood Plantation) and swamps are done in small minivans. Guides are multilin-gual.... *Tel 504/391–3544. Daily tours by appointment. Hotel pick-ups. Admission charged.*

Treasure Chest Casino. Docked across from the Pontchartrain Center in Kenner, this replica of a 19th-century paddle-wheeler is a three-decker with 25,000 square feet in which you can place your bets or put your quarters. Live entertain-ment, a snack bar, and an ice cream parlor are other *diver-tissements*.... *Tel 504/443–8000, 800/298–0711. 5050 Williams Blvd., Kenner; docked on Lake Pontchartrain across from the Pontchartrain Center. Admission free.*

Tulane University. Named for philanthropist Paul Tulane, this is Louisiana's largest private university, with a student body of more than 12,000.... *Tel 504/865–5000. 6823 St. Charles Ave.*

Woldenberg Riverfront Park. This 12-acre park, locally adored, is landscaped with shade trees and plenty of green spaces and park benches scattered here and there. It stretches along the Mississippi from the Aquarium of the Americas up to Jax Brewery.... *Tel 504/861–2537 (Audubon Institute, which administers the park).*

New Orleans Diversions

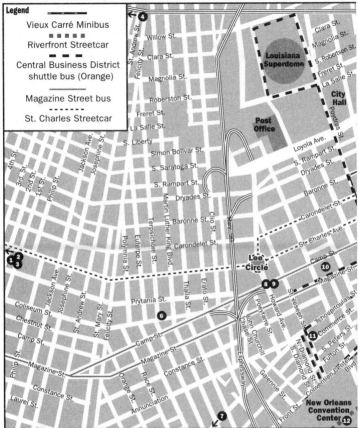

Legend

Vieux Carré Minibus

Riverfront Streetcar

Central Business District shuttle bus (Orange)

Magazine Street bus

St. Charles Streetcar

Aquarium of the Americas **18**	Gallier House **33**
Audubon Zoo **1**	Harrah's Casino **36**
Beauregard-Keyes House **32**	Hermann-Grima House **23**
Canal Street Ferry **16**	Historic New Orleans Collection **25**
City Park **37**	*John James Audubon* Riverboat **19**
Confederate Museum **8**	Lafayette Cemetery **6**
Contemporary Arts Center **9**	Lakelawn Metairie Cemetery **4**
Creole Queen Riverboat **14**	Louisiana Children's Museum **11**
Delta Queen Steamboat Co. **7**	Louisiana Nature and Science Center **12**
Flamingo Casino **15**	Louisiana State Museum (Cabildo) **27**
Folklife Center **30**	

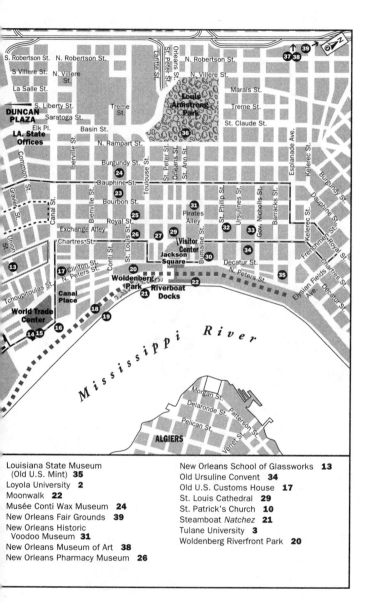

Louisiana State Museum
(Old U.S. Mint) **35**

Loyola University **2**

Moonwalk **22**

Musée Conti Wax Museum **24**

New Orleans Fair Grounds **39**

New Orleans Historic
Voodoo Museum **31**

New Orleans Museum of Art **38**

New Orleans Pharmacy Museum **26**

New Orleans School of Glassworks **13**

Old Ursuline Convent **34**

Old U.S. Customs House **17**

St. Louis Cathedral **29**

St. Patrick's Church **10**

Steamboat *Natchez* **21**

Tulane University **3**

Woldenberg Riverfront Park **20**

4

outside

It hasn't been all
that long since
New Orleans was
a city of satisfied
slobs for whom
the most strenu-
ous exercise was

buttering a chunk of hot French bread, downing a dinner of rich sauces and bananas Foster, then knocking back a few Dixies or Hurricanes. It was just like Italy, but without the strikes. A city well known as the cholesterol capital of the world, where the whole idea about being alive was to party and have as much fun as possible. As recently as the mid-eighties you'd see the odd jogger—"odd," assuredly—who'd run a block and then collapse on the nearest park bench or patch of grass to take a cigarette break.

But then along came Fitness as a Way of Life. Nowadays a person can't walk down the street—not even in the Quarter—without being passed by a half-naked blue streak in running shoes, or blissed-out Rollerbladers with so many protective pads Velcroed on to them that they look like Ninja warriors. And if you light a cigarette in Jackson Square, you'll draw the same sorts of censorious glares as if you were in San Francisco or L.A. The main problem with this new regime is that it's so darn hot down here. In the summer, you can work up a sweat just sitting on a balcony sipping a Sazerac in the late afternoon—just imagine what a noonday jog would do to you. If you're going to work out, stick to the early mornings (it can be 80° by 9am in summer) or early evening. You'll be even happier knocking yourself out in April and October, when the humidity is low enough that you can actually breathe.

The Lowdown

Stretching your legs... In the northeast part of the city, a 10-minute drive up Esplanade Avenue from the Quarter practically out to Lake Pontchartrain, **City Park** (park headquarters tel 504/482–4888, 1 Palm Dr.) is one of the nation's largest urban parks, with 1,500 acres of trails, gardens, and lagoons, and hundreds of majestic live oaks. This place is *huge*. Lope along the meandering pathways, or head for the **City Park Track**, a 400-meter polyurethane track just outside **Tad Gormley Stadium** (tel 504/482–4888, on Roosevelt Mall near the casino building, open daily dawn–dusk). There's an identical track inside the stadium, too, which was built for and used during the 1992 Olympic track and field trials.

A 10-minute drive in another direction from the Quarter, out through the Garden District, 400-acre **Audubon Park** (tel 504/861–2537, 6800 St. Charles

Ave., across from Tulane and Loyola Universities) can be reached via the St. Charles Avenue streetcar. Shaded by giant live oaks whose ancient boughs bend down and scrape the ground, there are miles of jogging, hiking, and biking trails, including a 2-mile par course laid out on a macadam path from the park entrance on St. Charles Avenue, all the way through to Magazine Street and the entrance to the zoo. (The par course's starting point is to the left of the golf course as you face the park.) Running through a bucolic area where swans and ducks cruise on a sleepy lagoon, you can stop along the way at 18 exercise stations (chin-up bars and the like—don't expect Nautilus equipment). Cars are banned on the park drives between St. Charles Avenue and Magazine Street, but even so you'll have to be nimble to navigate around the weekend swarms of bikes and Rollerblades.

Right in the CBD, the **Rivercenter Racquet and Health Club** (tel 504/556–3742, New Orleans Hilton Riverside Hotel, 2 Poydras St.) has an outdoor 1 1/4-mile jogging track where, for a small fee, you can clock your distance while taking in great views of the Mississippi, the riverboats, and the skyline. New Orleanians like to beat their feet beside the Mississippi River, especially along the levee. One of the most popular stretches is around **Riverbend**, the little pocket neighborhood where the river makes a spectacular bend, and St. Charles Avenue dead-ends at Carrollton Avenue. Take the St. Charles Avenue streetcar and get off at Carrollton Avenue to walk up on the levee, where you can stroll, run, jog, or fly a kite to your heart's content. Out in eastern New Orleans, about 20 minutes from the Quarter, the **Louisiana Nature and Science Center** (tel 504/246–5672, Joe Brown Memorial Park, 11000 Lake Forest Blvd.; closed Mon; admission charged) offers easygoing nature trails lacing through an 86-acre preserve of bottomland hardwood forest. This spot is better for walking than jogging—it'd be a pity to come this far from the tourist track and not commune with the ecosystem.

If you'd rather run with the pack and your timing is right, you can sign up for the **Crescent City Classic** (tel 504/861–8686, 8200 Hampton St., 70118; open weekdays 9–5), held in April. Some 30,000 runners head from Jackson Square downtown to the Audubon Zoo uptown, and in typical New Orleans style, there's plenty of jazz

NEW ORLEANS | GETTING OUTSIDE

and food to spirit them along. Check also with the **New Orleans Track Club** (tel. 504/482–6682, Box 52003, 70152; open 24 hours), which has its foot in about 45 club races annually, or **Southern Runner Productions** (tel 504/899–3333, 6112A Magazine St., 70118; open 10–6, closed Sat), which can tell you all about the **Hallowe'en Witches Run**, a 5K-event held the Friday night before Halloween. About 1,500 to 2,000 runners of both sexes usually show up in all sorts of outlandish costumes, and they all wind up at a big bash at whichever downtown hotel's hosting the event that year.

The tennis racket... For most active sports, the slickest venue for visitors is the **Rivercenter Racquet and Health Club** at the Hilton Riverside (tel 504/556–3742, 2 Poydras St.). It's right there in the CBD and is just about always open (Mon–Thurs 6am–10:30pm, Fri 6am–9pm, Sat 7–7, Sun 7–5). The only catch is that a fee is charged, and the tennis courts—eight indoor, three outdoor—may be all booked up. There are also three squash courts and four racquetball courts, tennis and racquetball instruction, and a pro shop where they'll not only string your racquet or rent one to you, but they'll also find you a game through the Match-Maker Service. A 10-minute car drive away from the French Quarter, the **City Park Tennis Center** (tel 504/482–4888, Victory Dr., City Park) has many more courts—36 lighted rubico and laykold courts, shaded by oaks and cypress trees—as well as equipment rentals and individual and group lessons by USPTA pros. It's open Mon–Thur 7am–10pm, Fri–Sun 7–7; there is a court fee, but you usually don't need to reserve ahead to get on a court. There are also 10 clay courts in **Audubon Park** (tel 504/861–2537, near the zoo at Henry Clay and Tchoupitoulas St.; fee charged), where you can usually drop by and get on a court with no fuss. They open at 8am and stay open pretty much until it's too dark to see the ball.

Par for the course... You can play golf year-round down here, and as a result there's a good supply of courses, though most of them are pretty flat—this is, after all, delta country. Since most locals who play golf belong to private clubs, there's usually no problem getting tee times on the public courses—just give them a call. Visiting golfers often head for City Park's **Bayou Oaks Golf Courses** (tel 504/483–9396, 1040 Filmore Dr.; greens fees $9–17, cart rental $16), where there are four—count 'em, four—18-holers, not to mention a 100-tee double-decker driving range, lit at night. Now there's a park that appreciates golf. There's also an 18-hole course in **Audubon Park** (tel 504/865–8260, 473 Walnut Dr.; greens fees $8–10, cart rental $8), which is par 68 for men, par 69 for women; and out in eastern New Orleans's Pontchartrain Park, about half an hour from the Quarter, the par-72 **Joe Bartholomew Golf Course** (tel. 504/288–0928, 6514 Congress Dr.; greens fees $7.75–10, cart rental $17.95) is worth the trek if you like long courses—it's 6,945 yards for men, 6,023 for women. Over on the West Bank of the river, the public courses are par-70 **Brechtel** (tel 504/362–4761, 3700 Behrman Place; greens fees $6.75–4.10, cart rental $12), par-69 **Plantation Golf Course** (tel 504/392–3363, 1001 Behrman Hwy.; greens fees $5.40–7.50, cart rental $10.80–14), and par-71 **Bayou Barriere Golf Course** (tel 504/394–9500 or 504/394–0662, 7427 Rte. 23, Belle Chase; greens fees $20–35 including cart), which actually has 27 holes, so you can vary the layout.

If you're a really dedicated golfer—and that's often a redundant term—you might want to drive up into the instep of this boot-shaped state to play the area's best course, designed by Arnold Palmer, at **The Bluffs at Thompson Creek** (tel 504/634–5222, Rte. 965, 6 miles east of U.S. 61; greens fees $45–55). Its signature hole number 17 is a stunning par-three atop one of the high bluffs that give the club its name. The par-72 course is wildly popular with St. Francisville duffers, but it's not impossible to get a tee time—nonmembers can call a couple of days in advance (not before Friday for weekend times) and reserve any times not already booked by members. To really make sure you can get on the course, reserve a room at the attached **Lodge at the Bluffs** (tel 504/634–3410), which has 39 fairly plush one-bedroom suites; lodge guests are guaranteed tee times and get discounts on the greens fee. Considering it's a 2-hour drive from New Orleans, staying over's not a bad idea anyway.

On a bicycle built for one... There are no hills to slow you down in this delta town, so pumping is easy; the humidity, however, can really get to you. At **Bicycle Michael's** (tel 504/945–9505, 918 Frenchmen St., Faubourg Marigny; open daily at 10) you can not only rent wheels but also pick up a touring map with the best bike routes. If you want to do more than just putter around in the city parks, Bicycle Michael himself, Mike Farrand, recommends this 25-mile route: from the French Quarter, head up Esplanade Avenue to City Park, loop along Lakeshore Drive, come back into Mid-City, spin through Audubon Park and the Tulane campus, then go along the levee at Riverbend, down through the Garden District, and along St. Charles Avenue back to the Quarter. Hardy cyclists can do it in an hour.

Back in the saddle... There is no place in the city where you can rent a horse and bolt off on your own. However, you can take a guided trail ride at **Cascade Stables** (tel 504/891–2246, 700 East Drive near the zoo; open 9–4; fee charged). You'll ride only for about 45 minutes, but the guide does lead you through some of the prettiest areas of the park. No trail rides are offered at **City Park Stables** (tel 504/282–9247, 1040 Filmore Dr.; open 9–5; fee charged), but you can take lessons there and attend an occasional horse show.

If you've got the time, however, the best experience on horseback in these parts has got to be the spectacular guided trail rides at the Nature Stables of the **Global Wildlife Center** (tel 504/624-WILD, Rte. 40 West, just outside of Folsom; open 10–sunset; admission charged; reservation required), across Lake Pontchartrain. One of only three such wildlife facilities in the country, the 900-acre center is a protected area for hundreds of endangered species; the animals roam free, while humans are the ones cooped up, in motorized covered wagons. On the horseback tours, though, you can get even closer to nature. Friendly giraffes, ostriches, camels, zebras, llamas, bison, and antelopes go about their business, while visitors snap pictures like mad and feed them tidbits provided by the tour guides. The countryside is lovely, all green and lush with hills, valleys, ponds, and wooded groves. You can even stay overnight at the Safari Lodge, a very rustic lodging on site; the package includes breakfast and dinner, a wagon tour, a horseback ride, and fishing, too, if you bring your own gear. To reach the Global Wildlife

Center, take the Lake Pontchartrain Causeway to I-12 West, turn right at the town of Robert (exit 47) onto Route 445, and drive 10 ¹/₂ miles to Route 40; turn right and drive for 1 mile.

Gone fishin'... The main fish in these parts are speckled trout and bass. Former TV weatherman Nash Roberts will run you out into the coastal marshes year-round through **Fishhunter Guide Service, Inc.** (tel 504/837–0702 or 800/887–1385, 1040 N. Rampart St., 70116), which provides everything you need for light tackle fishing and will even pick you up at your hotel. You'll need your own wheels for our other two options. **Co Co Marina** (tel 504/594–6626, 800/648–2626, 106 Pier 56, Chauvin, LA 70344) has its feet smack in the Gulf of Mexico; the drive down, about an hour from New Orleans, is splendid, especially in the spring, when colorfully decorated shrimp boats line the bayous. To get there, take U.S. 90 south from New Orleans and hitch up with Route 57 (routes 56 and 57 form a circular drive from and to Houma, so take Route 56 for the return drive). It should go without saying, but won't, that this is not really the place to be when hurricanes sweep up through the gulf. **Capt. Phil's Saltwater Guide Service** (tel 504/348–3264, 4037 Hugo Dr., Marrero) is operated by Captain Phil Robichaux, a familiar face to many Orleanians from a local fishing show hosted by sportsfisherman and TV personality Frank Davis. Equipment and artificial bait is provided; Captain Phil's four boats prowl the coastal marshes, setting off from the Lafitte Marina near the Barataria Unit of the Jean Lafitte National Historical Park. The park is about an hour's drive from downtown New Orleans. Follow Decatur Street across Canal Street, where it becomes Magazine Street, then cross the Crescent City Connection and take the West Bank Expressway (U.S. 90) to Barataria Boulevard (Route 45). Turn left on Route 45 and watch for the Barataria Unit signs.

In search of the yellow-toothed nutria... If you're at all inclined toward outdoorsy things, you really should not leave this area without visiting the aforementioned **Barataria Unit** of the **Jean Lafitte National Historical Park** (tel. 504/589–2330, Rte. 45 near Jean Lafitte; admission free; open daily 9–5), an 8,000-acre preserve

GETTING OUTSIDE | **NEW ORLEANS**

about an hour south of the city. Eight miles of paved nature trails wind through the wetlands, where you can see egrets, all sorts of slithery critters including the occasional gator, and those really hideous nutria—they're the giant rodents you've read about, the ones that are eating up the coastal wetlands. (Keep in mind what the rangers tell us: it's their home, not ours. We're the ones trespassing.) You can strike out on your own (ever mindful of whose home this is) or hook up with a ranger-guided tour. Trails lead through a hardwood forest and a picture-postcard Louisiana swamp with spectacular scenery and great bird-watching. At the nearby **Bayou Barn** (tel 504/689–2663 or 800/TO–BAYOU, junction. Rtes. 31, 34, and 45, near Crown Point; open 9–5), you can rent a canoe, either on your own or with a guide, and paddle off among the moss-draped cypresses that jut out of the water. Eerily beautiful. Be sure to ask about the schedule for moonlight canoeing, which usually happens about once a month. The Bayou Barn also serves up pretty fair gumbo and jambalaya, and has occasional *fais-do-do* (Cajun dances)—the friendly staff will show you how to jig and two-step, a really great way to shake a leg.

Boating and fishing for urban wimps... If you'd as soon forgo the nutria and gators, you can get some peaceful canoeing and pedal-boating done in **City Park** (tel 504/488–9371, 1 Dreyfous Dr.; Mon–Fri 8–5, Sat–Sun 7–7). Graceful white swans, ducks, and geese glide along 8 miles of artificial lagoons in a romantic setting of ancient oak trees. The lagoons are stocked with bass, catfish, and perch, who haven't a clue in the world that they're fair game. You'll have to bring your own fishing gear, but boats can be rented and fishing licenses obtained (you can't fish without one) in the Casino, a building within which there is not a trace of gambling.

Indoor fitness... The best health club in town that's available to visitors is the **Rivercenter Racquet and Health Club** at the New Orleans Hilton Riverside Hotel (tel 504/556–3742, 2 Poydras St., CBD; $8 for hotel guests, $10 for others), the same place we recommended above for tennis and racquetball. The exercise room here is stellar, too, with state-of-the-art Nautilus equipment, Keiser Cam II, and Universal gym stuff, as well as Bally computerized Lifecycles, handheld weights, and a rowing machine; there's also an aerobics rooms, and for those who prefer their fitness to be passive, a full-service unisex salon, saunas, whirlpools, a masseur, and a tanning bed. **Le Meridien's Health and Fitness Center** (tel 504/525–6500, 614 Canal St.; free to Le Meridien guests, $9 others) is less extensive than the Rivercenter—nobody in town beats the Rivercenter—but it has cardiovascular and Nautilus equipment (with a staff of trainers to see that you don't blow a gasket on one of those machines), a sauna, a Jacuzzi, an aerobics room, massages, and a heated rooftop pool. In contrast to these gleaming high-tech health clubs, the very old-line **New Orleans Athletic Club** (tel 504/525–2375, 222 N. Rampart St.; open daily; $20 fee) is a prestigious private club founded in 1872, which claims to be the nation's second-oldest athletic club. The big marble halls have been outfitted with all the modern stuff, however—Nautilus gear, a great swimming pool, a hot tub, a steam room—as well as an excellent restaurant, in the grand old men's-club tradition, though women are allowed. Out-of-towners are allowed to enter the hallowed halls for one day, for the fee.

If your tastes are more egalitarian, try the **Lee Circle YMCA** (tel 504/568–9622, 920 St. Charles Ave.; fee charged), the better equipped of the city's two Y's. It has an indoor half-mile running track, a swell 60-foot pool, sauna, steam room, whirlpool, weightlifting stuff, aerobics machines, racquetball, and tennis.

ping

Never doubt that
New Orleans is a
two-faced city—
just look at the
French Quarter,
where ritzy,
world-class

antique stores and art galleries sit cheek by jowl with some of the world's raunchiest T-shirt stands. Naturally, because it is the tourist center, the Quarter has an overabundance of really tacky souvenir shops. You won't have any trouble at all finding a "French postcard." On the other hand, you won't have trouble finding that rare gilded Napoleon III desk, either. This is not a hot retail-clothing market; there are plenty of clothing stores, of course, to serve style-conscious locals—you'll find Lord & Taylor, Saks Fifth Avenue, and Macy's—but no one comes to New Orleans from, say, New York or L.A. or even Dallas on a clothes-buying spree. The big-ticket items are to be found in antique stores, but there are also wonderful little gift shops, boutiques, bookstores, and record shops.

What to Buy

Rare is the person who leaves this town without buying at least one box of **pralines**—those luscious little candy patties made of sugar, butter, and pecans. They're sold in gift shops all over town, but Orleanians themselves like to pop into the Old Town Praline Shop on Royal Street to satisfy their sweet tooth. **Carnival masks** are also enormously popular souvenirs and gifts. Some are those horrible little ceramic harlequin masks you can buy anywhere, but others are handmade works of art—and they are not cheap. In addition to the masks, local crafts include marvelous handmade **dolls**—some of them of the antique persuasion, which makes them too expensive to play with. Locals like to buy the handpainted **ties** of Mike Fennelly, available at his restaurant, Mike's on the Avenue, where the artist is also the chef. Wembley Tabasco ties are also currently all the rage. Splashy **Mardi Gras and Jazz Fest posters** are popular take-home items. The sounds of New Orleans's world-class musicians are readily available on **records**, **CDs**, **and tapes** at places like Record Ron's, the Louisiana Music Factory, and the retail outlet of the GHB Jazz Foundation; they'll carry some recordings you couldn't hope to find in most other cities. There are even places that package New Orleans's **food**, either to take with you or have shipped. Speaking of which, **cookbooks** abound with regional recipes, and most of the top local chefs have produced at least one cookbook, including Emeril Lagasse, Paul Prudhomme, Kevin Graham, and Alex Patout (see "Really Cooking," below).

Target Zones

The largest concentration of malls, stores, and shops lies in the French Quarter and the Central Business District (CBD).

There's at least one shop on almost all of the Quarter's 96 blocks, hunkering for the most part in those charming little 19th-century buildings, town houses, and cottages; the great majority of the shops we list below are in the Quarter. The stroll-through **French Market**, a 200-year-old restored marketplace, is a five-block collection of genuinely quaint, pastel-painted low stone buildings containing open-air cafes and shops selling clothes, candy, T-shirts, and the like; it stretches from St. Ann Street to Barracks Street. Simply by virtue of being in the Quarter, it's full of tourists, but it isn't glitzy and the atmosphere is authentically New Orleans. The century-old-Café du Monde (see Dining and Diversions) is the upriver anchor (at St. Ann Street); at the Barracks Street end are the ramshackle **Old Farmers' Market** and **Community Flea Market**, two completely ungentrified shopping areas where locals go for produce and bargain items. The Jackson Brewery Corporation (locally called the Jax Brewery) has three indoor "festival market-places," which you can bet means they're tourist-oriented, geared mostly to sell food, entertainment, fashion, and impulse items: the **Jax Brewery** is in the restored 1891 Jackson Brewery; walkways connect it to its sister,

Code Words

If the baker tosses in one extra doughnut to make it 13, he's given you a baker's dozen. In New Orleans that little something extra is called **lagniappe** *(pronounced LAN-yap. Roughly). This may be the first of the code words you can forget; the custom is not nearly as prevalent as it used to be.* **Makin' groceries** *means going to the grocery store. The root of this ubiquitous phrase is the French word* faire, *which means "to do" or "to make." But Orleanians never "do" groceries. They say, "I gotta make groceries today...." You'll hear* praline *pronounced PRAY-leen a lot, but that's because the city is full of Yankees who don't know any better. It's PRAH-leen.*

the **Millhouse**; and two blocks toward Canal Street is the third Jax mall, the **Marketplace**. Though they have less New Orleans color than the French Quarter shops, the stores in the CBD are where Orleanians themselves go for their high-end shopping. **Maison Blanche** is a full-service department store with designer labels, housewares, appliances—the works. There are Maison Blanches all over the country now, but this turn-of-the-century store is the mother ship. Orleanians don't feel that Christmas season has officially started until the giant white effigy of a snowman named Mr. Bingle (based on a puppet from a now-forgotten 1950s kids' TV show) appears on the store's handsome cast-iron facade. Toward the river, **Canal Place** is a tony pedestrian mall set in a three-story marble-and-travertine atrium, starring Saks Fifth Avenue, Laura Ashley, Brooks Brothers, Williams-Sonoma, and Gucci, with 40 or so somewhat lesser lights. **Riverwalk**, with 200 shops, restaurants, and a food court, is another festival market-place alongside the river, with a plastic atmosphere not unlike the other Rouse Company developments in New York and Baltimore. The mix of tenants includes national chains (Banana Republic, The Disney Store, The Sharper Image) and local upscale shops (Yvonne LaFleur and Street Scenes). The **New Orleans Center** is a sleek, characterless atrium mall connected by walkways to the adjacent Superdome and Hyatt Regency Hotel. Leading lights here are Lord & Taylor and Macy's, but there are dozens of other chains, as well as a large food court.

The place to head for contemporary artworks is **Gallery Row**, on Julia Street in the Warehouse/Arts District, in which old aban-doned warehouses have been converted into galleries, apartments, and restaurants. Julia Street between St. Charles Avenue and the convention center is the hot stretch, so it's fairly conve-nient to CBD hotels. June, July, and August are the months for gallery openings, with festive doings the first Saturday night every summer month. Call the Contemporary

Good Reads

Anne Rice's fictional five-vol-ume Vampire Chronicles *are set in New Orleans and in her own Garden District homes. Other fiction set in New Orleans:* In the Land of Dreamy Dreams *by Ellen Gilchrist and* The Moviegoer *by Walker Percy. New Orleans dialects are done to a T in John Kennedy Toole's riotous Pulitzer Prize-winning* A Confederacy of Dunces. *Julie Smith, not an Orleanian, has written five books based here, most recently 1995's* House of Blues. *And homegrown novel-ist Nancy Lemann has cap-tured the city in her* Lives of the Saints *and* Ritz of the Bayou. *For nonfiction, Lyle Saxon's* Fabulous New Orleans *is fabulous; it was written long before 1936, when the preservationists began their rescue of the French Quarter, and gives you an entirely dif-ferent view of the old city. Saxon collaborated with Robert Tallant and Edward Dreyer for* Gumbo Ya Ya, *a collection of old folktales.* Voodoo *is revealed by Robert Tallant in* Voodoo in New Orleans. *John Churchill Chase's* Frenchmen, Desire, Good Children *has some fun insider stuff. Fans of Anne Rice will love* Haunted City: An Unauthorized Guide to the Magical, Magnificent New Orleans of Anne Rice *by Joy Dickinson.*

Arts Center at 504/523–1216 for information about openings; see "Gallery hopping" in the Diversions for a rundown of the best/trendiest/most interesting places. There are six miles or so of shops lining **Magazine Street**, which stretches upriver from Canal Street all the way to the Audubon Zoo. Many of the once-grand town houses and cottages that line this street are in a sad state of repair; nevertheless, various antique shops, bookstores, and used-clothing boutiques along here make it worth visiting. The surrounding neighborhood is seedy, though, so it's not very safe to wander around; your best bet is to take a cab to a specific address, or engage Macon Riddle (tel 504/899–3027) for a half- or full-day shopping expedition. A shopping consultant with a special interest in antiques, she keeps up to speed on what's where and how much it costs.

Riverbend is a pocket of shops tucked in beside the Uptown great bend in the river. You can reach it on the St. Charles streetcar—get off where the streetcar turns off St. Charles Avenue onto Carrollton Avenue. Trendy shops are tucked into Creole cottages scattered on tree-lined streets; you could easily spend a half day walking around browsing here.

Trading with the Natives

What with an annual onslaught of about eight million visitors, New Orleans's merchants are accustomed to packing and mailing. Don't expect such service from the vendors in the Community Flea Market, that jumble of stalls behind the Old Farmers' Market in the French Quarter, but many other places will ship. However, you *can* haggle for prices at the flea market—but don't embarrass yourself trying to bargain with the top-end antique dealers on Royal Street.

Hours of Business

Almost all shops downtown in the French Quarter and the CBD are open daily, but many shops uptown—in the Garden District, Riverbend, and on Magazine Street—are closed on Sunday. As a very general rule, New Orleans shops open around 9 or 10 and close at 5:30 or 6, but in the Quarter closing hours can depend upon how heavy the foot traffic is. Shops in the malls keep more reliable hours.

Sales Tax

The combined state and local tax comes to a whopping 9%. Louisiana's Tax-Free Shopping program helps, if you happen to be visiting from another country. The program applies to international visitors with valid passports and return tickets, and is available in stores that display the LTFS insignia. It works like this: When making a purchase, show your passport and request a refund voucher for the sales tax. You'll be charged full price, including sales tax. Keep your sales slip and refund voucher. When you arrive at the airport for your departure, go to the LTFS refund center and present the sales slip, tax refund voucher, your passport, and your return ticket. Refunds under $100 will be made in cash; amounts over $500 will be sent by check to your home address. A handling fee of $5 to $10 is deducted from your refund.

The Lowdown

Antiquities... The antique stores on Royal Street are ages-old establishments, most of them operated by a third or fourth generation of the founders, and accustomed to working with similarly venerable dealers in Europe and in this country. Obviously, there are different items in every store on the street, but they're all top quality, and if you're an antiques lover, you'll want to browse the whole strip. Expect prices to be high—and absolutely fair for what you're getting. The oldest on the street is **Waldhorn's**, established on June 4, 1880, by Moise Waldhorn and now run by fourth-generation owners. Stop here for the amazing display of American and English jewelry and silver. The owners of **Moss Antiques**, **Keil Antiques**, and **Royal Antiques** are all related, having descended from founders of The Royal Company, founded in 1899, and their stocks are also similar—precious old French and English furnishings and jewelry, with Royal tending a bit more toward country-style stuff. The **French Antique Shop** is the best place for Tiffany and Baccarat crystal chandeliers. **M. S. Rau**, begun in 1912 by Mendel Rau and his wife, Fanny, is operated now by their grandson and specializes in 19th-century American antiques, including lots of Victorian cut glass. One of the largest stores on Royal Street is **Dixon & Dixon**, owned by civic leader and art dealer David Dixon, who travels throughout this country and Europe buying estate jewels and collections of French, English, and Dutch furnishings, oil paintings, and Persian rugs. At **Gerald D. Katz Antiques**, the showcased collections contain jewelry, furniture, paintings, and objets d'art. **Diane Genre** focuses on exquisite examples of Asian art—lacquers, prints, and screens. Look in prestigious **Rothchild's Antiques** for fine custom-made jewelry and elegant 18th- and 19th-century French and English furnishings. **Manheim Galleries**, opened in 1910 and currently run by the second-generation owner, occupies a 19th-century bank building; the former director's conference room of the bank now holds the famous Manheim jade collection, and the gallery has also sewn up the local market on delicate porcelain Boehm Birds. Patrick Dunne's **Lucullus** (which is actually on Chartres Street, not Royal) is a very posh place to purchase 17th- to 19th-century cookware, furnishings, and paintings. Vintage timepieces are the specialty at **Jack Sutton**, though if you're into antique clocks, you'll want to detour from Royal Street and head Uptown to see the outstanding collection at **Kohlmaier and Kohlmaier**, off Magazine Street, as well as the clocks and watches at **19th Century Antiques**, on Magazine Street. And speaking of Magazine Street, a few other dealers up there definitely give the Royal Street merchants a run for their money. **Jon Antiques**, which occupies a historic 19th-century house, directly imports some very fine 18th- and 19th-century English and French furniture and furnishings; it's fairly nearby the aforementioned 19th Century Antiques, so you can do them on the same cab ride. **Accent Antiques** is a good place to go for European prints. **Blackamoor**, which handles furniture and American art, as well as porcelain and jewelry, has shops both on Magazine Street and in the Quarter (on Chartres Street).

Collectibles... You can brush up on military history while chatting up the knowledgeable folks at **Le Petit Soldier Shop**, which has two-inch-tall toy soldiers all lined up in rows. Look for the miniature Napoleon, an Eisenhower, both Lee and Grant, and even a Mussolini. The **Brass Monkey** absolutely shines with all its brass lamps, ceiling fans, and carousel horses (half or full-sized) carved of wood and trimmed with brass; collectors should make a beeline for the antique music boxes and walking sticks. A third generation operates **James H. Cohen & Sons**, a huge antique store that has everything from Civil War cannonballs to Confederate money, Frederic Remington bronco-busters, rare coins, antique firearms, and flags. **Manheim Galleries** is the local agent for Boehm Birds, delicate porcelains created by 19th-century American potter Edward Marshall Boehm and now much coveted by collectors.

Crafty things... At **The Idea Factory**, a marvelous place owned and run by the friendly Bacon family, you can watch them carve adorable tiny toys out of wood—and they'll carve your name on that toy airplane or whatever else you buy. Their prices aren't expensive, either. For sheer beauty, a better bet is the delicate, museum-quality flowers of handcrafted metal displayed (and sold) in the shop of **Takis**, a Greek who is a horticulturalist as well as an artisan. Check in at **RHINO**, a big, modern, well-lit store in the CBD, for upscale handcrafted jewelry and artworks by regional artisans. Head for **Crafty Louisianians** to see a wonderful collection of dolls, ranging from bisque to rag to voodoo; some of the lower-end merchandise, such as the totally inauthentic voodoo dolls, verges on kitsch, but there's good stuff here too. If you want a fine only-in-New-Orleans souvenir, though, visit **Umbrella Lady** Ann B. Lane at her studio, where she makes the colorful parasols that funeral parade-followers brandish in the joyous "second-lining" part of a jazz funeral. Lane herself often leads the second-lining at the French Market open-air cafes. And for those who want the *Architectural Digest* look, there are some really splendid high-priced garden ornaments—statuary and fountains of carved granite and marble—set out in the peaceful courtyard of **Coghlan Galleries**. At **Charbonnet & Charbonnet**, a Magazine Street antique store, the scent of sawdust hits you as soon as you walk in the door—the in-house cabinet shop custom-produces furnishings from relics of razed houses and buildings. Even if you're not in the market for furnishings, it's fascinating to witness this urban archaeology in action.

Diamonds are a girl's best friend... On the very upper end of the scale, Orleanian **Mignon Faget** creates elegant designs of bronze d'or and silver inspired by local architecture and nature—look for motifs such as banana leaves, palm fronds, even sea creatures. A smaller, funkier place is **Quarter Moon**, where husband-and-wife team Ellis and Michael Shallbetter fashion Mardi Gras masks and other New Orleans-related motifs into fun silver jewelry. For fine jewelry that doesn't necessarily show its Louisiana roots, try **Adler's**, an old-line CBD jeweler selling pricey baubles. Among the antique stores, **Waldhorn's** specializes in remarkable antique jewelry, and **Gerald D. Katz Antiques** sells some fine Victorian and Art Nouveau pieces. If all you want are cheap trinkets, of course, there's always the **Community Flea Market**.

Masking for Mardi Gras... While you can buy cheesy souvenir masks at gift shops throughout the Quarter, high-quality Carnival masks—which can cost anywhere from $20 to $3,000—are sold at these few stores. Master maskmaker Michael Stark's **Little Shop of Fantasy** may look like a hole in the wall, but inside it's brightened by fantastic leather and feather masks lining the walls and counters. More than 100 regional artists make the fabulous creations at **Rumors**, a more upscale store that sells jewelry as well as masks. At the **Mardi Gras Center** there is a grand conglomeration of masks, costumes, and accoutrements for Fat Tuesday doings—these aren't made as souvenirs but for Orleanians to wear during Carnival (if they can't make their own), so while some of them are gorgeous works of art, others are clever rubber or Latex disguises. For a Cajun spin on things, check out the Mardi Gras masks by Acadian artist Cathy Judice at **Crafty Louisianans**—her Masks of Mamou, made from painted window screens, resemble those worn by Cajun horsemen in the Courir du Mardi Gras, an ages-old race where masked riders gallop on horseback through the Cajun Country countryside. At Riverwalk, you can buy elaborate masks made of everything from ceramic to rubber in a small shop called **Masks & Make Believe**.

Incredible edibles... Do like all the tourists do and stop by **Aunt Sally's Praline Shop** on Decatur Street to watch the pralinemaking and browse through the cookbooks, aprons, and things—but go to the **Old Town Praline Shop**, as locals do, to buy your candies. (Orleanians avoid Aunt Sally's because it's always so crammed with tourists. Besides, the creamy candy patties at the Old Town Praline Shop just taste better.) Before you leave Old Town with your goodies, take a look at the delightful rear courtyard with its banana trees and subtropical greenery. **Creole Delicacies** also boasts of its pralines, which are perfectly fine, but the reason to come here is for one-stop shopping on gift packages of spices, rémoulade sauce, and hot peppers. **The New Orleans School of Cooking** conducts upbeat two-hour cooking demonstrations (here's where to learn how to make that perfect étouffée); you won't get your own hands floury and greasy, but you will get to taste the finished product. In the **Louisiana General Store**—its retail outlet—you can buy cookbooks, spices, rices, sauces, and other items to create your own Cajun and Creole culinary masterpieces. **Gumbo Ya Ya** has gift baskets of Louisiana foods, and at **Bayou to Go**, at the airport, you can get frozen seafoods packed to travel with you or be shipped. In the Garden District, stop by the **Li'l Fisherman**—a corner fish market where neighborhood folk go for their seafood—to order fresh fish for shipping.

Funky old stuff... Locals love to hang out at the **Community Flea Market** at the Old Farmers' Market, where tables and bins are loaded with all manner of items for sale. You can pick up Mardi Gras beads and doubloons (aluminum coins tossed from Carnival floats); jazz records, CDs, and tapes; stuffed toys; houseplants; maybe a fringed lampshade or even a fringed flapper dress from somebody's attic. The Farmers' Market itself is in rickety open-air sheds, where farmers have been bringing just-picked produce and fruit for about 200 years.

Exotic and erotic... You won't have any trouble at all finding the erotic. Just walk down Bourbon Street and look at all the X-rated undies and indefinables displayed in shop windows. What you see is what you get—all are of the same sleazy quality, and the shopowners are used to tittering tourists who gawk at the merchandise but never buy. **Second Skin Leather** is a bit off the beaten track (though still in the Quarter), but it delivers its exotica—leather, latex, and "sexual hardware"—with a welcome glint of humor.

The sounds of music... With its plethora of world-class music, New Orleans's record stores do a land-office business. **Record Ron's** is one of the largest—a couple of big, cluttered stores with narrow aisles and overflowing bins of recorded music in every genre. The **Louisiana Music**

Factory is a rollicking place during Jazz Fest, when jam sessions are a featured attraction. The **GHB Jazz Foundation** has a retail outlet where it sells the eight labels the foundation itself produces, as well as other companies' jazz recordings; the adjacent Palm Court Jazz Café, also owned by George and Nina Buck, is a great place for dinner accompanied by live traditional jazz. If you stop by **Preservation Hall** to hear the music—and you should—you'll probably have to wait in the carriageway, the whole purpose of which is to encourage you to browse through the bins for records and tapes of all the jazz legends who perform or have performed there.

Book nooks... A handful of locally owned bookstores are worth singling out for their special New Orleans flavor. In the Quarter, **Beckham's Bookshop** has been going strong for more than 25 years, its shelves sagging with thousands of used books; the **Librairie** is a branch of Beckham's that just stays open a little later. Both are generally crowded with browsers thumbing through old treasures, some of which sell for only a buck or two. Perhaps the city's most atmospheric bookstore is **Faulkner House Books**, on the ground floor of the apartment building in which William Faulkner wrote his first novel, *A Soldier's Pay;* green shutters open on to the cracked flagstones of Pirate's Alley. The staff here is helpful, knowledgeable, and tactful enough to let you browse for hours undisturbed. If you're familiar with Barnes & Noble, you'll recognize **BookStar** as soon as you step inside—big, brass-accented, and sterile, it's just like other branches of that discount bookstore chain. Its very size means it has loads of books in stock, and computers to help the cheerful–but–overworked staff find you what you're looking for. And you can't beat those discounted prices. Uptown, the **Maple Street Book Shop**, **DeVille Books and Prints**, and the **Garden District Book Shop** are all locally owned. Maple Street's Rhoda Faust is a veritable guru among local book lovers, known for helping readers locate hard-to-find books; the Garden District Book Shop's owner Britton Trice publishes his own limited editions of prominent local writers, including Anne Rice and Richard Ford, and the publication party for Rice's recent *Memnoch the Devil* was held here.

Dolls to ooh and aah over... If you're a collector—and collectible dolls are a big thing down here—there are three places to head for: **Oh, Susannah**, where the exquisite dolls are too pricey to play with; **Boyer Antiques & Doll Shop**, which also sells exceptional antique items and restored dolls and dollhouses; and **The Ginja Jar**, known for its wonderful bisque dolls. For actual dolls to play with, however, **Hello, Dolly** has all types of newer dolls for sale, and in the other half of the same cottage, **Crafty Louisianians** sells voodoo dolls and cornstalk dolls and other folk-art things. The **Little Toy Shoppe**—which despite its name is a large toy store—includes in its wide selection some lovely bisque dolls and creations by name dollmakers Madame Alexander and Peggy Nisbet.

A tip of the hat... Folks down here tend to wear hats a lot, especially panama hats. Custom-made ladies' hats—the sort Princess Di looks so good in, with ribbons, bows, and frilly froufrous—can be found at **Yvonne LaFleur's**, a Riverwalk shop that also carries sportswear, formal gowns, and bridal gowns. The same kinds of smart chapeaux in the shop windows at **Fleur de Paris** practically stop traffic on Royal Street. Local hatmakers Tracy Thomson and Ann Marie Popko make clever little novelty hats for women that you can find at **Quarter Moon** and the **Little Shop of Fantasy**, two pocket-sized boutiques in the French Quarter. **Rine Chapeaux**—another pint-sized shop, this one in Riverwalk—has racks of hats for men and women, ranging from chichi little numbers to cowboy hats. In-the-know Orleanian men go straight to long-established **Meyer the Hatter** in the CBD.

For your voodoo to-do... Do not be fooled by films such as *Angel Heart*—you're bloody unlikely to run across any bloodletting voodoo rites down here. There are an estimated 20,000 voodoo practitioners in New Orleans, but they consider it a religion and not a black-magic cult. (Occasionally someone will stage a cleansing ritual to publicly chase out bad spirits, but you can bet that's done as much for the P.R. value as anything.) Several shops in town cater to the tourists' curiosity about voodoo (or hoodoo, as it's sometimes called)—foremost among them the **New Orleans Historic Voodoo Museum**, which takes itself (and the tourist dollar) very seriously indeed. A dark and gloomy place, it displays and sells *gris-gris* (pronounced gree-gree, and meaning voodoo charms), various potions and powders, and operates voodoo tours to various "haunted" places around town. The **Witches' Corner**, only slightly better lit than the Voodoo Museum, is a murky little hole-in-the-wall devoted to witchcraft and voodoo accoutrements such as ju-ju bags, useful for warding off evil spirits.

Picking up the scent... New Orleans is home to a couple of very old-line perfumers, the oldest being **Bourbon French Parfum**. This tiny place, tucked in the lower Pontalba Apartments off Jackson Square, will sell you a fragrance, or custom-blend one just for you. Let them anoint you with a sample of Kus Kus, the very first scent created when the store was founded in 1843. A mere babe compared to Bourbon French Parfum—and with a much less friendly staff—**Hové Parfumeur** is the retail outlet for a New Orleans–based mail-order company that was founded in 1931. Although it's in a historic 19th-century Creole house, the place has about as much character as— well, as a mail-order catalog.

Really cooking... Almost all of the top-name chefs have produced a cookbook or two, among them Kevin Graham, Paul Prudhomme, Emeril Lagasse, and Alex Patout. There are tables full of local cookbooks at gift shops like **Aunt Sally's Praline Shop** and the **Old Town Praline Shop**, as well as at such bookstores as **BookStar**, the **Maple Street Book Shop** uptown, and the **Garden District Book Shop**.

Dressed to the nines... In a city where "costume" is a verb and cross-dressing an art form, you don't have to wait for Carnival to don outrageous garb. Only the tourists will do double-takes; we natives are accustomed to the costumed characters that roam around the Quarter. **Fred and Ethel's Vintage Clothing**, a cluttered, funky little shop across from the French Market, sells all manner of used clothing, some of it dating from the 1800s—crinoline petticoats, gentlemen's frock coats and waistcoats, 1950s taffeta cocktail dresses á la Kim Novak, or men's brocade smoking jackets á la Hugh Hefner. Both **MGM Costumes**, up on St. Charles Avenue, and **Broadway Bound** sell as well as rent costumes, ranging from ape suits to Scarlett O'Hara–style gowns.

The Index

Accent Antiques. Come here for imported English and European furnishings and prints.... *Tel 504/897–9466. 2855 Magazine St., Uptown.*

Adler's. In business since 1898, this elegant, dignified jewelry store glitters with diamonds, emeralds, and other expensive gems.... *Tel 504/523–5292, or 800/925–7912. 722 Canal St., CBD. Closed Sun.*

Aunt Sally's Praline Shop. You can watch the candymakers stirring up batches of pralines and buy boxes to take home or have shipped. The shop has all sorts of souvenir items, including T-shirts, aprons, cookbooks, chicory-laced New Orleans coffee, and beignet mix.... *Tel 504/524–5107. 810 Decatur St., French Quarter. Open 8–8.*

Bayou to Go. Fresh Louisiana seafoods—gumbo, jambalaya, crawfish étouffée—are prepared and wrapped to travel with you on the plane.... *Tel 504/468–8040. Concourse C, New Orleans International Airport. Open 7–7.*

Beckham's Bookshop. This creaky old two-story bookstore, a French Quarter fixture for more than 25 years, overflows with secondhand and rare books.... *Tel 504/522–9875. 228 Decatur St., French Quarter.*

Blackamoor. The stock here includes antique furniture and porcelain as well as American art and jewelry.... *Tel 504/ 523–7786, 324 Chartres St., French Quarter; tel 504/ 897–2711, 3433 Magazine St., Uptown.*

BookStar. This huge two-story bookstore stocks almost everything you're looking for, including books by local and regional authors (Anne Rice, Stephen Ambrose, 1993 Pulitzer Prize–winning novelist Robert Olen Butler), cookbooks, and guidebooks—and all at a discount, too. You may have to wait in line at the cash register.... *Tel 504/523–6411. The Marketplace, 414 N. Peters St., French Quarter. Open 10–midnight.*

Bourbon French Parfum. Your wildest perfume dreams can be fulfilled in this tiny shop carrying scores of fragrances with seductive names. The shop was founded in 1843 (on Bourbon Street, hence the name).... *Tel 504/522–4480. 525 St. Ann St., French Quarter.*

Boyer Antiques & Doll Shop. Toy lovers will adore the antique dolls, doll restorations, and small antiques to be found here.... *Tel 504/522–4513. 241 Chartres St. and 330 Chartres St., French Quarter. Closed Sun.*

Brass Monkey. The focus here is on brass and brass-trimmed items. Wood-carved carousel horses, antique walking sticks, and dressing-table accessories are specialties.... *Tel 504/561–0688. 235 Royal St., French Quarter.*

Broadway Bound. If MGM Costume Rentals (see below) is fresh out of fangs and capes, or low on boas, tiaras, and scepters, hie yourself to Broadway Bound, this costume-loving city's second-tier rent-a-costume emporium. Browsing is a kick, even if you don't buy anything.... *Tel 504/821–1000. 2737 Canal St., CBD. Closed weekends.*

Canal Place. This tony downtown mall has three levels of stores: Saks Fifth Avenue, Laura Ashley, Gucci, Ann Taylor, Williams-Sonoma, and Grand Cuisine, and about 40 other upscale tenants. The third level has a food court, three first-run movie theaters, and the Southern Repertory Theatre (see Entertainment).... *Tel 504/587– 0739. 333 Canal St., CBD. Mall open 10–midnight. Shops close at 6.*

Charbonnet & Charbonnet. As well as selling English and Irish country antiques, this store has an in-house cabinet shop for making customized furnishings using components from razed houses and buildings.... *Tel 504/891–9948. 2929 Magazine St., Uptown.*

Coghlan Galleries. Statuary, fountains, and charming garden ornaments—winged cherubs, tiny lambs, gargoyles, all carved by regional artisans—are displayed in a peaceful courtyard.... *Tel 504/525–8550. 710 Toulouse St., French Quarter.*

Community Flea Market. Racks of clothes, bins of books and records, stacks of T-shirts, and trays of jewelry and trinkets, as well as furniture of various descriptions, are sold by vendors in this outdoor flea market spread out in and around the Old Farmers' Market.... *Tel 504/596–3420. 1235 N. Peters St., French Quarter. Open 7–7.*

Crafty Louisianians. You'll find an assortment of Louisiana handicrafts here, including lots of folk-art dolls.... *Tel 504/528–3094. 813 Royal St., French Quarter.*

Creole Delicacies. The main draw is the pralines, but gift packages of spices, rémoulade sauce, and hot peppers are sold here, too.... *Tel 525–9508, 523 St. Ann St., French Quarter; tel 504/523–6425, Riverwalk, CBD. Riverwalk store open until 10.*

DeVille Books and Prints. This locally owned shop carries regional books, guidebooks, cookbooks, maps, posters, and prints.... *Tel 504/525–1846, 344 Carondelet St., CBD; tel 504/595–8916, Riverwalk. Carondelet St. store closed Sun.*

Diane Genre. Aficionados of antique Asian art lay down big money for the exquisite items here—Japanese woodblock prints, textiles, paintings, lacquer, and screens, as well as delicately handpainted Chinese chests and cabinets.... *Tel 504/525–7270. 233 Royal St., French Quarter. Closed Sun.*

Dixon & Dixon. The 20,000 square feet of this huge emporium are filled with antiques from the 17th to 19th centuries, estate jewelry, antique rugs, and European oil paintings.... *Tel 504/524–0282, 800/848–5148. 237 Royal St., French Quarter. Other stores at 301 Royal St. (tel 504/524–2630) and 321 Chartres St. (tel 504/528–3690), French Quarter.*

Faulkner House Books. Located in the building in which William Faulkner wrote his first book, this shop specializes in that author's works and books by other Southern writers.... *Tel 504/524–2940. 624 Pirate's Alley, French Quarter.*

Fleur de Paris. One the city's most elegant haute couture boutiques—with haut prices to match—Fleur de Paris features its own private-label collection of fine women's streetwear, tailored suits, cocktail dresses, formal gowns, and hats. The snooty sales staff will make you feel like you're in Paris, too.... Tel 504/525–1899. 721 Royal St., French Quarter. Closed Sun.

Fred and Ethel's Vintage Clothing. Plow through the mishmash of secondhand and antique clothes here to find that perfect costume.... *Tel 504/523–2942. 1215 Decatur St., French Quarter. Open Mon–Fri 1:30–7:30, Sat–Sun noon–7.*

French Antique Shop. Among the fine 18th- and 19th-century French furnishings in this lovely store are chandeliers, mirrors, marble mantels, porcelains, and bronze statues.... *Tel 504/524–9861. 225 Royal St., French Quarter. Closed Sun.*

French Market. A former Native American trading post, this restored five-block complex of shops, restaurants, and open-air cafes includes the long popular hangout Café du Monde and the Old Farmers' Market (see below), both of which are open 24 hours.... *Tel 504/522–2621. 1008 N. Peters St., French Quarter.*

Garden District Book Shop. Britton Trice and company have encyclopedic knowledge about book-related subjects, especially regional and hard-to-find volumes. The store is tucked into The Rink, a small mall in the Garden District.... *Tel 504/895–2266. 2727 Prytania St., Uptown. Closed Sun.*

Gerald D. Katz Antiques. This is the place to go for collections of Georgian, Victorian, Edwardian, Art Nouveau, Art Deco, and retro jewelry, in addition to 18th- and 19th-century furniture, paintings, and objets d'art.... *Tel 504/524–5050. 505 Royal St., French Quarter. Closed Sun June–Aug.*

GHB Jazz Foundation. Music lovers flock to this retail outlet, chock-full of traditional jazz, Dixie, and R&B records, CDs, and tapes from GHB's vast warehouse stock of their own and other labels.... *Tel 504/525–1776. 61 French Market Place, French Quarter. Open Mon–Fri noon–6.*

The Ginja Jar. The bisque dolls here are top-quality, handcrafted by national and local artists. Next door, Ginja Jar Too (607 Royal St., tel 504/523–7614) has some marvelous dollhouses, dollhouse furnishings, antique walking sticks, and much more.... *Tel 504/523–7643. 611 Royal St., French Quarter.*

Gumbo Ya Ya. Pralines, fudge, spices, and homemade sauces are among the take-home items at this singular Cajun food store.... *Tel 504/522–7484. 219 Bourbon St., French Quarter. Closed Sun.*

Hello, Dolly. Sharing half a cottage with Crafty Louisianians, this shop is awash with dolls, from fine bisque dolls to voodoo dolls and a line of soft sculptures (i.e., fabric dolls) called Enchanted Minikins.... *Tel 504/522–9948. 815 Royal St., French Quarter. Closed Sun.*

Hové Parfumeur. This retail outlet, flagship of a long-established catalog company (what kind of people shop for perfume by mail?), is a bit sterile; expect scented soaps, sachets, and perfumes with names such as Kiss in the Dark and Pirate's Gold.... *Tel 504/522–4480. 824 Royal St., French Quarter. Closed Sun.*

The Idea Factory. The Bacon family carves wonderful wooden paddle-wheelers, alligators, streetcars, roadster convertibles, signs, toy dump trucks and fire engines, miniature working mantel clocks, and scores of other items, from the large to the little.... *Tel 504/524–5195, 800/524–IDEA. 838 Chartres St., French Quarter.*

Jack Sutton. Vintage timepieces are the specialty at this elegant antique store, but there are also glass cases lined with delicate Dresden figurines, as well as small, intricately carved ivory figures and fine jewelry.... *Tel 504/522–0555. 315 Royal St., French Quarter. Closed Sun.*

Jackson Brewery. Three large indoor pedestrian malls in the French Quarter are run by the Jackson Brewery Corporation. The flagship Jax Brewery mall occupies a historic 19th-century building where Jax beer was once brewed. Since Planet Hollywood bought it in 1994, only a few other small retail shops remain. Adjacent to the brewery on Decatur St. is the four-story Millhouse, which houses several shops and push-cart vendors. Two blocks toward Canal St. (400 block of Decatur St.t, between St. Louis and Conti sts.), the Marketplace contains BookStar, Tower Records and Video, the Hard Rock Cafe, and not much else.... *Tel 504/586–8015. 620 Decatur St. All 3 malls open Sun–Thurs 10–9, Fri–Sat 10–10.*

James H. Cohen & Sons. A wooden Indian guards the front door of this large, fascinating store, open since 1898. Antique weapons and flags hang on the walls, and glass cases are filled with rare coins, Frederic Remington bronzes, Civil War cannonballs, and much, much more.... *Tel 504/522–3305, 800/535–1853. 437 Royal St., French Quarter.*

Jon Antiques. Well deserving its fine reputation, Mrs. Jon Strauss's antique shop deals in 18th- and 19th-century English and French furniture, mirrors, lamps, porcelains, and tea caddies.... *Tel 504/899–4482. 4605 Magazine St., Uptown. Closed Sun.*

Keil Antiques. Since 1899, Keil's has specialized in French and English antiques, including jewelry, marble mantels, gold-leaf mirrors, and chandeliers.... *Tel 504/522–4552. 325 Royal St., French Quarter. Closed Sun.*

Kohlmaier and Kohlmaier. Antique clocks are the specialty—longcase and mantel clocks, the rare and the unusual. Ruppert Kohlmaier's cabinetmakers also reproduce period furnishings, sold here.... *Tel 504/895–6394. 1018 Harmony St., Uptown.*

Le Petit Soldier Shop. You'll marvel at the miniature toy soldiers here, with fine detailing in uniforms, weapons, and horses.... *Tel 504/523–7741. 528 Royal St., French Quarter.*

Librairie. A branch of the venerable Beckham's Bookshop (see above), this, too, is a big, musty old place with racks, stacks, and shelves of used books. The small staff will not exactly overwhelm you with offers of assistance, but with time and patience you may find some out-of-print treasures.... *Tel 504/525–4837. 823 Chartres St., French Quarter. Open 10–8.*

Li'l Fisherman. This corner fish market prepares very fresh Louisiana seafoods to go—shrimp, crawfish, blue crabs, speckled trout, whatever's in season—at reasonable prices.... *Tel 504/897–9907. 3301 Magazine St., Uptown.*

Little Shop of Fantasy. Michael Stark makes the unusual and exotic masks sold in this tiny hole-in-the-wall, while Tracy Keller and Jill Kelly produce the delightful cloches, tall top hats and stovepipes, bonnets, and Mad Hatters with over-sized crowns.... *Tel 504/529–4243. 523 Dumaine St., French Quarter.*

Little Toy Shoppe. This large store is the place to go for toys of all types—tops, puzzles, kites, toy airplanes, and blocks—but it has an exceptional collection of bisque dolls, dressed in organdy, velvets, and lace.... *Tel 504/522–6588. 900 Decatur St., French Quarter.*

Louisiana General Store. The retail outlet at the New Orleans School of Cooking is a spacious place with tables and shelves full of south Louisiana condiments, Cajun spices, rice, cookbooks, packages of shelled pecans, and aprons.... *Tel. 504/525–3034. 620 Decatur St., French Quarter. Open Sun–Thurs 10–9, Fri–Sat 10–10.*

Louisiana Music Factory. The focus here is on jazz, Cajun, zydeco, R&B, and other south Louisiana sounds.... *Tel 504/523–1094. 225 N. Peters St., French Quarter. Open 10–7.*

Lucullus. Proprietor Patrick Dunne named his gallery for Lucius Licinius Lucullus, who was a wealthy Roman general famous for his lavish banquets. The feast here includes 17th-, 18th-, and 19th-century culinary antiques, including cookware, silverware, china, furnishings, and objets d'art.... *Tel 504/528–9620. 610 Chartres St., French Quarter. Closed Sun.*

Macon Riddle. She's a shopping consultant, who can be engaged for half- and full-day antiquing excursions replete with expert up-to-the-minute advice and commentary.... *Tel 504/899–3027. By appointment.*

Maison Blanche. Now the flagship of a national chain, the Canal St. original is a home-grown department store carrying everything from Donna Karan to kitchen appliances. There are branches in several suburban malls.... *Tel 504/566–1000. 901 Canal St., CBD.*

Manheim Galleries. The local agent for Boehm Birds, Manheim also has a remarkable jade collection and an extensive selection of antique European and Oriental furnishings and decorative art—17th- and 18th-century English, French, and Continental furniture, as well as fine 18th- and 19th-century paintings and porcelains.... *Tel 504/568–1901. 403 Royal St., French Quarter. Closed Sun.*

Maple Street Book Shop. Owned by Orleanian Rhoda Faust, there's the original store on Maple Street, a fine children's bookstore adjacent, and other branches around the city. These well-stocked stores will search for hard-to-find books.... *Tel 504/866–4916. 7523 Maple St., Uptown. Closed Sun.*

Mardi Gras Center. Those Orleanians who don't make their own masks and costumes get them here, where there are literally hundreds of costumes, masks, and other Mardi Gras makings.... *Tel 504/524–4384. 831 Chartres St., French Quarter. Closed Sun.*

Marketplace. See Jackson Brewery, above.

Masks & Make Believe. The vivid creations here range from small ceramic wall decorations to feathery eye-masks to rubber full-face masks of everyone from George Bush to Yoda.... *Tel 504/522–6473. Riverwalk, CBD.*

Meyer the Hatter. In business since 1894, the Hatter has Panama straws, western Stetsons, fine men's headwear, and even major league baseball caps.... *Tel 504/525–1048. 120 St. Charles St., CBD. Closed Sun.*

MGM Costume Rentals. A favorite stop for locals who wish to be incognito, it has thousands of costumes from the old MGM studio....*Tel 504/581–3999. 1617 St. Charles Ave., Open Mon—Fri 9–5:30, Sat 9:30–5, Closed Sun.*

Mignon Faget. Mignon Faget finds inspiration in her native New Orleans for the jewelry she makes of 14K gold, silver, and bronze d'or—imaginative earrings, cufflinks, tie clasps, and bracelets.... *Tel 504/524–2973. Canal Place, 1st level, CBD. Closed Tues.*

Mike's on the Avenue. This restaurant (see Dining) is not a shop, but chef Mike Fennelly is also an artist—the restaurant's walls are covered with his paintings—and his splashy $55 hand-painted ties are for sale here.... *Tel 504/523–1709. 628 St. Charles Ave., CBD. Closed Sun.*

Millhouse. See Jackson Brewery, above.

Moss Antiques. Top-of-the-line antique jewelry, crystal chandeliers, and decorative arts are showcased in this handsome store.... *Tel 504/522–3981. 411 Royal St., French Quarter. Closed Sun.*

M. S. Rau. Royal Street's venerable antique store specializes in American antiques, jewelry, music boxes, silver, porcelain, and glass....*Tel 504/523–4662, 800/544–9440. 630 Royal St., French Quarter.*

New Orleans Center. Adjacent to the Superdome and the Hyatt Regency Hotel, this large and rambling modern mall's two biggest tenants are Macy's and Lord and Taylor. There are dozens of other shops (The Gap, County Seat, and other national chains), as well as restaurants and a food court.... *Tel 504/568–0000. 1400 Poydras St., CBD. Open Mon–Sat 10–8, Sun noon–6.*

New Orleans Historic Voodoo Museum. In the cramped front room of this only-in-New-Orleans institution, studiedly spooky-looking folk will chat to you about their religion and then sell you various powders, potions, and charms to ward off evil spirits, bring you true love, or make an enemy dead.... *Tel 504/523–7865. 724 Dumaine St., French Quarter. Open daily at 10, closes when it gets even darker outside than it is inside.*

New Orleans School of Cooking. Cooking demonstrations are held here; reservations are required, and when you call, ask what's to be prepared—it may be an étouffe, jambalaya, shrimp creole, or some other dish for which Louisiana is famous. Attached is the Louisiana General Store (see above).... *Tel 504/525–2665. 620 Decatur St., French Quarter. Cooking demonstrations 10–1, closed Sun.*

19th Century Antiques. Rare and unusual clocks, cut glass, china, bisque dolls, bric-a-brac, and antique watches are among the many choices here.... *Tel 504/891–4845. 4838 Magazine St., Uptown. Closed Sun.*

Oh, Susannah. The shop's exquisite collection of old-fashioned dolls, as well as African American, Asian, and baby dolls, are all dressed in beautifully crafted clothing.... *Tel 504/586–8701. 518 St. Peter St., on Jackson Square, French Quarter.*

Old Farmers' Market. Tumbledown open-air sheds house this almost always crowded fruit and vegetable market at the downriver end of the French Market (see above). Farmers have been bringing fresh produce here for 200 years (not the same farmers the whole time, of course).... *Tel 504/596–3420. 1235 N. Peter St., French Quarter. Open 24 hours.*

Old Town Praline Shop. A local favorite for pralines, this quaint little house was where opera goddess Adelina Patti stayed during her 19th-century peformance tour in New Orleans.... *Tel 504/525–1413. 627 Royal St., French Quarter. Closed Sun.*

Preservation Hall. Only open at night when the bands are playing, the Hall has for sale several bins of records by Preservation Hall veteran recording stars.... *Tel 504/523–8939 (night). 726 St. Peter St., French Quarter. Open 8pm–midnight.*

Quarter Moon. New Orleans motifs, such as tiny Mardi Gras masks, show up in the cufflinks, rings, and brooches sold here, all handmade by Michael Shallbetter and his wife, Ellis. The hats made by Tracy Thomson and Ann Marie Popko are decorated with feathers and plumes and all manner of frou-frous.... *Tel 504/524–3208. 918 Royal St., French Quarter.*

Record Ron's. The wide selection of music here by local and international artists embraces country, Cajun, rock, zydeco, and slews of obscure records, CDs, and tapes by local and regional artists.... *Tel 504/524–9444, 1129 Decatur St.; tel 504/522–2239, 407 Decatur St., French Quarter. Both stores open 10–7.*

RHINO. The acronym stands for "Right Here In New Orleans," and all of the crafts in this nonprofit shop are indeed made right here. More than 70 artists create the furnishings, paintings, apparel, and decorative items. A very upscale place.... *Tel 504/523–7945. Canal Place, 333 Canal St., CBD.*

Rine Chapeaux. At this small shop, filled with headgear for men and women, you'll have access to everything from cowboy hats to old-fashioned ladies' bonnets.... *Tel 504/523–7463. Riverwalk, 1 Poydras St., CBD.*

Riverwalk. A riverside mall that stretches from the foot of Poydras St. upriver to Julia St., the Convention Center, and the Warehouse District, this complex has 200 or so shops and restaurants including Abercrombie & Fitch, Banana Republic, and The Sharper Image, as well as local stores like Yvonne LaFleur and Street Scenes and a huge food court.... *Tel 504/522–2555. 1 Poydras St., CBD. Open Mon–Thur 10–9, Fri–Sat 10–10, Sun 11–7.*

Rothchild's Antiques. This prestigious store handles antique English and French furniture, estate jewelry, crystal chandeliers, marble mantels, silver, and porcelain.... *Tel 504/523–5816. 241 and 321 Royal St., French Quarter.*

Royal Antiques. Since 1899, this store has carried unusually high-quality 18th- and 19th-century country French and English furnishings, chandeliers, and brass and copper accessories.... *Tel 504/524–7033, 307–09 Royal St.; tel 504/525–6646, 715 Bienville St., French Quarter.*

Rumors. Using leather, feathers, beads, and sequins, more than 100 artists create the delightful, very fantastical masks here (and at Rumors Too, tel 504/523–0011, 319 Royal St.).... *Tel 504/525–0292. 513 Royal St., French Quarter. Open Sun–Thur 9:30–6, Fri and Sat until the traffic thins.*

Second Skin Leather. "Purveyors of leather, latex, sexual hardware, and erotica for men and women," the shop proclaims, and it lives up to its claims in this Quarter sidestreet sexual emporium.... *Tel 504/561–8167. 521 St. Philip St. Open noon–10, Sun until 6.*

Street Scenes. Master woodcarver Kay Glenn creates scenes of New Orleans and regional culture, showing plantations, jazz bands, parades, and riverboats.... *Tel 504/595–8865, 800/845–0650. Riverwalk, 1 Poydras St., CBD.*

Takis. This craftsman makes lovely museum-quality metal sculptures of flowers.... *Tel 504/522–6361. 638 1/2 Royal St., French Quarter. Closed Sun.*

Umbrella Lady. Ann B. Lane often leads the second-lining at the French Market open-air cafes. When she isn't doing that, she's making the colorful parasols that are part and parcel of the parading.... *Tel 504/523–7791. 1107 Decatur St., French Quarter. By appointment.*

Waldhorn's. The oldest store on Royal St., Waldhorn's was established in 1880 and has been going strong ever since, selling an extensive collection of antique American and English jewelry and silver, and 18th- and 19th-century English furnishings and porcelains.... *Tel 504/581–6379. 343 Royal St., French Quarter. Open 9–4:30. Closed Sun.*

Witches' Corner. Self-proclaimed witches operate this dimly lit little shop devoted to witchcraft and voodoo.... *Tel 504/ 522–7730. 521 St. Philip St., French Quarter. Closed Sun.*

Yvonne LaFleur. New Orleans fashion-plate LaFleur carries a line of upmarket women's ready-to-wear; she also custom-designs hats, party dresses, and wedding gowns, and even produces a private-label fragrance. Nothing in this boutique is cheap, in any sense of the word.... *Tel 504/866–9666. 8131 Hampson St., Riverwalk. Closed weekends.*

tlife

6

One thing's for
sure: You won't
leave this town
without knowing
that jazz was born
in New Orleans.
No way can you

forget it. Music is all over the city, blaring from dingy dives, sleek rooms, frilly riverboats, and, lately, casinos. The city has produced a long roster of world-class musical luminaries, among them Louis Armstrong, Fats Domino, Louis Prima, Jelly Roll Morton, and of course the acknowledged originator, Buddy Bolden, who trilled the first riffs in the genre a century or so ago. While jazzologists generally agree on how it all started, they debate as to the exact year it actually became "jazz." (Just like Orleanians—they love to bicker and split hairs, especially about the exact dates of historical happenings and superlatives—which exactly is the oldest building in town, which restaurant serves the best rémoulade...)

Locals also get all worked up over New Orleans funk, a sultry sound that mixes Afro-Caribbean with R&B, but they also get their clocks pretty well cleaned jigging to zydeco, a zippy soulmate of Cajun. Cajun music itself ranges from languid waltzes to red-hot jigs—zydeco is just red-hotter. And second-lining is second-nature here. (At jazz funerals, a hand-clapping foot-stomping "second line" behind the musicians celebrates the release of the deceased's soul.) It is entirely possible, even preferable, to second-line without a funeral.

You may have heard of Bourbon Street. If not, welcome to the planet. The city's most famous street is virtually riddled with funky hole-in-the-wall music clubs where you can hear everything from karaoke to bagpipes. And jazz, of course. They're all lined up in a row, some of them with carny-type barkers out front drumming up trade. Sure, it's overrun with tourists, but Bourbon runs through a neighborhood—the French Quarter—which has some 5,000 residents, local people who work and play and cross-dress and belly up to bars here, too. Neighborhood entertainers have names like the Neville Brothers, the Iguanas, Walter "Wolfman" Washington, Marva Wright, Charmaine Neville, the Meters, and Li'l Queenie, and you're damn right locals turn out to hear them. Outside the Quarter the music scene is played out in a much larger arena, not as concentrated as in the Quarter. Except for a couple of pockets—notably in the Warehouse District and in Riverbend—outside the Quarter you'll have to do your bar-hopping on wheels.

The French Quarter has a highly visible, very nearly militant gay community, with a pack of hopping bars to support the scene. The annual gay costume competition on Burgundy Street is a dazzling affair on Fat Tuesday. And you'll know you're not in Kansas anymore if you're anywhere in the French Quarter during Southern Decadence Day—still known in other places as Labor Day. The drag parade will knock your socks smack off your feet, and gay bars like Café Lafitte in Exile and the Golden Lantern have outrageous Easter Bonnet Contests.

You may question this city's reputation as a laid-back kind of town once you get a load of the locals working up a lather on a dime-sized dance floor. Orleanians are big on grungy dives, the grungier the better. The trick is to avoid slipping on all the "glow" dripping off faces onto the floor.

Of course, virtually none of the rules apply during Mardi Gras or Jazz Fest. During those events, thousands of people pour into New Orleans, a goodly portion of them headed for the French Quarter. Hours change, prices change (upward), and schedules change as the entire city battens down for the onslaught.

Sources

The editors of *Gambit*, a weekly newspaper, keep up to speed on the music scene. The paper is free and can be picked up at newsstands, grocery stores, and bookstores, as well as in some hotels and restaurants. *Offbeat* magazine, another freebie, offers news, views, and reviews of the hot and the not. Friday's *Times–Picayune* carries "Lagniappe," a tabloid section detailing the weekend's best bets, including a detailed listing of what's doing around town. And *Ambush*— "a flamboyant tabloid"—is a free, adults-only publication

Of Craps and Cocktails

New Orleanians adore legends, and among the favorites is the one about the origins of the game of craps. Count Bernard de Marigny (around whom legends swarm like locusts) was a wealthy 19th-century French Creole who inherited a fortune when he was only 15 and proceeded to fritter it away. He traveled frequently to Europe, and brought back home from France a game of chance that involved the throwing of dice. The American riffraff living in New Orleans referred to the Creoles as crapauds—frogs—and called the game they played "craps." Another cherished legend has it that the world's very first cocktail was served in New Orleans. A French Quarter chemist named Antoine Amedée Peychaud mixed a bit of bitters with Sazerac-de-Forge cognac and absinthe to create a hair-of-the-dog stomach remedy. He served it to his customers in little egg cups, for which the French word was coquetiers. The word was soon anglicized to "cocktails," and another legend was born. Peychaud bitters is the only original ingredient still used to concoct the cocktail—absinthe has been illegal in this country since not longer after Peychaud made his bitters. Local mixologists use a made-in-New Orleans substitute called Herbsaint.

NEW ORLEANS | NIGHTLIFE

with news about gay and lesbian happenings. Tune in, too, to **WWOZ-90.7 FM**, a radio station devoted to playing local music and broadcasting local music calendars.

Storyville and the Blue Book

Local lore has it that in 1744 a French officer complained— or was that applauded?—that there were not 10 women of blameless character to be found in the colony. By most accounts, it seems that prostitution began to flourish almost as soon as the French settlers settled. Various means were employed to control it, all to no avail. Then, in 1897, a city alderman named Sidney Story introduced an ordinance that would restrict bordellos to a 20-block area behind the French Quarter. The legislation passed and, to the horror of the alderman, the neighborhood was dubbed "Storyville." Stories about the old red-light district abound in this legend-loving city—about the "sporting houses," the jazz musicians who played in the parlors (notably, Jelly Roll Morton), and the spasm bands (ragtag bands, often kids, using makeshift instruments) that played on the street corners. The Blue Book was a listing of all the houses and the girls who worked in them. Today, it's a pricey collector's item, selling in antique stores for upward of $150. It's the only remaining trace of Storyville—the district was shut down in 1917 on orders of the United States Navy, and a housing project now sprawls over the site.

Schedules can change between the time the newspaper calendars are put together and the times of the performances, though, so call ahead to double-check.

Liquor Laws and Drinking Hours

New Orleans's nightlife happens around the clock. There are no legal closing hours, no curfew; the general ambience seems to encourage partying all night. Closing hours often depend upon the flow of traffic, especially on Bourbon Street. But engrave this on the palm of your hand: Do not go wandering around on deserted streets, and certainly not in the middle of the night. Stick to Bourbon Street between St. Ann and Bienville Streets once it gets late. Heaven knows it's enough of a sight to see, and if you stay reasonably sober you probably won't get rolled.

Before you dive into a Bourbon Street dive, ask about the minimum and the cover charge—there's often a two-drink minimum per set. You can buy liquor in grocery stores and drugstores, and you may do so whenever the doors are open for business, even on Sundays and election days. The legal drinking age is 21.

New Orleans's best-known adult beverage is the Hurricane, a potently sweet concoction of rum and fruit juices. The Sazerac is made with bourbon and bitters and served in a glass coated with ersatz absinthe. Both beverages should be approached with caution and plenty of respect.

The Lowdown

Only in New Orleans... Touristy though it is, **Preservation Hall** should not be missed. Called locally "the Hall," Preservation Hall is really a single boxlike room. The name is a throwback to the turn of the century, when early jazz bands played around town in halls that had names like Funky Butts, the Odd Fellows, and Perseverance Hall. In the early 1960s, the late Allen Jaffe, a jazz buff and tuba player from Pennsylvania—a man much loved and highly respected among musicians—set up Preservation Hall in order to replicate those old music halls, to preserve the tradition of jazz bands, and to give the old-time legends a regular place to play. The small, dingy, cramped room has no creature comforts, only a few hard benches and some filthy cushions scattered on the floor, where you can sit at the feet of the musicians. If you're standing in the back, as you'll probably have to do, you won't be able to see the musicians unless you're tall. You won't have any trouble hearing them, however, even though there's no sound system, because the hall is so small. The band plays 10- or 15-minute sets, then takes a break while a hawker comes in to hawk records. Many people leave after the first set, either because they're uncomfortable or because they think they have to (in fact, you don't have to leave until the place closes at midnight). Those in the back who opt to stay can then move forward, aiming for the hard benches. After you've been standing awhile, those benches look real cozy. Admission is $3, and you can stay for 10 minutes or four hours, depending upon your physical stamina. Best advice: If you don't like traditional jazz, stay away. It is touristy—locals avoid it because there's no bar or dance floor—but $3 for four hours doth not a trap make. Funky as they come, **Tipitina's**—an Uptown club with a down-home soul—is a local institution for New Orleans funk, R&B, reggae, rock, and Cajun. (Tip's is getting stiff competition from the **House of Blues**, which offers the same lineup in classier surroundings.) **Lafitte's Blacksmith Shop** is not a predominantly bar, but gays as well as straights are drawn to the sing-along bar and the Old New Orleans atmosphere. And then there's the **Old Absinthe Bar** (at 400 Bourbon Street) and Tony Moran's **Old Absinthe House** (at 240 Bourbon Street), which are distant relatives though not jointly owned. According to local lore, shortly after the feds shut down the Old Absinthe House Bar during Prohibition in the 1920s, someone broke into the place and gutted it, stealing everything from the cash register to the clock. It all turned up sometime later at a bar down the street, which came to be called the Absinthe Bar.

C'mon get happy... **City Lights**, a dance club in the Warehouse District, is a munch-along place before the discs begin spinning. A big, high-ceilinged room with a horseshoe-shaped bar and six-foot video screens, it gets the thirtysomethings who live in the Warehouse District.

Isn't it romantic?... If troths be still plighted, a splendid place for doing so is the **Victorian Lounge**, with its wood-burning fireplace, pressed-tin ceiling, velvet-covered chairs, and wood paneling. Many people swoon over the **Napoleon House**, albeit the place is all but falling apart at the seams—there's something about the candlelight flickering off those sepia walls. Romance is in the air, in the velvet banquettes, and in the white-lace cloths in the **Sazerac Restaurant**, a fit place for cheek-to-cheeking.

Most outrageous clubs... The revues at **The Mint**, just outside the Quarter, are designed to raise eyebrows and draw a raucous mix of gays and straights. Perennial favorites Becky Allen and Ricky Graham do fast-paced revues that are heavy on double entendres. But if it's really eye-popping stuff you're looking for, the gay and lesbian clubs are the places to be (see "Gay and Lesbian Scene," below). If you're a cowboy hankering to dance with another cowboy, head for **Rawhide**.

Where the locals go... Anyplace there's good music, which means a whole raft of places. Young uptowners flood **Carrollton Station**, which has a bit more in the way of decor than most dives. It's next door to **Jimmy's Club**, where rock pops till very late. Funky **Tipitina's**

uptown has to compete now with the **House of Blues** for local favors. Uptown, Oak Street swings with a crowd moving back and forth between the **Maple Leaf Bar** and **Muddy Waters**. Downtown, the forlorn-looking storefront **Cafe Brasil** is a Bohemian outpost for the young and the disillusioned; Julia Roberts and Lyle Lovett came here on their first date. Check out **Checkpoint Charlie's**, on the fringe of the Quarter, for loud late-night blues and pool (not to mention the on-premises Laundromat). Right in the Quarter, try the **Old Absinthe House Bar** for blues, and in the Warehouse District **Howlin' Wolf** for alternative and punk music. Without a doubt the least-publicized place in all New Orleans, the grungy, shoebox-sized **Dungeon** draws locals in-the-know, plus every with-it celebrity that comes to town. The only live music they have is disco. It's almost hidden between Molly's and the Tropical Isle on Toulouse Street, and it doesn't open until midnight, but things keep on till the early morning light. **Tropical Isle Bourbon** and **Tropical Isle Toulouse** are both after-hours clubs that really zing during Jazz Fest. Imported from Carmel, California, the Chartres Street branch of Clint Eastwood's **Hog's Breath Saloon & Cafe** is a popular hang-out place for Quarterites, some of whom have been known to add their undies to those dangling from the upstairs rafters. **Donna's**, a little bar and grill that showcases nothing but brass bands, is grungy enough to appeal to local tastes. A 24-hour haven that bills itself as a Coffeehouse Museum (displays of antique coffee machines back up its claim), **Kaldi's** has the flavor of the sixties and the occasional trio soothing folks into the wee hours. New Orleans's sizeable Irish population—very much in evidence during the city's three St. Patrick's Day parades—toss back the Guinness at **O'Flaherty's Irish Channel** pub, where the flavor is authentically Celtic.

Where the locals don't go... Many Quarterites, miffed at the changing face of their beloved neighborhood, vow to boycott **Planet Hollywood**, yet another outpost of the Bruce Willis/Sylvester Stallone/Arnold Schwarzenegger chain. **Chris Owens Club** plays primarily for the tourist trade, as do the **544 Club** and the **Famous Door** just down the street. Most of the patrons at **Pete Fountain's Club**, which is in the New Orleans Hilton Riverside, are guests checked into that hotel, though Pete is a local icon. Locals rarely darken the door of **Preservation Hall**, and the only ones that frequent **Pat O'Brien's** are college kids. (O'Brien's invented the Hurricane cocktail and serves it up in 29-ounce glasses shaped like hurricane lamps, which countless tourists have bought to take home.) The **Cajun Cabin** is another Bourbon Street trap, where drinks with names like Swamp Water and Cajun Sunrise come in 16-ounce souvenir glasses. The **Maison Bourbon**, the **Krazy Korner**, the **Hard Rock Cafe**, and **Maxwell's** are loaded with tourists, and usually avoided by locals. And far be it from an Orleanian to go cruising off on the *Creole Queen* or the **Steamboat** *Natchez*. Orleanians love the Mississippi, but they tend to take it for granted, along with the boats that float on it. Locals seem drawn to dime-sized dance floors, which may explain why they tend not to take to the plenty-big one at **Rhythms**; otherwise, the place fits the Orleanian taste for loud, live blues.

Cajun and zydeco dancing... Across the street from the Convention Center, **Mulate's** is an old-fashioned dance hall where feet fly to beat the band. Nearby, **Michaul's Live Cajun Music Restaurant** is pretty much what the name says, with instructors on hand for free two-stepping lessons. A lot of fun—so what if it's loaded with tourists and conventioneers? The Sunday night fais-do-dos at **Tipitina's** are great ways to work up a sweat. On Thursdays, you have a tough choice between the **Mid-City Bowling Lanes Rock 'n' Bowl** and the **Maple Leaf**—look for Rockin' Dopsie, Jr. (pronounced "doop-sie," by the way), Filé, and Beausoleil, all south Louisiana Cajun and zydeco bands. Whichever you choose you'll have good local company.

For urban cowboys... On Sundays, **Howlin' Wolf** goes country—don't arrive fashionably late, or you won't get any of the barbecued ribs. **Rawhide** is the place for gays who like C&W (and a raw place it is, indeed). **Mustang Sally's** is a chain, but the local branch draws suburban cowboys to its big dance floor, for live music and occasional line-dance lessons.

Music and munchies... In addition to **Preservation Hall**, the **Palm Court Jazz Cafe** does great traditional jazz and serves food and booze along with it, all in the comfort of a smart cafe. Soul food is super at the cavernous **Praline Connection Gospel & Blues Hall** in the Warehouse District. Celebs came out in full force to open **Planet Hollywood** (opened May 1995) and the **House of Blues** (opened Mardi Gras 1994), both of which have restaurants attached; the Planet Hollywood one makes a special effort to give a Louisiana spin to the food, though that still hasn't managed to endear the place to locals. **Jimmy Buffett's Margaritaville** is a lively spot in the lower Quarter, where the food pays tribute to Key West (Key lime pie, conch burgers, etc.). There are great burgers at **Snug Harbor**, though the jazz and food are served up in separate sections. Standard burgers and fries are served up at the **Hard Rock Cafe**; the real point of coming here is the rock-and-roll decor, of interest chiefly to teenagers. With so many branches, the chain must be running low on rock memorabilia by now; this one features a Rolling Stones standing bass used to record "Ruby Tuesday," part of Fats Domino's piano, a jacket that belonged to Professor Longhair, and Dr. John's cape, top hat, and cane.

Where to pick up someone else's spouse... Hotel lounges seem to provide the right aura for possibly illicit behavior, maybe because both parties know that, should matters progress, there are bedrooms available not so far away. At any rate, the Fairmont Hotel's darkly romantic **Sazerac Bar**, with its long wooden bar and handsome murals, is a fine place to pull up a barstool and chat up your fellow imbiber. The **Esplanade Lounge** in the marbled halls of the Royal Orleans hotel has soft piano music, flaming desserts, and a cozy ambience. Uptowners and guests at the Pontchartrain Hotel love to hang out at the hotel's **Bayou Bar** and listen to the piano. Things are very chic at **Jazz Meridien**, in the atrium lounge of Le Meridien, where traditional jazz takes up the slack if conversation lapses.

The college scene... Kids from Tulane and Loyola, among several other local colleges, are all over the place. Uptown, check out the **Maple Leaf**, **Jimmy's Club**, **Tipitina's**, and **Carrollton Station**, among others. In the Warehouse District, young people don't seem to mind the crowds and cramped quarters at **Howlin' Wolf**, for alternative music, and **Vic's Kangaroo Cafe** for blues. And

NIGHTLIFE | NEW ORLEANS

college kids seem impervious to the general theory that **Pat O'Brien's** is just for tourists—they belly up for the Hurricanes there, too. The **House of Blues** is phenomenally popular with all ages.

The gay and lesbian scene... The oldest and most famous of the men's gay bars is **Café Lafitte in Exile**, so named because the late owner felt "exiled" after losing Lafitte's Blacksmith Shop, a mostly straight bar just down the street. At Lafitte in Exile, Wednesday is the Hump Night Pool Tournament, Thursday Crown Royal Night ("Wear your tiara and drink your crown"). The leather and Levi's scene is played out at **Rawhide**, where the music is country-and-western. Thursday night Calendar Boy shows at **Oz** are a big draw; so are the Sunday tea dances at **Bourbon Pub/Parade**, a glitzy dance club with lasers and lights. Female impersonator T. T. Thompson's club, appropriately named **T.T.'s Club**, and the **Golden Lantern** do determinedly outrageous drag shows—scheduled and unscheduled. Gay black men turn up for DJ dancing at **Wolfendale's**. The area's only predominantly lesbian bar, **Charlene's**, is just slightly off the beaten track on the fringe of the Quarter.

Where to meet people outside the clubs... Open dances with big bands are sponsored by the **Airline Lions Club**, but you have to be really dedicated to go there: it's way out in Metairie. Uptown, open square-, folk-, and contra dances are regularly scheduled by the **GNO Folk Society**; their dancing takes place in the First Presbyterian Church Fellowship Hall. The church hall is usually the setting, too, for gatherings of the **Crescent City International Dancers**, another group that sponsors open folk dances, with instructors to make sure it isn't all Greek to you—or Irish, or whatever the case may be.

NEW ORLEANS | NIGHTLIFE

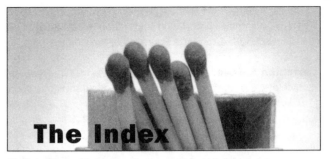

The Index

Airline Lions Club. Regularly scheduled big band dances, open to the public, are held at this Metairie club. Usually BYOB.... *Tel 504/888–5376. 3110 Division St., Metairie. Admission.*

Bayou Bar. Uptowners and celeb guests of the Pontchartrain frequent this sophisticated piano bar with leather banquettes and murals of Caribbean scenes.... *Tel 504/524–0581. Pontchartrain Hotel, 2031 St. Charles Ave., Garden District.*

Bourbon Pub/Parade. A popular gay men's club, the Parade has lasers, videos, a good dance floor, and a decorous tea dance every Sunday afternoon.... *Tel 504/529–2107. 801 Bourbon St., French Quarter. Cover.*

Cafe Brasil. There are no tables inside—just dancing and hanging out—and the crowd collapsed over the sidewalk tables nursing espressos and liqueurs is very young and devoutly Bohemian. Rare is the tourist who wanders in here. Art exhibits, poetry readings, and live music all come in many different flavors; check newspaper listings for what's up—the only phone here is a pay phone that may or not be answered.... *Tel 504/947–9386. 2100 Chartres St., Faubourg Marigny. Opens at noon. Small cover Fri and Sat after 11pm.*

Café Lafitte in Exile. Headquarters for the annual Gay Pride Day festivities, this has been a popular gay men's bar since the early fifties. Unsuspecting passersby on Bourbon are sometimes startled by the hoots emanating from enthusiastic revelers hanging over the second-floor balcony.... *Tel 504/522–8377. 901 Bourbon St., French Quarter.*

Cajun Cabin. Tops with tourists, who think they've died and gone to Acadiana, the rollicking Cabin opens its doors wide and spills its little heart right out onto Bourbon. The music is live every night; the chef is Cajun, and the food's not bad at all.... *Tel 504/529–4256. 501 Bourbon St., French Quarter.*

Carrollton Station. A snug little joint dressed up in decorator colors, the Station rocks till very late. Sunday night's open acoustic mike is a big hit with locals, who come in all ages and descriptions. Jimmy's Club (see below) is just a holler away.... *Tel 504/865–9190. 8140 Willow St., Uptown.*

Charlene's. On the fringe of the Quarter, the area's only lesbian bar has been around since the 1970s. There's music upstairs and down in this two-story spot; happy hour's from 5 until 8.... *Tel 504/945–9328. 940 Elysian Fields Ave., French Quarter. Closed Mon.*

Checkpoint Charlie's. If you're in a pool-shooting mood in the wee small hours, take a cue from this dive on the fringe of the French Quarter. You can even take your dirty clothes and do them in the Laundromat. Open 24 hours, it draws a funky crowd for ear-splitting rock and blues.... *Tel 504/947–0979. 501 Esplanade Ave., Faubourg Marigny.*

Chris Owens Club. Ms. Owens is a legend on Bourbon St., which mainly means she's been around for a spell. Notwithstanding those sexy posters plastered outside, Chris isn't a stripper—a tease, maybe, but not a stripper. All a-shimmer and a-glitter, she performs a one-woman variety show, singing and dancing renditions of the Top 40, show tunes, blues, a little Latin stuff. If you've never seen a glitzy one-woman show, it's worth seeing, but those who've been to Vegas may not be too dazzled. A trio backs her up and plays for your dancing pleasure between shows. Heavyweight trumpet player Al Hirt blasts the evening off, his early sets followed at 10:30 by Owens' revue.... *Tel 504/523–6400. 500 Bourbon St., French Quarter. Closed Sun. Cover.*

City Lights. The young and trendy from the Warehouse District dude themselves out (there's a strict dress code—you can't get in if you're wearing tennis shoes, T-shirts, jeans, or shorts) to chat each other up during happy hour. Those who linger dance to DJ music; the music goes live Fridays at 9.... *Tel 504/568–1700. 310 Howard Ave., Warehouse District. Closed Sun–Tue. Cover after 9.*

Creole Queen Riverboat. The various cruises of the great white riverboat include "Dinner on the River & All That Jazz"—a nice outing if you're looking for something the whole family can enjoy. Tons of food (New Orleans specialties), plus traditional jazz.... *Tel 504/524–0814. Canal St. Wharf, CBD. Boarding buffet begin at 7pm; cruise 8–10. Admission covers the works.*

Crescent City International Dancers. This social club sponsors regularly scheduled folk-dance sessions, with the public invited to join in. There's an instructor to put you through the right paces.... *Tel 504/738–6914. First Presbyterian Church Fellowship Hall, 5401 S. Claiborne Ave., Uptown. Admission.*

Donna's Bar & Grill. A strictly no-frills (and no tourists) bar devoted solely to brass bands. The best of them play here—the Rebirth, the Chosen Few, the Little Rascals, the Soul Rebels. A blast—a *loud* blast. It's on the fringe of the Quarter, across from Harrah's.... *Tel 504/596–6914. 800 N. Rampart St., Treme.*

The Dungeon. If you're wondering where the Rolling Stones and other superstars hang out after the concert, this is it. Hard-core grunge decor; don't expect elbow room. The entrance is squeezed between Molly's and the Tropical Isle.... *No phone. About 738 Toulouse St., French Quarter. Opens at midnight.*

Esplanade Lounge. Marble floors, Oriental carpeting, and cushy drawing-room seating add up to a swell place to wind down. Desserts and coffee are served to the tune of the grand piano.... *Tel 504/529–5333. Omni Royal Orleans Hotel, 621 St. Louis St., French Quarter.*

Famous Door. The French Quarter was little more than a run-down slum when the doors opened on this club in 1934. The decor is rinky-dink, tables are miniscule, and the music loud—R&B and traditional jazz are on tap. There's a rear patio, but you'll still be breathing in the stench of Bourbon St.... *Tel 504/522–7626 or 504/524–4009. 339 Bourbon St., French Quarter. 2-drink minimum.*

544 Club. A Bourbon Street honky-tonk, the 544 has held down this corner of Bourbon for ages. Gary Brown and Feelings

NIGHTLIFE | **NEW ORLEANS**

play pop and R&B with pizzazz.... *Tel 504/566–0529. 544 Bourbon St., French Quarter.*

GNO Folk Society. Check with this friendly group to find out when the next square, folk, and contra dances are scheduled.... *Tel 504/866–3257 or 504/895–9227. First Presbyterian Church Fellowship Hall, 5401 S. Claiborne Ave., Uptown. Admission.*

Golden Lantern. The Quarter's second-oldest gay men's bar (only Café Lafitte in Exile, see above, is older), the GL is one of the main drags, so to speak, for the annual Southern Decadence Day doings. Drag shows and a daily 5–9 happy hour are among the draws.... *Tel 504/529–2860. 1239 Royal St., French Quarter. Open 24 hours.*

Hard Rock Cafe. There's usually a line waiting to get into the New Orleans outpost of the Hard Rock. The big bar is guitar-shaped, and the de rigueur rock and pop iconography is on display.... *Tel 504/529–5617. 440 N. Peters St., French Quarter.*

Hog's Breath Saloon & Cafe. "A hog's breath is better than no breath at all" saith the T-shirts. This is primarily a hangout place, with occasional live music upstairs. There's a burger-and-fries cafe downstairs, and a Sunday-afternoon all-you-can-eat crawfish buffet served with live country music.... *Tel 504/522–1736. 339 Chartres St., French Quarter. Upstairs open Wed–Sat, starting at 9pm.*

House of Blues. The very best that $7 million can buy, the New Orleans edition of HOB is a rambling high-tech place with a 260-seat restaurant overlooking the cavernous concert hall. The whole place is done up with an overkill of folk art. Dan Aykroyd opened the place up with his blues band. Top names and local talent take the stage; live shows are telecast on Fridays on TBS, weekly radio shows on CBS. Check your local listings, as the saying goes.... *Tel 504/529–2624. 225 Decatur St., French Quarter.*

Howlin' Wolf. Alternative, rock, and punk dominate and draw twentysomethings to this Warehouse District hotspot. Nothing disguises the fact that this building was once a warehouse. Neither the bar, the stage, nor the dance floor is of what you'd call epic proportions.... *Tel 504/523–2551. 828 S. Peters St., Warehouse District.*

Jazz Meridien. If you like traditional jazz but can't stand the stablelike Preservation Hall, hie yourself over to the atrium in Le Meridien. There are no more tourists and conventioneers here than there are at the Hall, the seats are soft, and the champagne flows like wine.... *Tel 504/525–6500. 614 Canal St., CBD. 1-drink minimum.*

Jimmy Buffett's Margaritaville. Paradise for Parrotheads (Buffett buffs), New Orleans's answer to Key West is a barnlike place in the lower Quarter, where the decor runs toward pictures of Jimmy. Apart from an occasional appearance by Buffett himself, the featured artists are Zachary Richard, Mari Serpas and the Instigators, and a lineup of laid-back live local bands.... *Tel 504/592–2565. 1104 Decatur St., French Quarter. Music kicks off at 10:30. 1-drink minimum.*

Jimmy's Club. An uptown version of Preservation Hall, at least as far as comfort is concerned, though the sound is usually hard rock. Walls are black, and that's it for decor. Local and national bands have split the eardrums of the young and the restless.... *Tel 504/861–8200. 8200 Willow St., Uptown. Cover.*

Kaldi's. A very mixed bag of gospel, jazz, and blues are served up from time to time—usually on weekends—in a big turn-of-the-century building that once housed a bank. It doesn't keep banking hours anymore. The mood is definitely laid-back sixties.... *Tel 504/586–8989. 940 Decatur St., French Quarter.*

Krazy Korner. As loud as they come, this tiny hole-in-the-wall is aslosh with tourists shakin', rattlin', and rollin' on a dance floor not much bigger than a phone booth. Red-hot mamas belt out blues to beat the band.... *Tel 504/524–3157. 640 Bourbon St., French Quarter. 2-drink minimum per set.*

Lafitte's Blacksmith Shop. An institute of higher imbibing, Lafitte's—not to be confused with Café Lafitte in Exile—is a dark grungy bar in a ramshackle cottage that's been here since 1772. It is bandied about that this was once the blacksmith shop of brothers Jean and Pierre Lafitte, and a front for their freebooting endeavors. Locals have been

NEW ORLEANS | NIGHTLIFE

singing along at the piano bar for ages.... *Tel 504/523–0066. 941 Bourbon St., French Quarter.*

Maison Bourbon. When the jazzmen are on the bandstand, the doors are flung wide, and you can hang out on Bourbon St. and listen to Wallace Davenport, Tommy Yetta, and Steve Slocum laying out hot licks. This is a tiny bar with not much in the way of decoration, beyond a few tables loaded with tourists, a long, busy bar, and the raised bandstand at the rear facing the street.... *Tel 504/522–8818. 641 Bourbon St., French Quarter. 2-drink minimum.*

Maple Leaf Bar. A pressed-tin roof hovers over this madly popular place, where hordes of mostly young locals in cutoffs and tank tops shout and gyrate on a dance floor the size of a pinhead. There's a rear patio where you can gasp what passes for fresh air in these parts. The live music is R&B, rock, or reggae; the Thursday night Cajun and zydeco bands are something to see. Things quiet down on Sunday afternoons for poetry readings.... *Tel 504/866–9357, concert line 504/866–LEAF. 8316 Oak St., Uptown. Open daily at 1pm. Cover.*

Maxwell's. Dolled up with second-line parasols, big-and-brassy Maxwell's is the home base of Jimmy Maxwell, who fronts the city's best-known society orchestra. They play Dixieland and traditional jazz on Sunday nights, alternating with Banu Gibson and her New Orleans Hot Jazz band. Harry Connick, Sr., sings here when not occupied as New Orleans's district attorney; on rare occasions, his renowned son, Harry Connick, Jr., stops by to croon a tune or two, but don't make a special trip here hoping to hear him.... *Tel 504/523–4207. 615 Toulouse St., French Quarter. Cover.*

Michaul's Live Cajun Music Restaurant. Real-live Cajun bands loosen things up in this dance hall, where a whole lot of two-stepping gets done and instructors offer free dance lessons. The music and dancing are a whole lot better than the food.... *Tel 504/522–5517. 840 St. Charles Ave., Warehouse District. Doors open at 6, music starts at 7:30. Closed Sun.*

Mid-City Bowling Lanes & Sports Palace. A bowling alley with a twist. And a turn. And a whirl. The home of the locally famous Rock 'n' Bowl is well worth the climb up those stairs, and the accents are all New Orleans's.... *Tel 504/ 482–3133. 4133 S. Carrollton Ave., Mid-City.*

The Mint. Revues here are studiedly outré and the mixed crowd of gays and straights loves every minute of it. It all happens—the drag shows, the bawdy songs, the double entendres—in a big 19th-century building on the fringe of the Quarter.... *Tel 504/525–2000. 504 Esplanade Ave., Faubourg Marigny. Shows Thur–Sat at 11, Sun at 3. Cover.*

Muddy Waters. Marva Wright often belts out the blues in this neighborhood bar and grill, but there's always a boisterous crowd jukin' up a storm to whoever's on the stand. Mix it up on the tiny dance floor, or take the longer view from the upstairs balcony.... *Tel 504/866–7174. 8301 Oak St., Uptown. Cover.*

Mulate's. A rustic place with a lot of cypress, Mulate's is a spin-off of a madly popular Cajun dance hall in Breaux Bridge, deep in the heart of Cajun country to the west of New Orleans. Live Cajun music encourages foot-stomping, two-stepping, and jigging. The 400-seat cafe turns out pretty good Cajun food. Not the place for a quiet tête-à-tête.... *Tel 504/522–1492. 201 Julia St., Warehouse District.*

Mustang Sally's. Cowboy hats and boots abound at this branch of the national country-music chain.... *Tel 504/443–2925. 3406 Williams Blvd., Kenner.*

Napoleon House. The music is canned and classical, but this ancient sepia-colored bar is revered by Orleanians. The building dates from 1797 and shows its age. Sip a Pimm's Cup by candlelight here to cap off the night.... *Tel 504/524–9752. 500 Chartres St., French Quarter.*

O'Flaherty's Irish Channel. A cavernous tavern "Where the Celtic Folk Meet," the Irish Channel was the brainchild of two true sons of Erin—Danny and Patrick O'Flaherty. A lot goes on here, what with nightly music by the Celtic Folk, bagpipe and jig lessons, and the occasional concert by visiting icons like Tommy Makem and Paddy Reilly.... *Tel 504/529–1317. 508 Toulouse St., French Quarter. Occasional cover.*

Old Absinthe Bar. Dark, cramped, and dingy, the Absinthe Bar (a different animal from the Old Absinthe House Bar down the street) churns out really hard-driving blues. Things tune up and take off around midnight or so. A favorite with Quarterites.... *Tel 504/525–8108. 400 Bourbon St., French Quarter. 2-drink minimum.*

Oz. Gay men—mostly young—gather to dance together and swoon over the Thursday-night Calendar Boy revues. Otherwise, Oz is a cruisin', boozin', dancin' kind of place.... *Tel 504/593–9491. 800 Bourbon St., French Quarter.*

Palm Court Jazz Cafe. A very New Orleans place, with tile floors, cafe curtains, and a noise level befitting Bourbon St., the Palm Court showcases many of the Preservation Hall greats, plus things like chairs and white-clothed tables that you don't get at the Hall itself. Jazz authorities Nina and George Buck run the place, as well as producing several record labels stocked and sold in the adjoining store.... *Tel 504/525–0200. 1204 Decatur St., French Quarter. Opens for dinner at 7. Closed Mon and Tue. Cover at tables.*

Pat O'Brien's. All those zillions of tourists lined up on St. Peter St. are waiting to get into either Preservation Hall or Pat O'Brien's, or both. Going strong since the 1930s, Pat's mixed up the very first Hurricane, the now-ubiquitous beverage made of rum and fruit juices. There's a raucous piano bar to the right of the entrance and a splendid courtyard in the rear.... *Tel 504/525–4823. 718 St. Peter St., French Quarter.*

Pete Fountain's Club. New Orleans's clarinet legend plays traditional jazz and Dixie in a swank red-velvet room at the Hilton. The beloved native son tours a lot; when he's away the cats still play, so when you call to make the (required) reservation, be sure to ask if he'll be performing. His shows are at 10:15.... *Tel 504/523–4374. New Orleans Hilton Riverside Hotel, CBD. Closed Sun and Mon. Stiff cover.*

Planet Hollywood. Demi and Bruce and Sly, plus your proverbial galaxy of stars, were out in full force for the big bash that opened this branch of the ever-lengthening chain in 1995. Hard to believe it all happened right here on Planet Earth. It's all dolled up with the usual movie memorabilia. The Louisianan chefs have seen that the food is worthy of

New Orleans.... *Tel 504/522–7826. Jax Brewery, 620 Decatur St., French Quarter.*

Preservation Hall. The definition of grunge (and creature discomfort), the Hall is nevertheless the place to hunker down and hear the world's best traditional jazz. If you don't get in line by about 7:30 you may have to hunker down while standing up, but true jazz buffs don't mind.... *Tel 504/523–8939 (night), 504/522–2841 (day). 726 St. Peter St., French Quarter. Cover.*

Praline Connection Gospel & Blues Hall. Not hard to spot—what with the outside walls splashed with jazzy paintings—the cavernous 9,000-square-foot hall is big enough to hold the facades of a couple of houses and still have room for the 50-foot bar. That's the gospel truth. Soul food is served along with the music.... *Tel 504/523–3973. 907 S. Peters St., Warehouse District.*

Rawhide. Gays of the leather and Levi's persuasion dance with each other to country-and-western music in a roughhewn bar. It's boisterous, raw, and not for the faint of heart.... *Tel 504/525–8106. 740 Burgundy St., French Quarter.*

Rhythms. Live blues blares out of this 500-seat covered courtyard. In a departure from local tradition, the dance floor is actually big enough for dancing.... *Tel 504/523–3800. 227 Bourbon St., French Quarter. 2-drink minimum.*

Sazerac Bar. A sleek hangout for the suits, the Fairmont's bar is small and intimate, with discreet lighting, a long polished wood bar, colorful murals of Louisiana scenes, and barstools loaded with high-rollers, homegrown and otherwise. The house drink, not surprisingly, is the Sazerac, touted as the world's first cocktail. Cheek-to-chic dancing is done to a sophisticated trio in the adjacent **Sazerac Restaurant**. Great place for a romantic rendezvous.... *Tel 504/529–7111. Fairmont Hotel, 123 Baronne St., CBD.*

Snug Harbor. Locals flock to this rambling and rustic two-story place, where modern jazz icons like Ellis Marsalis hold forth. You get a better view of the stage from the second-floor balcony and can almost carry on a conversation up there. But the heavy-duty action is downstairs. Pretty good burgers and ham steaks are served in the restaurant.... *Tel 504/ 949–0696. 626 Frenchmen St., Faubourg Marigny. Cover.*

Steamboat Natchez. Tourists get carried away by this big white sternwheeler, which does evening excursions featuring banjo-thumping traditional jazz and Dixie and a lavish buffet of local specialties. A tame evening for the kids. Locals wouldn't be caught dead here.... *Tel 504/ 586–8777, 800/233–BOAT. Toulouse St. Wharf, French Quarter. Boards at 6pm at Toulouse St. Wharf, cruise 7–9. Admission covers the whole works.*

T.T.'s Club. The home court of female impersonator T. T. Thompson is wildly popular with gays.... *Tel 504/523– 9521. 820 N. Rampart St., Treme.*

Tipitina's. An institution, Tip's ambles around upstairs and down, with a couple or three bars and yards of cutoffs jukin' on a dime-sized dance floor. New Orleans funk reigns, along with rock and reggae. The Sunday night Cajun fais-do-do usually features Bruce Daigrepont and his band of Cajuns.... *Tel 504/895–8477 or 504/897–3943. 501 Napoleon Ave., Uptown. Cover.*

Tony Moran's Absinthe House. A historic building—it dates from 1805—houses the seedy Old Absinthe House bar, whose very seediness seems to appeal to an older crowd of dedicated drinkers—there's no music here, that's in the Absinthe Bar down the street, and the only "attractions" are the football helmets dangling from the ceiling and the international business cards that paper the peeling walls.... *Tel 504/523–3181. 240 Bourbon St., French Quarter.*

Tropical Isle Bourbon. The house drink is called the Hand Grenade, but by itself the rock and pop packs a wallop. This is a hard-driving dive with a lineup of local bands. Like most places in this neck of the woods, the two Tropical Isles are wild and raucous during Jazz Fest.... *Tel 504/529–4109. 721 Bourbon St., French Quarter.*

Tropical Isle Toulouse. The Bourbon Street branch was a spin-off from this late-night den. The sounds and sensibilities are about the same in each place. Very loud, very late.... *Tel 504/525–1689. 738 Toulouse St., French Quarter.*

Vic's Kangaroo Cafe. Best known as home base for harmonica player Rockin' Jake, this long skinny cafe also lines out good gutbucket (that's lowdown, mean blues). The overflow spills out to the few tables scattered on the sidewalk. The owner's an Aussie, and a short menu showcases some Down Under dishes.... *Tel 504/524–GDAY. 636 Tchoupitoulas St., Warehouse District.*

Victorian Lounge. The dark, romantic Victorian Lounge seduces loads of locals with its wood-burning fireplace, clubby velvet-upholstered chairs, and pressed-tin ceiling. Live and sultry modern jazz adds to the mood, but only on Thursday.... *Tel 504/899–9308. Columns Hotel, 3811 St. Charles Ave., Uptown.*

Wolfendale's. In-the-know black gays have been doing the Wolfendale's scene for more than a decade. The daily happy hour happens from 4 until 9, when the drinks are cheap. The Rampart Revue is an outré Thursday happening. Dancing is done to whatever the DJ spins.... *Tel 504/524–5749. 834 N. Rampart St., Treme.*

7

nment

Truth to tell, the big scenes in New Orleans are played in music clubs and restaurants. There is no big-time theater, except for road shows that play the Saenger Performing Arts Center; locally, there is only one professional Actors Equity company, the Southern Repertory Theatre, and it focuses on new works, primarily by southern playwrights. Major concerts are booked into the Superdome, and top-name nightclub acts come into the Kiefer UNO Lakefront Arena, but those acts don't necessarily have any local flavor—you're likely to catch the same shows in Cleveland or Salt Lake City. You'll have to check out the Nightlife chapter for the stuff that really makes New Orleans swing.

Used to be, the local artsy crowd would wring their collective hands, deploring the fact that New Orleans was not New York. They loved New Orleans—wouldn't live anywhere else on the planet, to be sure—but, still, they suffered from a bit of an inferiority complex. "Well, New York has this…," they said, "and New York does that." They constantly compared the Big Easy to the Big Apple and found the latter tastier, at least as far as the arts were concerned. Okay, so New York is not very big on Mardi Gras, and Jazz Fest can certainly hold its own against New York's JVC Jazz Festival. But after that… Then they stopped wringing their hands, got themselves together, and created what they like to refer to as the "SoHo of the South"—the Warehouse/Arts District. The centerpiece of that arty district is the Contemporary Arts Center, the CAC, which includes an avant-garde theater. It's the shrine in which all local alternative artists worship.

Sources

Frankly, if you're still in the planning stages of your trip to New Orleans, don't worry about scoping out the culture scene beforehand—you'll be able to get tickets easily enough once you're in town. (The one exception to this is Jazz Fest—for the scoop on that, see Diversions.) Pick up "Lagniappe," the *Times-Picayune*'s weekend entertainment tabloid, which comes out with the paper every Friday; it gives a pretty trustworthy rundown on what's doing around town in theaters, art galleries, music clubs, and so forth. *Gambit*, a free weekly paper available at newsstands and bookstores, also has listings of current events, though it's not as knowledgeable on the theater scene as it is on the music clubs. Most hotels have copies lying around of *This Week in New Orleans* and *Where*, both of them free (and fairly uncritical) magazines with calendars of events, feature articles, shopping news, and such.

Getting Tickets

The only really tough tickets in town are for the occasional major pop concerts, like Pearl Jam or the Stones. Tickets for events at the **Louisiana Superdome**, the **Kiefer UNO Lakefront Arena**, and the **Saenger Performing Arts Center** are sold through **Ticketmaster**, either by phone (credit-card charge line tel 504/522–5555 or 800/488–5252) or at the box office on the third floor of the **Maison Blanche** department store (same telephone number, 900 Canal St., open Mon–Sat 10 until 5:30). If you go in person to the box-office counter at Maison Blanche, you'll probably have to wait in line, but at least you'll be able to see the various venues' seating plans before purchasing your tickets—not a bad idea considering how huge the Dome, the Keifer arena, and the Saenger are (the smallest is the Saenger, which has 2,800 seats). The other local theaters, however, are all small enough that any seat gives a decent view. The administrative offices of the city's opera, ballet, and symphony are staffed, usually weekdays from 9 until 5, if you need to call for information, but theater box offices are only open during the run of a show.

Code Words
*You'll never be far away from the term **second line**. Second-liners are parade-followers; the term derives from jazz funerals, during which mourners fall in line behind the jazz band. The band plays dirges on the walk to the cemetery, but after the graveside services, joyful songs ring out in celebration of the release of the deceased's soul. White handkerchiefs and parasols pump up and down, hands clap, feet dance, and a whole lot of shakin' goes on. A **looker-after** is a New Orleans institution. She is the intimate and lover of a jazz musician, whom she...looks after. Looker-afters are treated with great respect. The story is told of an old-time jazz legend who lay dying in the ICU, with visitors strictly restricted to family members. A white woman was barred by nurses from entering the room until she said, merely, "It's okay. I'm his looker-after." She was ushered right in.*

Tickets for community-theater productions are in the $8–15 range; opera tickets are $30–80; ballet, concerts, and road shows can range anywhere from around $15 to 100. Tickets for Saints games start at $30.

The Lowdown

The play's the thing... New Orleans has only one Equity theater company: **Southern Repertory Theatre**, which puts on a season of plays by known and unknown southern playwrights in its plush and intimate 150-seat theater on the third level of the Canal Place mall. The quality of its productions can be pretty uneven; in the past few seasons, for example, Lillian Hellman's *Toys in the Attic* was well received, but their all-black version of Tennessee Williams's *The Rose Tattoo*, with its African American Serafina, was almost laughed out of town, and the interracial *The Glass Menagerie* was also panned. Try to find out what the *Times-Picayune*'s critic had to say about whatever's on the marquee when you get to town. The Southern Rep's theater is also the occasional venue for traveling shows, so don't expect everything that plays in this mall-top theater to fit the Southern Rep's criteria. If you're looking for the avant-garde, look first to the **Contemporary Arts Center**. The CAC got off the ground in 1976 after a local corporation donated a warehouse for the use of a group of struggling alternative artists. The large two-story erstwhile warehouse, its exterior painted dark red, evokes an airy feeling of freedom, with its 10,000 square feet of space and big windows that let in the sunlight. The center has grown as it has been renovated, and now absolutely adores itself for its outrageousness, its outlandishness, and its ability to shock the socks off Uptown Orleanians with various nudities and obscenities, but self-involved as it may be, it does attract some notable talent. In 1995 Edward Albee directed the regional premiere of his play *Fragments*, using only local actors. Up until very recently, the prestigious theater in New Orleans, locally speaking, was **Le Petit Théâtre du Vieux Carré**. Claiming to be the oldest continuously operating community theater in the country, Le Petit used to do solid top-quality productions of mainstream plays and musicals—the CAC crowd thought these were far too staid and conservative, but they were still quite professionally done. But in the last three or four years, Le Petit productions have not been nearly as polished, and their ticket subscriptions have been dropping off. It's almost worth the price of a theater ticket, though, just to see the building—a charming restored 18th-century building on Jackson Square, built around a courtyard— and as a bonus, good coffee is served entr'acte. In a corner of the building, **Teddy's Corner** presents well-attended children's plays. Contemporary plays are performed in a pocket-sized theater in Faubourg Marigny called, appropriately enough, **Theatre Marigny**. Marigny's plays are pretty inconsistent, but this theater loves taking risks. When they staged episodes of *The Honeymooners*, Ralph Kramden was played by a woman; the same actress played Willy Loman's wife in their *Death of a Salesman* production, which was locally applauded, at least for effort and chutzpah. **True Brew** is a funky little coffeehouse in the Warehouse/Arts District where some very good plays, usually one-acts by local playwrights, are performed. Orleanians adore True Brew—it has the flavor of Greenwich Village in the 1960s—and the arts crowd likes to hang out here even if there's no play on the boards at the moment.

Classical sounds... Emeril's restaurant, to name just one popular eatery, gets better local support than does classical music around here. New Orleans's only symphony orchestra is the **Louisiana Philharmonic Orchestra (LPO)**, whose season runs from September through April. The Classics Concerts include works by the standard classical composers—Mendelssohn, Prokofiev, Tchaikovsky, and the gang; audiences dress more casually for the Beethoven in Blue Jeans series, which mixes Beethoven with 20th-century artists like Copland, Bernstein, and Gershwin. In December, Handel's *Messiah* is always performed, and in January, the LPO shows off its chamber music skills with three Basically Bach concerts in **Roussell Hall** at Loyola University. Playing in the ornate old **Orpheum Theatre** (129 University Place), the LPO is a fine orchestra, which ends up playing the same standards year after year because it can't count on a more adventurous audience. It is for the most part made up of dedicated musicians from the defunct New Orleans Symphony, which struggled for years and finally went belly-up in 1991. The longtime conductor, Maxim Shostakovich, son of the famous composer, was forced to resign because of the company's financial difficulties—in plain terms, they couldn't pay him. He does return engagements occasionally, wielding his baton in front of the LPO.

Grand opera... Opera was first performed in this country in New Orleans in 1796—the French opera *Sylvain* was the production. A permanent opera company was established here in 1813, and the city's present company, the **New Orleans Opera Association**, was formed in the 1940s. From 1859 until 1919, the French Opera House at the corner of Toulouse and Bourbon Streets in the Quarter was the scene of lavish operas and balls. But despite the Orleanian love of opera, the opera house was not rebuilt after fire destroyed it, and its lot sat vacant until the 1960s, when a hotel was built there (at 541 Bourbon Street). These days, celebrity conductors and national and international opera stars perform with the New Orleans Opera Association in four annual productions, running from October through March. It ain't the Met, but the operas are handsomely mounted and fairly well attended by locals. They take place in the **Mahalia Jackson Theatre of the Performing Arts**, with its red plush seats and lovely sparkling crystal chandeliers; it's the only remaining performance space in the city's Cultural Center in Armstrong Park, which used to include the Municipal Auditorium. In 1995, that auditorium was converted into a casino, so there goes the neighborhood—at least as far as culture is concerned.

Men in tights... As is the case with the symphony, New Orleans does not have what you would call a good track record in terms of The Dance. There is no professional dance company. The **New Orleans Ballet Association** is essentially a producer—or "dance presenter," as it is defined by the National Endowment for the Arts— bringing to town guest companies, both classical and modern, such as the Royal Winnipeg Ballet and the Chicago Dance Theater. It also promotes the **New Orleans Ballet Ensemble**, a multi-ethnic troupe of non-professional dancers performing school outreach programs—a worthy community program but not much of a dance asset for visitors. The association evolved—or should we say devolved—from the New Orleans City Ballet, which, from 1983 until 1991, did split seasons with the Cincinnati City Ballet, with the two cities sharing artists and repertoire. Ballet and other dance performances take place in the **Mahalia Jackson Theatre of the Performing Arts** in Armstrong Park between September and June. If you love dance, it's worth checking the papers once you hit town to see whether a notable national company is performing during your stay; you can pretty well depend on tickets being available.

Revues and cabarets... There are "cabarets" galore on Bourbon Street, if the term is quite loosely applied to the sundry topless, bottomless, and "burlique" (otherwise known as burlesque) establishments. The longest running and best known of them all is **Big Daddy's**, though the current star stripper of the day, who calls herself GiO, struts her stuff at a place called **Bourbon Burlesque**. Somewhat more respectable, and well away from the Bourbon Street hustle, is **The Mint** in Faubourg Marigny, a legit cabaret appealing to a predominantly gay crowd, though straights are not strangers there either. The revues and shows strive to be outrageous and shocking, though they lean mostly on sexual double entendres and drag shows, tongue-planted-firmly-in-cheek. Mainstays at the Mint are the very popular Becky Allen and Ricky Graham, whose risqué comedy-and-song routines are always received with enthusiastic hoots and hollers.

The big game... Well, how 'bout dem Saints? as dey say locally. The beleaguered **New Orleans Saints** of the National Football League play their home games on Sundays—and on the occasional Monday night—in the almost overpoweringly big **Louisiana Superdome**. Saints fans tend to be wildly demonstrative, especially so when the team is losing, as it does all too often. But passionate as these fans are, there aren't so many of them that they sell out the Dome (it's a pretty big place, after all); tickets are readily available—especially when the team has a record of, say, 2 and 9 for the season. (That's when you'll see the fans in the stands pull paper sacks over their heads, as if ashamed to show their faces.) Half-time is a colorful event, with Dixieland and marching bands putting on a gaudy, high-spirited show. Home games of the **Tulane Green Wave** are played on Saturdays during the season in the Dome, which is also home to the **Sugar Bowl**, one of the oldest of the college bowl games, played either on New Year's Eve or New Year's Day. Around Sugar Bowl time, the French Quarter is mobbed with shrieking, not altogether sober college kids, and nobody sobers up or becomes any more subdued inside the Dome. On January 28, 1997, the **Super Bowl** will be played in the Dome, and New Orleans will be aslosh—*aslosh*—with football fans, sportscasters, and celebrities, not to mention a couple of pro football teams; Fat Tuesday falls on February 11 that year, so you can bet it's going to be your proverbial madhouse in New Orleans. If you haven't made your hotel reservation and bought your ticket by now, you may be out of luck. Still, it may be worth a try; contact the New Orleans Metropolitan Convention & Visitors Bureau for information.

If you're a baseball fan, you might enjoy catching the breeze out on the lakefront and watching the **New Orleans Zephyrs Baseball Club** play ball at Privateer Park at the University of New Orleans campus (admission charged). The AAA club, affiliated with the Milwaukee Brewers, manages to hold its own somewhere in the middle of the American Association's won/lost rankings. Think small-town Americana and you've captured the ambience. The way major-league baseball's going these days, there's something appealing and refreshing about a AAA game.

New Orleans has no professional basketball team, but that doesn't deter contemplation of an $84-million sports arena adjacent to the Superdome for that purpose, the thinking apparently being "if you build it, they will come...." The city is in the throes of building such a complex—Orleanians always go into throes about these things—though neither construction date nor completion nor even approval of the project has yet been announced.

The Index

Big Daddy's. The longest-running of Bourbon St.'s raunchy burlesque clubs.... *Tel 504/581–7167. 522 Bourbon St. Open 3pm–4am. Cover charge.*

Bourbon Burlesque. A strip club on the Bourbon St. strip... *Tel 504/561–8057. 327 Bourbon St. Cover charge.*

Contemporary Arts Center. The hottest spot in town for experimental and avant-garde theater, the CAC has two spaces at its Warehouse District headquarters. Both mount plays of regional playwrights, as well as traveling shows, national and international.... *Tel 504/523–1216, box office 504/528–3800. 900 Camp St. Season Sept–June.*

Kiefer UNO Lakefront Arena. Performances as diverse as Frank Sinatra and the Scots Guards are held in this rather soulless 10,000-seat auditorium on the east campus of the University of New Orleans. During his 1987 visit, Pope John Paul II celebrated a huge outdoor mass in a specially constructed gazebo on the grounds.... *Tel 504/286–7222. 6801 Franklin Ave. at Lakeshore Dr., Lakefront.*

Le Petit Théâtre du Vieux Carré. One of the nation's oldest continuously operating community theaters, Le Petit performs musicals, plays, and productions for children in a historic building on Jackson Square in the French Quarter. Children's shows are presented weekends in Teddy's Corner, in the same building as Le Petit during the season.... *Tel 504/522–2081 or 504/522–9958. 616 St. Peter St. Season Sept–June.*

Louisiana Philharmonic Orchestra. Classics and pops are performed in the Beaux Arts Orpheum Theatre in the CBD.... *Tel 504/523–6530. 821 Gravier St. Season Sept–Apr.*

Louisiana Superdome. The seating arrangement in the Dome, the largest facility of its kind, can be shuffled around like a deck of cards to provide seating for almost anything, from football games (the New Orleans Saints, the Tulane Green Wave) to rock concerts.... *Tel 504/587–3800. 1500 Sugar Bowl Dr. Football season Oct–Dec. Admission charged for tours of the Dome and for the games. Saints tickets start at $30.*

Mahalia Jackson Theatre of the Performing Arts. The New Orleans opera and visiting ballet companies perform in the sophisticated theater, with red plush seats, crystal chandeliers, and warm wood paneling. It's on the fringe of the French Quarter, in Armstrong Park, a few steps from Harrah's New Orleans Casino.... *Tel 504/565–7470. 801 N. Rampart St.*

The Mint. Outrageous revues play here to a mixed crowd of gays and straights in a big 19th-century building on the fringe of the Quarter.... *Tel 504/525–2000. 504 Esplanade Ave., Faubourg Marigny. Shows Thur-Sat at 11, Sun at 3. Cover charge.*

New Orleans Ballet Association. Classical ballets are performed by visiting companies in the Mahalia Jackson Theatre for the Performing Arts.... *Box office tel 504/565–7470. Performances at 801 N. Rampart St. Ballet office tel 504/522–0996. 639 Loyola Ave. Season Sept–May.*

New Orleans Opera Association. Opera—grand and comic—is performed at the Mahalia Jackson Theatre for the Performing Arts.... *Box office tel 504/565–7470. Performances at 801 N. Rampart St. Opera office tel 504/529–2278. 333 St. Charles Ave. Season Oct–Mar.*

New Orleans Saints. The Crescent City entry in the National Football League plays home games on Sunday afternoons, and occasionally on Monday nights, in the Louisiana Superdome (see above). The hapless Saints have yet to get a firm foothold in the playoffs, but the devoted "who dat" fans keep hoping.... *Ticket office tel 504/522–2600. 1500 Poydras St. Season Aug–Dec.*

New Orleans Zephyrs Baseball Club. A triple-A club affiliated with the Milwaukee Brewers, the Zephyrs play home games at University of New Orleans Privateer Park.... *Tel 504/282–7666. 139 Robert E. Lee Blvd. Season Apr–Oct.*

Orpheum Theatre. An ornate, acoustically fine, 1,700-seat theater with a Beaux Arts facade, this auditorium was built in 1918, and was on the Old Orpheum vaudeville circuit; these days, it's home to the Louisiana Philharmonic Orchestra.... *Tel 504/524–3285. 129 University Place.*

Roussell Hall. The Louisiana Philharmonic occasionally performs in this recital hall on the campus of Loyola University. For information, contact the LPO administration office (see above).... *6363 St. Charles Ave.*

Saenger Performing Arts Center. Where the big acts play. Touring companies of Broadway shows and top-name nightclub acts perform in this 2,800–seat Italian Renaissance theater built in the 1920s and dramatically decorated with statuary and ersatz stars in a midnight-blue ersatz sky. The Saenger offers an annual subscription series (individual tickets are also sold) of six or seven shows, which have included *Cats*, *Grand Hotel*, and *Fiddler on the Roof*.... *Tel 504/ 524–2490. 143 N. Rampart St.*

Southern Repertory Theatre. The city's only Equity theater troupe performs plays by southern playwrights, the known and the unknown, in a plush 150-seat theater on the third level of the Canal Place mall.... *Tel 504/861–8163. Canal Place. Season Mar–Sept.*

Theatre Marigny. In a tiny and rustic pocket-sized playhouse, the company performs plays by Tennessee Williams, Arthur Miller, and experimental works, none of them to great critical acclaim.... *Tel 504/944–2653. 616 Frenchmen St., Faubourg Marigny. Season Sept–June.*

True Brew. Some of the city's most popular plays have been— and are—performed in this very casual coffeehouse in a renovated warehouse, in (naturally) the Warehouse District.... *Tel 504/522–2907. 200 Julia St.*

Tulane Green Wave. On Saturday afternoons, Tulane University's football eleven plays home games in the Superdome.... *Tel 504/865–5506 (sports information line). 1520 Sugar Bowl Dr.*

ENTERTAINMENT | NEW ORLEANS

hotlines & other basics

Airports... Soaring four feet above sea level, **New Orleans International Airport** *(tel 504/464–3547)*, a.k.a. Moisant Field, is in Kenner, a small town about 15 miles west of downtown New Orleans. All domestic airlines drop in, as well as several international carriers. **Airport Shuttle** *(tel 504/522–3500)*, as you might surmise, operates minivans from and to the airport, one-way fare $10 per person. At the airport, you just walk out of the terminal and board one. Your hotel will make the (necessary) reservations for your return to the airport. **Louisiana Transit** *(tel 504/737–9611)* operates a bus between the airport and Elk Place in the CBD for exact fare, $1.10. The trip takes 45 minutes to an hour. If you call **United Cab Company** *(tel 504/522–9711, 800/323–3303)* and reserve in advance, a United cab will pick you up at the airport; give them your name and arrival particulars (flight date, time, airline). There is no additional fee above the regular fare from the airport: $21, whether there are one, two, or three of you. Four or more is $8 per person extra.

Baby-sitters... Both **Accent Child Care** *(tel 504/524–1227)* and **Dependable Kid Care** *(tel 504/486–4001, 800/862–5806)* offer in-hotel sitters, and if you like, they'll run the kids out on specially designed kiddie-type tours while you're knocking back Sazeracs somewhere.

Buses... **Greyhound Bus** shares Union Passenger Terminal *(1001 Loyola Ave.)* with Amtrak. Greyhound's phone number is 800/231-2222. City buses and streetcars are operated by the **Regional Transit Authority**. Call the 24-hour RideLine *(tel 504/248-3900)* for information about routes. Fare on the buses and the St. Charles streetcar is $1; the Riverfront streetcar costs $1.25. The **St. Charles streetcar** rumbles up St. Charles Avenue from the CBD past Audubon Park and Tulane and Loyola Universities; at the river's bend, where St. Charles Avenue dead ends, it hangs a right on Carrollton Avenue and runs on to Palmer Park. The **Riverfront streetcar** runs parallel with the river—though not exactly on the river's bank—from Esplanade Avenue on the lower border of the French Quarter, past the French Market, Jax Brewery, Riverwalk, and the Ernest N. Morial Convention Center in the Warehouse District. A **VisiTour pass** gives you unlimited rides on city buses and streetcars, $4 for one day, $8 for three days; they're sold in hotels and shopping centers.

Car rentals... All of the major car rental companies have outlets at the airport and downtown: **Avis** *(tel 504/523-4317, 800/331-1212; 2024 Canal St.; after 5pm, emergency tel 504/464-9511)*; **Budget** *(tel 504/527-2277, 800/527-0700; 1317 Canal St.)*; **Dollar** *(tel 504/467-2285, 800/421-6868; 1208 Canal St.)*; **Hertz** *(tel 504/568-1645, 800/654-3131; 901 Convention Center Blvd.)*. **Sears** *(tel 504/465-8785, 800/527-0770, 1245 Airline Dr.)* and **Value** *(tel 504/469-2668, 1701 Airline Hwy.)* do not have downtown outlets.

Convention center... One of these years, expansion of the **Ernest N. Morial Convention Center** *(tel 504/582-3000, 900 Convention Center Blvd., CBD)* will have to stop because they'll simply run out of land. Phase Three of the ongoing development is scheduled to be finished in 1998, adding to several zillion existing square feet of "contiguous space." It's one of the largest such facilities in the country, and New Orleans being a favorite party place, conventions are booked well into the millennium. The Sunday night before Fat Tuesday, Bacchus has its big bash in the center, replete with marching bands and floats. Giant floats (and very exuberant float riders) lumber round and round the floors amidst a shrieking throng of some 2,000. The boys of Bacchus save up their best beads to heave at their families and friends. Sorry, it's a members-only event.

Dentists... For referrals, call the **New Orleans Dental Association** *(tel 504/834–6449, 2121 N. Causeway Blvd., Metairie).*

Doctors... All of the major hospitals have referral services for specialists, or you can contact the **Tulane University Professional/Physicians Referral Group** *(tel 504/588–5800)* or **Touro Infirmary** *(tel 504/897–7011).*

Driving around... Interstate 10 is the major east–west artery through town; I-55 runs north–south, connecting with I-10 west of town. U.S. 90 (a.k.a. the Old Spanish Trail) loops through town, and I-12 runs east–west on the north shore of Lake Pontchartrain. I-59 is a north–south artery that connects with I-10 east of the city. Don't look for a French Quarter exit off I-10; it's called Vieux Carré, and it's exit 235A. Exit at Poydras Street to reach the Central Business District (CBD). Outside of the CBD and the French Quarter, New Orleans has a real problem with street signs—they're hard to spot, let alone read. And Orleanians are notoriously whimsical lane-switchers. One more note: If you're driving around town during Mardi Gras and innocently block a parade route, you'll be fined $100. Now you've been warned.

Code Words

*In any normal city, the strip running down the center of a boulevard is called a median. In New Orleans, a median is called the **neutral ground**. The term harks back to when the city was divided between Creoles and Americans. Creoles took it as real tacky when the Americans came to town, and they gave the "barbarians" a royal snubbing. The Americans began building their homes on the upriver side of a broad dirt strip that bordered the French town. Fistfights frequently broke out between the French and the Americans, and the dirt strip became a sort of DMZ—a neutral ground—between them. The drainage canal that was to be built on the strip never happened, and now Canal Street runs over it—a wide street with city buses and streetcars wheezing through the "neutral ground." A sidewalk is a **banquette**, a French word that dates from colonial days. However, it's pronounced here to rhyme with "blanket."*

Emergencies... Dial **911** for emergency assistance. Hospitals with 24-hour emergency rooms are **Tulane University Medical Center** *(tel 504/588–5711, 1415 Tulane Ave., CBD)*; **Touro Infirmary** *(tel 504/897–8250, 1401 Foucher St., Uptown)*; or the **Medical Center of Louisiana** *(tel 504/568–2311, 1532 Tulane Ave., CBD)*, which everyone locally calls Charity Hospital.

Festivals and special events... To mention only the major events:

January: **The Sugar Bowl** Classic is played in the Louisiana Superdome on either New Year's Eve or New Year's Day (it can vary from year to year), with attendant basketball tournament, sailing, tennis, swimming, and flag football championship games. Contact: Sugar Bowl Classic, 1500 Sugar Bowl Drive, New Orleans, LA 70112, tel 504/525–8374. Carnival season begins annually on January 6, and in 1997 expect bedlam: **The Super Bowl** game will be shot out in the Dome (January 28) and that year Fat Tuesday falls on February 11. Big-time bedlam.

February–March: **Mardi Gras** takes place in February or March, depending upon the date of Easter: Fat Tuesday, the final day of the Carnival season, falls 40 days before Easter Sunday, not counting Sundays. On **Lundi Gras**, the Monday before Mardi Gras, the city throws a free masked ball on Spanish Plaza, with live music, fireworks, and big crowds. *(For Mardi Gras and Lundi Gras information, contact the New Orleans Metropolitan Convention & Visitors Bureau, tel 504/566–5011, 1500 Sugar Bowl Dr., New Orleans, LA 70112)*. Other March events whose dates can fluctuate are the **New Orleans Writers' Conference** and the **Tennessee Williams New Orleans Literary Festival** *(for both, contact Metro College Conference Services ED-122, tel 504/286–6680, University of New Orleans, New Orleans, LA 70148)*. There are always at least two **St. Patrick's Day** parades, one in the Irish channel—a working-class neighborhood near the Garden District *(Irish Channel St. Patrick's Day Parade, tel 504/565–7080, 1300 Perido, New Orleans, LA 70112)*—and another in the French Quarter *(contact Jim Monaghan, Molly's at the Market, tel 504/525–5169, 1107 Decatur St., New Orleans, LA 70116)*. **St. Joseph's Day** is March 19, but the related Italian-American parade and celebration falls on the second Saturday of the month *(American Italian Renaissance Foundation, tel. 504/522–*

7294, 1608 South Salcedo St., New Orleans, LA 70125). The **Black Heritage Festival** honors contributions of African Americans, with festivities at the Audubon Zoo, Riverwalk, and the Louisiana State Museum *(Black Heritage Foundation, tel 504/286–8867, P.O. Box 60131, New Orleans, LA 70160)*. The **Freeport McDermott Golf Classic**—a PGA event with a million-dollar purse and live television coverage—is played annually at the English Turn Country Club *(Tournament Coordinator, Freeport McMoRan Golf Classic, tel 504/831–4653, 110 Veterans Blvd., Suite 170, Metairie, LA 70005)*.

April: The first weekend in April, the French Quarter Festival is a block-party blast covering several blocks, including Jackson Square, and the French Market *(French Quarter Festivals, Inc., tel 504/522–5730, 100 Conti St., New Orleans, LA 70130)*. **Spring Fiesta** kicks off the Friday following Easter, with a parade through the Quarter featuring horse-drawn carriages, belles, and bands; the five-day festival includes tours of private historic homes and courtyards all aglow with candles *(Spring Fiesta, tel 504/581–1367, 826 St. Ann St., New Orleans, LA 70118)*. About 30,000 runners take part in April's **Crescent City Classic**, a 10,000-meter race from Jackson Square to Audubon Park, with plenty of attendant hoopla and hype *(Crescent City Classic, tel 504/861–8686, 8200 Hampson St., Suite 217, New Orleans, LA 70118)*. The dust has scarcely settled before it's time for the **New Orleans Jazz & Heritage Festival**, the second biggest event after Mardi Gras. Dates fluctuate, since it zings from the last weekend in April until the first weekend in May *(Jazz Fest, tel 504/522–4786, P.O. Box 53407, New Orleans, LA 70153)*.

May: The **Greek Festival** is a charmer, centered around the Hellenic Cultural Center and the lovely Greek Orthodox church near City Park. Greek music, dancing, and food, of course, are featured *(Holy Trinity Cathedral, tel 504/282–0259, 1200 Robert E. Lee Blvd., New Orleans, LA 70122)*.

June: June brings the **Great French Market Tomato Festival** *(tel 504/522–2621, French Market Corporation, P.O. Box 51749, New Orleans, LA 70151)*; the **Reggae Riddums Festival** in City Park *(Orpus Entertainment Corporation, tel 504/367–1313, P.O. Box 6156, New Orleans, LA 70174)*; and **Carnaval Latino**, a four-day music and food fest in Woldenberg Riverfront Park *(Hispanic Heritage*

Foundation, tel 504/523–9540, P.O. Box 2664, New Orleans, LA 70176).

July: **Go 4th on the River** is the big Independence Day blowout on the Mississippi, with enough fireworks to rattle the Ole Man right out of his sluggishness *(Visitor Marketing, tel 504/528–9994, 610 S. Peters St., Suite 301, New Orleans, LA 70130).*

August: In August we sweat.

September: The next to-do is the **Swamp Festival** at Audubon Zoo and Woldenberg Riverfront Park—a four-day event celebrating Louisiana bayou country with Cajun music, food, and crafts *(Special Events Dept., Audubon Institute, tel 504/861–2537, ext 366, 6500 Magazine St., New Orleans, LA 70118).*

October: The **New Orleans Film & Video Festival** is a film buffs' bash at Canal Place, with local premieres and such *(New Orleans Film & Video Festival, tel 504/523–3818, 108 Royal St., New Orleans, LA 70112).* **Halloween** is celebrated in grand style in this city—we Orleanians love to don costumes.

November: The annual **Bayou Classic** at the Superdome pits Grambling State University against Southern University in an end-of-the-season grudge match *(Louisiana Superdome Ticket Office, tel 504/587–3663, P.O. Box 50488, New Orleans, LA 70150).* Thanksgiving is the beginning of the **Thoroughbred racing season** at the Fair Grounds *(Fair Grounds Race Course, tel 504/944–5515, 1751 Gentilly Blvd., New Orleans, LA 70119).* The day after Thanksgiving, **Celebration in the Oaks** begins, when millions of lights illuminate 1,500-acre City Park—and millions of people, it seems, line their cars up to drive through the park *(Director of Public Relations, City Park, tel 504/482–4888, 1 Palm Dr., New Orleans, LA 70124).* The lights are lit until the first week in January. Papa Noel parades into town in December, ushering in **A New Orleans Christmas** (the name of which was until recently "A Creole Christmas") and discounted hotel rates. The celebration lasts the whole month, with historic houses dolled up in 19th-century style, food demonstrations (surprise!), a bonfire on the river, and many restaurants featuring Reveillon menus. (It was the Creole custom to have lavish dinners—called Reveillons—after midnight mass on Christmas Eve.) For information, contact New Orleans Christmas, tel.

504/522–5730, 100 Conti Street, New Orleans, LA 70130. **New Year's Eve** is celebrated in grand style, with booming, sizzling fireworks rousing the Ole Man again. And then danged if it ain't New Year's Day, and the whole thing starts all over again.

Gay and lesbian resources... The hotline of the **NO/AIDS Task Force** *(tel 504/945–4000)* is staffed 24 hours a day; its Drop-In Center is at 1407 Decatur Street in the Quarter, tel 504/524–8334. The **Gay & Lesbian Community Center** is at 816 N. Rampart Street, on the fringe of the French Quarter, tel 504/522–1103. *Ambush Magazine* and *Impact Gulf South Gay News* chronicle the area's news and events from a gay perspective.

Jazz hotlines... Shocking though it may be, the city in which jazz originated has no jazz hotline. But there you have it—there is no such animal.

Newspapers... The only daily paper is the *Times-Picayune*, which carries local, national, and international news with a liberal slant. The paper is owned by the Newhouse publishing conglomerate, but publisher Ashton Phelps is a New Orleanian. In the Quarter, **Matassa's Market** *(tel 504/525–9494, 1001 Dauphine St.)* and **Sidney's Newsstand** *(tel 504/524–6872, 917 Decatur St.)* both carry the *New York Times*. The largest newsstand is in Riverbend, where **Lenny's News** *(tel 504/866–5127, 622 S. Carrollton Ave.)* carries the likes of the London *Times* as well as local monthlies like the *Jewish Civic Press*, *Aqui New Orleans* (a Spanish-language paper), the *New Orleans Tribune* (African American), and *Ambush Magazine* and *Impact Gulf South Gay News* (both of which are gay- and lesbian-oriented). *Gambit* is a free weekly paper covering local news and happenings, with especially knowledgeable music listings, and *Offbeat* is a free weekly magazine with news and reviews of the music scene, available in bookstores, on newsstands, and in some hotels and music clubs.

Opening and closing times... Normal business hours are weekdays from 9 until 5. Banks are open from 9 until 3 or 4 on weekdays. Banks are closed on New Orleans's two indigenous holidays, November 1 (All Saints Day) and Mardi Gras (Fat Tuesday). On Fat Tuesday, all offices close as well.

Parking... It makes the hair turn white just to contemplate parking in the French Quarter. The French Quarter is a very small residential area—a small town that everyone and his, her, or their brother (or sister) wants to visit. Quarter residents are issued parking permits—those who have cars that is; a slew of them don't have cars and never leave the Quarter anyway. It is not necessary to have a permit in order to park in the Quarter, but parking places are very scarce, and nobody—nobody—understands the signs. Parking in the considerably less-congested CBD and other parts of the city is much less of a hassle. But you must always beware of the tow-truck drivers (a term that strikes terror in the hearts of Orleanians). A government blue ribbon panel should do a study to ascertain what it is that makes these people relish their work so much. They move at lightning speed—locals have been seen flinging themselves across the hoods of their cars to prevent them from being towed away. Towed cars are taken, swiftly, to the **Claiborne Auto Pound** *(tel 504/565–7450, 400 N. Claiborne Ave.)*. Precious few hotels in town offer free parking. In the Quarter, secured indoor pay parking is at **Dixie Parking** *(tel 504/524–5996, 911 Iberville St.)*, **Solares Garage** *(tel 504/524–5994, 721 Iberville St.)*, and in the **Maison Blanche Building** *(entrance on Dauphine St. between Canal and Iberville Sts.)*. There is a large open pay lot at the **Jax Brewery** *(Decatur St. between Toulouse and St. Louis Sts.)* and **behind the French Market** *(between Dumaine and Toulouse Sts.)*. Outside the Quarter, Dixie Parking operates **Clarke Garage** *(tel 504/525–8630, 930 Gravier St.)*, **Saratoga Garage** *(tel 504/524–3789, 222 Loyola Ave.)*, and **Poydras Center** *(tel 504/525–6911, 650 Poydras St.)*. And there is a huge indoor garage at the **Superdome** *(tel 504/587–3663, main office: 1550 Sugar Bowl Dr.)*.

Pharmacies... Pharmacies open 24 hours are **K&B** *(tel 504/895–0344, 3401 St. Charles Ave.)* and several **Walgreens**, including 3311 Canal Street *(tel 504/822–8073)* and 3057 Gentilly Boulevard *(tel 504/282–2621)*. There is also a Walgreens, open daily but not 24 hours, at 900 Canal Street *(tel. 504/523–3875)*.

Post office... The main office of the **U.S. Postal Service** is at 701 Poydras Street in the CBD *(tel 504/589–1111)*. There is a branch in the French Quarter at 1022 Iberville Street *(tel 504/524–0072)*. In the heart of the Quarter, the **French Quarter Postal Emporium** *(tel 504/525–6651, 940 Royal St.)* is a private mail service that sells stamps and offers most services Uncle Sam provides, at a slightly higher price. They'll also wrap packages for shipping; sell you postcards, maps, and envelopes; and let you use their photocopying and fax machines—for a fee, of course.

Radio stations... For lots of talk, tune to **WSMB 1350AM**; talk plus news is on **WWL 870 AM**. National Public Radio is on **WWNO 89.9 FM**, which also has late-night jazz. **WWOZ 90.7FM** is the community radio station, with lots of jazz and news of musical happenings. Oldies are on **KQLD 106.7 FM**, country is on **WNOE 101.1 FM**, and rock and gospel are on **WYLD 940 AM**.

Restrooms... Downtown, there are clean public restrooms in the malls (**Jax Brewery**, **Millhouse**, **Canal Place**, **New Orleans Center**, and **Riverwalk**) and in the **World Trade Center** at 2 Canal Street. There are also public restrooms (note the absence of the adjective "clean") in the **900** and **1200** blocks of the **French Market** and at St. Louis Street in

Getting to Know the NOPD

In 1993, a tourist staying in a CBD hotel got in her rental car, struck off down Canal Street, and made an illegal left turn—something that's all too easy to do on a street where turning left is a minor art form. She was forthwith arrested and taken to Central Lockup, where she was fingerprinted, strip-searched, deloused, and tossed in the clink. She was forced to spend the night there before frantic out-of-town relatives could spring her. Okay, besides making an illegal turn, this "criminal" was also driving without a license. Still, the poor woman will probably never recover from the ordeal. The New Orleans Police Department defended themselves, however, by saying she was treated no differently from any other persons who likewise break the law. That's a relief, isn't it? All of which is by way of introduction to the NOPD, a body of folks who are almost never referred to as "New Orleans's finest." They do play hardball, and seem to vie with local tow-truck drivers and meter maids in their zeal. Knowing this, it's wise to exercise extreme caution: don't speed, don't drive without a license, do not drive while drinking, and obey all traffic signs. Or else.

NEW ORLEANS | HOTLINES & OTHER BASICS

Woldenberg Riverfront Park. In **City Park**, there are facilities in the casino building, at 1 Dreyfous Avenue (where you pick up your City Park fishing permits and rent pedalboats), and in Audubon Park, at the tennis courts

(Henry Clay and Tchoupitoulas Sts.). Now, about Mardi Gras. The city's public facilities are perfectly adequate at all other times, except on Fat Tuesday. On Fat Tuesday, you have a million or so beer-swilling people milling around Downtown. The city sets up portable toilets in the CBD and in the Quarter, but not nearly enough of them. In self-defense, local hoteliers and restaurateurs—who are accustomed to anything during Mardi Gras—post signs proclaiming "Restrooms for customers only." Let's call a spade a spade here. Drunks treat the city like one giant latrine, particularly in the Quarter, and it's disgusting. Think about that before you start picking beads and doubloons up off the street.

Smoking... If you're a nonsmoker, you'll be pleased to note that New Orleans has most of the same restrictions that apply in other cities. If you're a smoker, you'll be just as mad as you are anywhere else. Smoking is prohibited in all public buildings, in doctors' offices, hospitals, and theater lobbies, in the Superdome (except for the corridors, and they will probably become "smoke-free" as well), on streetcars and buses. Most taxicabs also post No Smoking signs. Bars have not yet banned smoking, and most restaurants have separate sections for smokers.

Taxes... Combined local and state **sales tax** comes to 9%. Hotels are worse: the **hotel tax** is 11%, but the city imposes an additional $1 to $3 per room per night, depending on how many rooms are in the property. The bigger the hotel, the bigger the bite. This little fund-raiser for the city coffers takes a lot of visitors by surprise. The state offers some relief for visitors from out of the country in its **Louisiana Tax-Free Shopping** program *(tel 504/568–5323)*. International visitors can get a sales tax refund by following the bouncing ball thusly: Buy stuff in a store that displays the LTFS insignia and save your sales receipt. Just before your departure from the city, present the receipt at the LTFS refund office at the airport, along with your passport and round-trip airline ticket of less than 90 days' duration. Refunds of up to $500 will be made in cash on the spot. Refunds in excess of that will be mailed to your home address.

Taxis and limos... The most reliable taxi company is **United Cab Company** *(tel 504/522–9711, 800/323–3303)*; if you can't get through to United—the phone sometimes rings off the hook—call **Checker-Yellow**

Cabs *(tel 504/943–2411)*. Many local cabs accept plastic; ask in advance for a car that accepts the cards you're carrying. Don't be startled by the local cabdrivers' custom—usually—of leaping out to open the back door. In-town fare starts at $2.10, plus 20 cents for each one-sixth of a mile or 40 seconds, plus $1 for each additional passenger. I.e., if there are two of you, the fare jumps to $3.10 first crack out of the box. For traveling in style, call **London Livery** *(tel 504/831–0700)*, **A Touch of Class** *(tel 504/522–7565)*, or **Carey Bonomolo** *(tel 504/523–5466)*.

Tipping... New Orleans is not typically American, except in the tipping department. If you can find an airport skycap, tip a buck per bag. Cabdrivers get about 10% of the fare. Tip 15% to 20% in restaurants, and leave $2 to $3 per night for the hotel maid. This is as good a place as any to mention the proliferation of street hustlers in the Quarter who approach tourists with "I bet I know where you got dem shoes." You can fend them off with the proper response: "I got 'em on my feet."

Trains... Amtrak trains arrive and depart at **Union Passenger Terminal** *(tel 800/872–7245, 1001 Loyola Ave., CBD)*. The *City of New Orleans* ambles down from New York and the northeast, the *Crescent City Limited* chugs from Chicago and the Midwest, and the *Sunset Limited* stops in New Orleans on its cross-country trips from Florida to Los Angeles.

Travelers with disabilities... Somewhat surprisingly, since the city has only recently roused itself from its 19th-century slumber, there are a number of advocacy groups for people with disabilities. Some of the more active are the **Advocacy Center for the Elderly and Disabled** *(tel 504/522–2337, 800/960–7705, voice or TDD; 210 O'Keefe Ave., Suite 700, 70112)*; **New Orleans Resources for Independent Living** *(tel 504/522–1995, voice or TDD; NORIL, 1001 Howard Ave., Suite 300, 70113-2005)*; the **Deaf Action Center** *(voice line tel 504/525–7911, TDD 504/566–1815, 800/947–5277 for TDD 24-hour relay, 504/566–1822 for TDD 24-hr recorded message; 1231 Prytania St., 2nd floor, 70130)*; and the **Easter Seal Society of Louisiana for Children and Adults with Disabilities** *(tel 504/455–5533, voice or TDD, or 800/695–SEAL; 4937 Hearst Plaza, Suite 2L, Box 8425, Metairie, 70011)*.

TV channels... There is presently underway a shake-up involving network affiliations, but as of this writing, here are things as they stand: the local NBC affiliate is **WVUE TV/Channel 6**; CBS is **WWL-TV/Channel 4**; ABC is **WDSU-TV/Channel 8**; Fox is **WNOL/ Channel 38**; and PBS is **WYES-TV/Channel 12**. On Fat Tuesday, local anchors on channels 4, 6, and 8 usually provide live coverage decked out in costumes and beads. Good luck with WYES, incidentally, unless you're in a giving mood. The number of pledge drives they conduct is a local joke.

Visitor information... For information before you take off, write to the **New Orleans Metropolitan Convention and Visitors Bureau** *(tel 504/566–5011, 1500 Sugar Bowl Dr., 70112)*. After you've hit town, head for the bureau's **New Orleans Welcome Center** on Jackson Square *(tel 504/566–5011, 529 St. Ann St.)* to load up on free maps, brochures, and advice. The **Folklife Center of the Jean Lafitte National Historical Park** *(tel 504/589–2636, 916-18 N. Peters St., French Market)* has information about the French Quarter (which is under the auspices of the Park Service), as well as about the parks at Chalmette Battlefield and Barataria (see Diversions).

FROMMER'S COMPLETE TRAVEL GUIDES

*(Comprehensive guides to sightseeing, dining and accommodations,
with selections in all price ranges—from deluxe to budget)*

Acapulco/Ixtapa/Taxco, 2nd Ed.	C157	Italy '96 (avail. 11/95)	C183
Alaska '94-'95	C131	Jamaica/Barbados, 2nd Ed.	C149
Arizona '95	C166	Japan '94-'95	C144
Australia '94-'95	C147	Maui, 1st Ed.	C153
Austria, 6th Ed.	C162	Nepal, 3rd Ed. (avail. 11/95)	C184
Bahamas '96 (avail. 8/95)	C172	New England '95	C165
Belgium/Holland/Luxembourg, 4th Ed.	C170	New Mexico, 3rd Ed.	C167
		New York State, 4th Ed.	C133
Bermuda '96 (avail. 8/95)	C174	Northwest, 5th Ed.	C140
California '95	C164	Portugal '94-'95	C141
Canada '94-'95	C145	Puerto Rico '95-'96	C151
Caribbean '96 (avail. 9/95)	C173	Puerto Vallarta/Manzanillo/ Guadalajara, 2nd Ed.	C135
Carolinas/Georgia, 2nd Ed.	C128	Scandinavia, 16th Ed.	C169
Colorado '96 (avail. 11/95)	C179	Scotland '94-'95	C146
Costa Rica, 1st Ed.	C161	South Pacific '94-'95	C138
Cruises '95-'96	C150	Spain, 16th Ed.	C163
Delaware/Maryland '94-'95	C136	Switzerland, 7th Ed. (avail. 9/95)	C177
England '96 (avail. 10/95)	C180		
Florida '96 (avail. 9/95)	C181	Thailand, 2nd Ed.	C154
France '96 (avail. 11/95)	C182	U.S.A., 4th Ed.	C156
Germany '96 (avail. 9/95)	C176	Virgin Islands, 3rd Ed. (avail. 8/95)	C175
Honolulu/Waikiki/Oahu, 4th Ed. (avail. 10/95)	C178	Virginia '94-'95	C142
Ireland, 1st Ed.	C168	Yucatán '95-'96	C155

FROMMER'S $-A-DAY GUIDES

(Dream Vacations at Down-to-Earth Prices)

Australia on $45 '95-'96	D122	Ireland on $45 '94-'95	D118
Berlin from $50, 3rd Ed. (avail. 10/95)	D137	Israel on $45, 15th Ed.	D130
		London from $55 '96 (avail. 11/95)	D136
Caribbean from $60, 1st Ed. (avail. 9/95)	D133	Madrid on $50 '94-'95	D119
Costa Rica/Guatemala/Belize on $35, 3rd Ed.	D126	Mexico from $35 '96 (avail. 10/95)	D135
Eastern Europe on $30, 5th Ed.	D129	New York on $70 '94-'95	D121
England from $50 '96 (avail. 11/95)	D138	New Zealand from $45, 6th Ed.	D132
Europe from $50 '96 (avail. 10/95)	D139	Paris on $45 '94-'95	D117
Greece from $45, 6th Ed.	D131	South America on $40, 16th Ed.	D123
Hawaii from $60 '96 (avail. 9/95)	D134	Washington, D.C. on $50 '94-'95	D120

FROMMER'S COMPLETE CITY GUIDES

(Comprehensive guides to sightseeing, dining, and accommodations in all price ranges)

Amsterdam, 8th Ed.	S176	Miami '95-'96	S149
Athens, 10th Ed.	S174	Minneapolis/St. Paul, 4th Ed.	S159
Atlanta & the Summer Olympic		Montréal/Québec City '95	S166
Games '96 (avail. 11/95)	S181	Nashville/Memphis, 1st Ed.	S141
Atlantic City/Cape May,		New Orleans '96 (avail. 10/95)	S182
5th Ed.	S130	New York City '96 (avail. 11/95)	S183
Bangkok, 2nd Ed.	S147	Paris '96 (avail. 9/95)	S180
Barcelona '93-'94	S115	Philadelphia, 8th Ed.	S167
Berlin, 3rd Ed.	S162	Prague, 1st Ed.	S143
Boston '95	S160	Rome, 10th Ed.	S168
Budapest, 1st Ed.	S139	St. Louis/Kansas City, 2nd Ed.	S127
Chicago '95	S169	San Antonio/Austin, 1st Ed.	S177
Denver/Boulder/		San Diego '95	S158
Colorado Springs, 3rd Ed.	S154	San Francisco '96 (avail. 10/95)	S184
Disney World/Orlando '96		Santa Fe/Taos/	
(avail. 9/95)	S178	Albuquerque '95	S172
Dublin, 2nd Ed.	S157	Seattle/Portland '94-'95	S137
Hong Kong '94-'95	S140	Sydney, 4th Ed.	S171
Las Vegas '95	S163	Tampa/St. Petersburg, 3rd Ed.	S146
London '96 (avail. 9/95)	S179	Tokyo '94-'95	S144
Los Angeles '95	S164	Toronto, 3rd Ed.	S173
Madrid/Costa del Sol, 2nd Ed.	S165	Vancouver/Victoria '94-'95	S142
Mexico City, 1st Ed.	S175	Washington, D.C. '95	S153

FROMMER'S FAMILY GUIDES

(Guides to family-friendly hotels, restaurants, activities, and attractions)

California with Kids	F105	San Francisco with Kids	F104
Los Angeles with Kids	F103	Washington, D.C. with Kids	F102
New York City with Kids	F101		

FROMMER'S WALKING TOURS

(Memorable strolls through colorful and historic neighborhoods, accompanied by detailed directions and maps)

Berlin	W100	San Francisco, 2nd Ed.	W115
Chicago	W107	Spain's Favorite Cities	
England's Favorite Cities	W108	(avail. 9/95)	W116
London, 2nd Ed.	W111	Tokyo	W109
Montréal/Québec City	W106	Venice	W110
New York, 2nd Ed.	W113	Washington, D.C., 2nd Ed.	W114
Paris, 2nd Ed.	W112		

FROMMER'S AMERICA ON WHEELS

(Guides for travelers who are exploring the U.S.A. by car, featuring a brand-new rating system for accommodations and full-color road maps)

Arizona/New Mexico	A100	Florida	A102
California/Nevada	A101	Mid-Atlantic	A103

FROMMER'S SPECIAL-INTEREST TITLES

Arthur Frommer's Branson!	P107	Frommer's Where to	
Arthur Frommer's New World		Stay U.S.A., 11th Ed.	P102
of Travel (avail. 11/95)	P112	National Park Guide, 29th Ed.	P106
Frommer's Caribbean		USA Today Golf	
Hideaways (avail. 9/95)	P110	Tournament Guide	P113
Frommer's America's 100		USA Today Minor League	
Best-Loved State Parks	P109	Baseball Book	P111

FROMMER'S BEST BEACH VACATIONS
*(The top places to sun, stroll, shop, stay, play, party, and swim—with each
beach rated for beauty, swimming, sand, and amenities)*

California (avail. 10/95)	G100	Hawaii (avail. 10/95)	G102
Florida (avail. 10/95)	G101		

FROMMER'S BED & BREAKFAST GUIDES
*(Selective guides with four-color photos and full descriptions of
the best inns in each region)*

California	B100	Hawaii	B105
Caribbean	B101	Pacific Northwest	B106
East Coast	B102	Rockies	B107
Eastern United States	B103	Southwest	B108
Great American Cities	B104		

FROMMER'S IRREVERENT GUIDES
*(Wickedly honest guides for sophisticated travelers and
those who want to be)*

Chicago (avail. 11/95)	I100	New Orleans (avail. 11/95)	I103
London (avail. 11/95)	I101	San Francisco (avail. 11/95)	I104
Manhattan (avail. 11/95)	I102	Virgin Islands (avail. 11/95)	I105

FROMMER'S DRIVING TOURS
*(Four-color photos and detailed maps outlining
spectacular scenic driving routes)*

Australia	Y100	Italy	Y108
Austria	Y101	Mexico	Y109
Britain	Y102	Scandinavia	Y110
Canada	Y103	Scotland	Y111
Florida	Y104	Spain	Y112
France	Y105	Switzerland	Y113
Germany	Y106	U.S.A.	Y114
Ireland	Y107		

FROMMER'S BORN TO SHOP
*(The ultimate travel guides for discriminating
shoppers—from cut-rate to couture)*

Hong Kong (avail. 11/95)	Z100	London (avail. 11/95)	Z101

irreverent notes